Takeuchi Yoshimi

CORNELL EAST ASIA SERIES

The Cornell East Asia Series is published by the Cornell University East Asia Program (distinct from Cornell University Press). We publish affordably priced books on a variety of scholarly topics relating to East Asia as a service to the academic community and the general public. Standing orders, which provide for automatic notification and invoicing of each title in the series upon publication, are accepted.

If after review by internal and external readers a manuscript is accepted for publication, it is published on the basis of camera-ready copy provided by the volume author. Each author is thus responsible for any necessary copy-editing and for manuscript formatting. Address submission inquiries to CEAS Editorial Board, East Asia Program, Cornell University, Ithaca, New York 14853-7601.

STUDIES OF THE WEATHERHEAD EAST ASIAN INSTITUTE
COLUMBIA UNIVERSITY

The Weatherhead East Asian Institute is Columbia University's center for research, publication, and teaching on modern and contemporary Asia Pacific regions. The Studies of the Weatherhead East Asian Institute were inaugurated in 1962 to bring to a wider public the results of significant new research on modern and contemporary East Asia.

TAKEUCHI YOSHIMI

Displacing the West

RICHARD F. CALICHMAN

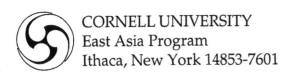

CORNELL UNIVERSITY
East Asia Program
Ithaca, New York 14853-7601

Number 120 in the Cornell East Asia Series

Published by the Cornell University East Asia Program, and included in Columbia University's Studies of the Weatherhead East Asian Institute.

Contents

Preface

Takeuchi Yoshimi (1910-1977) was both a foremost scholar of Chinese literature and culture and one of the major leftist critics of the postwar generation. His writings (which occupy seventeen volumes in his *Collected Works*) cover a vast range of subject material, extending from the Chinese writer Lu Xun to the American philosopher John Dewey, from Japanese culture of the Nara period to China's controversial nuclear testing in 1964. Today Takeuchi's place in twentieth-century Japanese intellectual history appears cemented by his sustained attention to the question of Japan's relations with Asia, and especially China. He was largely responsible for bringing about a change in intellectual focus in the postwar period away from western cultural phenomena to that of Asia, thereby provoking debate over Japan's own social and cultural identity. This work formed an important part of Takeuchi's challenge to the Japanese to more critically rethink the country's relation to the West so as to better evaluate the ramifications of western-style modernization. Having experienced firsthand the horrors of Japan's Fifteen-Year War (1931-1945), it can justifiably be said that all of Takeuchi's work was directed toward fostering a critical spirit of resistance on the basis of which, he hoped, repetition of this violence would henceforth be avoided. In his view, such a spirit of resistance must necessarily begin by reexamining Japan's place vis-à-vis the historical division between East and West.

As Takeuchi would later recount, the real reason behind his decision to study Chinese literature had surprisingly little to do with the fact that he himself chose this field in 1931 upon enrolling in the Chinese Literature department at Tokyo Imperial University. Truth be told, this decision was motivated by the department's reputation as the easiest to enter in the university. Instead what most determined Takeuchi's course of study was a journey to mainland China he took the following year, for it was then that he first saw the link between the reading he pursued in Tokyo and the actual people he saw all around him in Beijing living their everyday lives. Deeply inspired, Takeuchi returned to Japan and helped form the "Chūgoku bungaku kenkyūkai" [Chinese Literature Research Society], which soon began publishing a small journal, the *Chūgoku bungaku geppō*, to which he contributed essays and translations.[1]

Takeuchi's first book, *Ro Jin* [Lu Xun], was published in 1944, yet he had in fact completed the manuscript a year earlier while waiting to be drafted for military service. This work is at one and the same time an introduction to Lu Xun's thought and literature *and* an attempt on Takeuchi's part to begin to think through some of the questions that would haunt him throughout his life, such as those of ethics, action, subjectivity and revolution. In 1946 he finally returned from China, where he had fought and served as an interpreter. Refusing a faculty position at Tokyo University as well as invitations to join both the Japan Communist Party and the leftist "Shin Nihon bungakkai" [New Japanese Literature Association], Takeuchi energetically set to work writing and translating, and quickly became known on the postwar intellectual scene through his participation in various debates and round-table discussions.

The years that immediately followed saw the publication of several additional books on Lu Xun as well as the extremely influential essay "Kindai towa nanika" [What is Modernity?] (originally titled "Chinese Modernity and Japanese Modernity") (1948). In this piece Takeuchi criticized Japan's facile acceptance of western modernity, suggesting that this modernity and its history of colonial expansion was directly responsible for the country's own expansionism leading to the Fifteen-Year War. Rejection of such modernization was not to be achieved by an aggressive militarism, he argued; rather what was required was a more fundamental questioning of the nature of progress and historical change. The success of the Communist Revolution in China in 1949 brought increased attention to Takeuchi's writings. In 1953 he joined the faculty of Tokyo Metropolitan University and shortly thereafter was appointed chair of the "Shisō no kagaku kenkyukai" [Institute of the Science of Thought], whose members included the philosopher-critic Tsurumi Shunsuke and the political scientist Maruyama Masao.

Taking up some of the themes surrounding Japanese postwar identity that he had previously introduced in his *Nihon ideorogii* [Japanese Ideology] (1952), Takeuchi published the volumes *Kokumin bungaku ron* [On National Literature] and *Chishikijin no kadai* [The Task of Intellectuals] in 1954. Several years later he undertook a reexamination of the wartime

---

1. These early essays dating from the 1930s on such figures as Yu Dafu (on whom Takeuchi wrote his senior thesis), Mao Dun, Lu Xun and Zhou Zuoren (Lu Xun's younger brother) can be found in *Takeuchi Yoshimi zenshū* (Tokyo: Chikuma Shobō, 1980), vol. 14 (hereafter referred to as *TYz*).

"Kindai no chōkoku" [Overcoming Modernity] symposium in his essay of the same name. This article was especially well received, and did much to reopen debate on the question of Japanese resistance to western modernity at a time when the Japanese government was actively pursuing negotiations with the United States over a new Security Treaty (*Ampo*). The Treaty was infamously forced through by the ruling Liberal Democratic Party in 1960, prompting Takeuchi's immediate resignation from his teaching position as a sign of protest. He continued writing well into the decade of the seventies and died of cancer at the age of sixty-seven.

****

My reading of Takeuchi's text takes as its "key" or "clue"—*tegakari*, a word that occupies an important place in his thinking—Takeuchi's own unique manner of reading. From his earliest writings on Lu Xun, Takeuchi reveals a profound dissatisfaction with the methods of traditional scholarship in its emphasis on such values as detachment, thematization and objectivity. Doubtless these values cannot simply be eliminated from scholarship altogether, and yet they can (and indeed should, as Takeuchi argues) be put in their proper perspective, or reconceived in such a way as to allow for a *different* relationship to things to take place. Scholarship errs in assuming that these values are natural, as for example can most obviously be seen in the field of historiography. Here the scrupulous attention to the past and sensitivity to context unfold entirely within the framework of objectivity, which itself remains exempt from historicization in its apparent naturalness. In this refusal to question the very premises upon which it is grounded, historiography reveals an unflinching self-complacency. History of course receives the highest priority in historiography, and yet it is not difficult to see that this prioritization represents what is in fact a radical reversal in the relation between man and history: rather than being acknowledged as the universal or general element within which all human activity necessarily takes place (as for example the activity of scholarship), history is instead reduced by historiography to the mere status of thematized object. For Takeuchi, such objectification of history represents what he famously called the "decadence of scholarship" (*gakumon no daraku*).[2] What this scholarship forgets is that the rules under which it operates are historical through and through. In its objectification of history, historiography posits itself as in some sense detached or isolated from its object—and yet this is of course impossible given man's thoroughly historical nature, or what might be called his *inscription within* history. Takeuchi does not hesitate in pointing

---

2. "Kindai towa nanika (Nihon to Chūgoku no baai)," in *TYz*, vol. 4, p. 146. First published in 1948.

out the essential shortcomings of such scholarship, but even more than this he attempts to locate its historical emergence in the era of modernity. It is in modernity, he suggests, that the relation between man and things first comes to be transformed into one of objectification.

Hence in his reading of texts from modern Japanese and Chinese literature and intellectual history, Takeuchi will seek to go beyond a mere thetic relation so as to allow these texts to speak more urgently to contemporary problems, problems which cannot but bespeak our own status as moderns. This manner of reading is very explicitly set forth by Takeuchi in terms of the notion of "resistance" (*teikō*), for which he is perhaps best known in Japanese intellectual circles today. In the first place, this resistance poses itself against the methods of scholarship in Japan (which, let us note, Takeuchi saw as virtually identical to the methods employed by Japanese literature), which in the manipulation of various research objects remained shut off from the wealth of possibilities opened up by this latter, for these possibilities naturally threatened or placed in question one's own identity as subject. Takeuchi was not surprisingly attacked for his readings on the part of scholars who, recognizing his critique of objectification, accused him conversely of "subjectifying" his scholarship, that is, of sacrificing intellectual detachment for the sake of his own self-interests. Thus his work *Ro Jin* was seen by many as having in a certain sense less to do with Lu Xun than with Takeuchi himself.[3] However, such attacks reveal their true nature when one understands that the subject and object are, far from being mutually exclusive, in fact correlative with one another, that in other words the object is necessarily an *object* for a *subject*. It was primarily in order to call this relationship into question, we believe, that Takeuchi first turns to philosophy. This approach can be seen most visibly in his early works, where he attempts, in what is really an extraordinary gesture, to bring the thought of Nishida Kitarō to bear on the various problematics that emerged in his readings of Japanese and Chinese literary texts.[4] By thus introducing a range of philosophical concerns to literary discourse, Takeuchi hoped to provoke a manner of questioning which would go beyond mere inquiry into the object to include reflection on the very grounds of such inquiry. Only in this way could literature be released from the hold of a scholarship that, despite or rather precisely because of its prodigious attention to literary phenomena in

---

3. This attitude can be glimpsed even in the English-language scholarship on Takeuchi. Thus Lawrence Olson writes, in what is otherwise a fine introduction to Takeuchi's life and thought, "*Rojin* is the book of a young man not yet very sure of himself. Why [Takeuchi] found himself in Lu Xun is not entirely clear, but seems to have been an accident of his education and his travels as much as anything else." *Ambivalent Moderns: Portraits of Japanese Cultural Identity* (Savage, Maryland: Rowman & Littlefield, 1992), p. 53.
4. Takeuchi recounts this move in a 1975 autobiographical essay titled "Waga kaisō," in *TYz*, vol. 13, p. 263.

a restricted sense (authors, genres, movements, techniques, influences, etc.), yet remained utterly indifferent to the ways in which literature might also *resist* such phenomenologization. However, it is important to point out that this introduction of philosophy to literature was in no way an incorporation of something that existed simply outside of literature to begin with. Indeed, the thematization that so powerfully governed literary discourse in Japan was for Takeuchi *already* reflective of a certain philosophical interpretation of the world, however hidden or implicit. What was thus required was the making-explicit of this prior interpretation, for in so doing another relation to literature and the world might be allowed to come forth.

More generally, however, Takeuchi's resistance to the conventions of Japanese scholarship represented a resistance against modernity itself, which in turn must be understood as a form of resistance against the West. As with many other thinkers of his time, both inside and outside Japan, Takeuchi saw the emergence of modernity as principally grounded upon a crystallization of dualistic modes of thought, in which such differences as those between self and other, body and mind, etc. came now to be determined strictly in oppositional fashion. For Takeuchi, one of the most significant of these oppositions was that between East and West, which itself was historically indivisible from the opposition between the premodern (or feudal) and the modern. In modernity, he argued, the West first came into being as a kind of disembodied self that opposed itself to the "Orient," which was thereby reduced to the status of spiritless (or material) premodern other. Here we see that the fundamental change in man's relation to the world, which is now conceived in the barest or most impoverished of terms as a subject confronting ob-jects that stand against it, is essentially related to the modern West's colonial violence against the East. It is in this sense that Takeuchi determines the modern period as the process of the West's self-formation, a self-formation that is effected by the gradual absorption or appropriation of the alterity of the non-West.[5]

To speak of Takeuchi's texts under the heading of "displacing the West," then, is to suggest that his thought must be understood on both a historical and philosophical level. It is historical in that Takeuchi seeks at all times to respond to the exigencies of his present situation. Yet this situation was of course rooted in a past that for him was most immediately marked by the West's violence against the East in its ongoing westernization, or modernization, of the world. We have tried in the following pages to sketch out what was at stake in Takeuchi's response to this East-West problematic by following, as attentively as possible, the movement of his thinking in all the richness of its nuances and implications. Naturally there

---

5. For Asia's response to this movement of appropriation, see for example the 1957 essay "Ajia ni okeru shinpo to handō: Nihon no shisōteki jōkyō ni terashite," in *TYz*, vol. 5, pp. 57-81.

were other very specific historical situations within which Takeuchi found himself caught up and which he sought to address, as for instance Japan-China relations in the postwar era or the debate around "national literature" that took place in the 1950s. Although we discuss Takeuchi's thinking of some of these topics and events, at times quite extensively, we have nevertheless chosen to focus our primary attention on this question of the East-West relation. Here it will always be a matter of seeking to undo this relation by displacing the very terms upon which it is founded. And yet it must be forewarned that such displacement is *not* effected simply in view of a historical reversal of the East over the West—as Takeuchi himself, if we can say this, both knew and did not know. Rather what is required is a more fundamental and indeed more critical rethinking of these terms so as to not merely reproduce the cycle of East-West power relations.

Such a more fundamental thinking, let us emphasize, must begin where empirical understandings of history necessarily leave off. Because this latter fails to submit to any rigorous questioning the conceptual tools with which it analyzes historical data, it invariably repeats, in one form or another, the East-West power dynamic. This explains in part why we have not modeled our reading of Takeuchi on the various forms of historiography so common in the field of Asian Studies, whether this be biography, contextual studies, or the more sophisticated commentaries of intellectual history. Our interest in history has rather led us to seek out those points in Takeuchi's text where thinking may be said to *first open up* to historical singularity, which in our view is the most urgent and forceful manner of historical thinking. No doubt this approach will expose us to charges of formalism from various critics in the field. We hope to pursue this debate elsewhere, but in defense let it here suffice for us to declare that our intent is to do nothing more than draw out or elaborate upon Takeuchi's own sustained critique of *sekaishi*, or "world history," in all the falseness of its limited universalism.[6] The need to rethink history on a more originary basis than that provided by empiricist historiography emerges for us at precisely this point.

It is in this context that Takeuchi's attention to the historical may be said to touch upon something like philosophy. For the displacement of the West that Takeuchi undertakes in his textual practice creates a kind of domino effect in which many of the major concepts historically linked with the West (through which the West identifies *both* itself *and* its other) come to be unsettled. Chief among these are the concepts of subjectivity, theory,

---

6. For more recent critiques of "world history," in which the attention to historical singularity pursues paths that very much resemble our own, see Takahashi Tetsuya, *Kioku no echika: sensō, tetsugaku, Auschwitz* (Tokyo: Iwanami Shoten, 1995), pp. 175-236; and Sakai Naoki and Nishitani Osamu, *"Sekaishi" no kaitai: honyaku, shutai, rekishi* (Tokyo: Ibunsha, 1999), pp. 225-303.

experience, feeling and alterity, to name only the most important. It must be borne in mind that Takeuchi's critique of the West—and so by extension of Japan, which he viewed as now almost thoroughly westernized—was articulated on the basis of a more immediate experience of the world, and especially of other people. This experience was one of overwhelming *anxiety* for the self, since in its encounters it was forced to suffer the difference that the world presented to it. Before all else, Takeuchi maintained, this difference was registered corporeally; it marked the self as situated in a place that was not of its own making, thereby binding it to other things and other people in ways that exceeded the limits of its conscious understanding. In order to think this binding in all of its strange force, Takeuchi sought to reconceive the self not as the traditional subject of epistemology (*shukan*) but rather, far less grandly, as *shutai*, or what can be translated here as the agent of praxis. The effects of such a reconceptualization can in no way be exaggerated, and we have tried throughout our reading to give them their proper weight. In our view, Takeuchi's resistance to modernity and its entire conceptual apparatus can only begin to be understood by taking into account the enormity of the stakes involved in this transition from knowledge to action.

What Takeuchi once wrote of Lu Xun can very much be applied to himself, as he too perhaps was aware: "Lu Xun is not what one might call a 'thinker.' It is extremely difficult to extract (*toridasu*) his thought in the sense of an object (*kyakutai*), for there is nothing systematic (*taikeiteki*) about him."[7] This difficulty of extraction derives from the fact that things do not exist in isolation, but rather are what they are only by virtue of their position within a more general space, one which consists of an ever shifting series of elements. The act of extraction therefore effects an irreversible change upon things, it introduces them to a completely different and new set of elements with which they are now forced to participate. Thus in our reading of Takeuchi, we have tried to underscore that which in his thought refuses any simple extraction of it, for this thinking can in no way be reduced to a set of clear-cut themes or concepts. At the same time, however, the response to Takeuchi that a reading of his text entails cannot but produce a change in that very text itself. In contrast to the still dominant belief that thinkers of the past can only be understood in the identity of their thought, or perhaps in the identity of their immediate historical context, we have attempted what can only be called an *engagement* with Takeuchi's thinking. The necessity for such an engaged reading comes from Takeuchi himself, as much from his determination of man as being fundamentally engaged with, or tied to, the world, as from his own highly distinct manner of interpretation in which the limits of detachment and objectification come disturbingly

---

7. "Shisōka toshite no Ro Jin," in *TYz*, vol. 1, p. 158. First published in 1949.

to the fore. Doubtless these two aspects are inseparable, but what we would also like to point out here is that this notion of engagement is essentially directed toward the future. To be involved in the world is to in effect submit oneself to a future that produces transformation. Taking its cue from Takeuchi, an engaged reading of his text must accept and even, we believe, *embrace* the fact that there is no way to avoid such transformation, that change takes place in the very response of the future to its past. However, this does not in the least mean that the interpretive act is thus released from the hold of past texts; in other words, that now anything goes. Directly to the contrary, it means that the text assumes infinitely greater importance than it does in traditional scholarship, where it is reduced, as we indicated, to the mere status of object. In order to truly engage Takeuchi's thinking, then, his text cannot be taken at face value, but must instead be minutely scrutinized so as to uncover its hidden logic, its hesitations and—what is no less important—its inconsistencies.[8] For this reason, we have on occasion been forced to give certain passages and statements in Takeuchi's text what might appear to be an inordinate amount of weight, and yet this was done so as to bring forth as fully as possible the depth of meanings contained therein. Like Lu Xun, Takeuchi is not a systematic thinker.[9] But this lack of systematicity should not deceive us into treating his text lightly, for it is much more a question of learning to apprehend his thought in ways that do justice to its complexity, not despite but precisely because of its resistance to systematic understanding. The series of individual readings that we have undertaken here represents our attempt to allow some of that complexity to begin to come forth.

---

8. As Derrida writes, "If deconstruction is possible, this is because it mistrusts any sort of periodization and moves, or makes its gestures, lines and divisions move, not only within the corpus in general, but at times within a single sentence, or a microscopic element of a corpus. Deconstruction mistrusts proper names: it will not say 'Heidegger in general' says thus or so; it will deal, in the micrology of the Heideggerian text, with different moments, different applications, concurrent logics, while trusting no generality and no configuration that is solid and given. It is a sort of great earthquake, a general tremor, which nothing can calm. I cannot treat a corpus, or a book, as a coherent whole, and even the simple statement is subject to fission. At bottom, this is perhaps what writing is." Jacques Derrida and Maurizio Ferraris, *A Taste for the Secret*, trans. Giacomo Donis (Malden, Massachusetts: Polity Press, 2001), p. 9.

9. In so saying, however, it should be noted that recognition of his work can be found in the *Tetsugaku shisō jiten*, ed. Hiromatsu Wataru et al. (Tokyo: Iwanami Shoten, 1998), p. 1030.

Acknowledgments

This book owes a considerable debt both to the work and friendship of Naoki Sakai, and I am happy to record my gratitude here. Brett de Bary, Victor Koschmann and Karen Brazell provided wisdom and encouragement throughout my graduate career, and I consider myself fortunate to have studied with them. Sincere thanks go to Kyoko Selden for her expert suggestions regarding translations. Tom Lamarre, who acted as one of the book's reviewers, offered valuable criticisms and comments; the work is better as a result.

I am grateful to my colleagues in both the Asian Studies Program and the Department of Foreign Languages and Literatures at the City College of New York for their kind support. Despite her extremely busy schedule, Carol Gluck has unstintingly given of her time, energy and sagacity, and for this I am thankful. The Japan Society for the Promotion of Science provided me with a generous postdoctoral fellowship in Tokyo, during which time part of the manuscript was rewritten. Finally, I would like to thank Madge Huntington of the East Asian Institute at Columbia University for her institutional support of the manuscript; and Karen Smith at the Cornell East Asia Program for her assistance in preparing the text for publication.

The book is dedicated, with great warmth and affection, to M.

An earlier version of chapter three appeared in *positions: east asia cultures critique* 8:2 (Fall 2000). The Introduction was first published in the journal *Gendai shisō* 29:8 (July 2001) under the title "Takeuchi Yoshimi ni okeru teikō no mondai."

INTRODUCTION
Resistance and Translation: The Question of the Institution

In the United States as well as elsewhere, the institution of Asian Studies can be seen to be structured by a broad epistemological framework in which the Asian object of knowledge is opposed, more or less straightforwardly, by the western subject of knowledge. The western scholar writes on Asia, and in this way Asia comes to be presented to the West. Historically, this presentation has enabled a kind of self-reflection on the part of the West, which comes to understand itself in negative fashion as that which Asia is not. What this means, ultimately, is that no West can truly be said to have preceded the course of this self-reflection, that western identity first came into being by virtue of such reflection. In the necessary dependence of self-reflection upon reflection of an other, external entity, we can see that subjective identity is strangely divided from itself: the essential oneness and unity of the West which distinguishes it from all other entities is found to be present not within the West itself but rather within the Asia that opposes it, or at the very least within the relation that the West maintains with this outside. Which is to say, to speak paradoxically, that what is most proper to the West is its very impropriety, its alterity vis-à-vis itself. The notion of western identity does not have its source in a unified space called the West. Directly to the contrary, this notion refers most originally to a multiplicity of spaces, spaces which appear to be negated in the coming into being of the West qua West. Of course this is not to say that the notion of the West is simply senseless or absurd, a matter of false consciousness, as it were; only that the unity or oneness that is represented through it derives in its entirety from that which belongs properly outside of it. Only by denying that outside is this notion of the West at all intelligible.

1

It will be clear in the following pages just how much such type of thinking owes to the postwar Japanese thinker and sinologist Takeuchi Yoshimi, all of whose writings touch in one form or another upon this central question of the relation between the West and its outside. Even our concern with the representation of this relation by academic institutions or disciplines can be said to echo in a particular way Takeuchi's own concern. In for example the 1961 essay "Hōhō toshite no Ajia" [Asia as Method], Takeuchi attacks what he calls the "dead scholarship" of Japanese sinology, which, as he critically writes of his own research before the war, took as its "aim the [mere] rectification of the gaps and errors in knowledge of China on the part of the Japanese people."[1] What is so revealing in this statement are the words *Nihonjin no Chūgoku ni taisuru ninshiki*, or, literally, "the knowledge of China on the part of the Japanese people." Specifically, Takeuchi desires to call attention here to the oppositionality (*ni taisuru*) characteristic of the operation of knowledge, the fact that an entity must in some sense posit (or position) the other as existing *against* or *toward* itself so that it may come into presence and assume meaning. Prior to this positing the other exists strictly outside of the subject; its difference or alterity is not of the nature of oppositionality, which represents rather the active transformation of itself at the hands of the subject. In this instance, it is the positing of China in *tai suru* fashion—and here we may glimpse the essential relation between positionality and oppositionality—that first effects the presentation of this other qua China. And so as well, of course, the presentation of the subject Japan qua Japan. Precisely as we remarked in the case of the West, neither Japan nor China can be said to preexist this moment. Significantly, Takeuchi attempts to explain this act of presentation on the part of the knowing subject through the opposition between life and death. For him, the coming into presence of the object, or its being as such, is equivalent to death—and in this respect, his remark on the "dead scholarship" of sinology reveals itself to be far more than just a metaphor. The other is most full of life when its difference is given free play, when it is allowed the greatest range of movement so as to become virtually anything. This protean quality of the other is what above all constitutes its force, a force which is for Takeuchi literally its life-force. (And we should point out in this connection that both of these terms, "life" (*seikatsu*) and "force" (*chikara*), appear constantly and in privileged fashion throughout Takeuchi's writings). It is this force of alterity that works to disrupt the simple opposition between the subject and object of knowledge, whether in the institution of Japanese sinology or that of Asian Studies as practiced in the so-called "West." By necessity, the other's vital difference from the subject exceeds all attempts

---

1. In *Takeuchi Yoshimi hyōronshū* (Tokyo: Chikuma Shobō, 1973), vol. 3, p. 400 (hereafter referred to as *TYh*).

at its objectification. Takeuchi will even suggest that the subject's activity of presenting this other in object form takes place only derivatively, as a response to the force that this other first exerts upon the subject, and which the subject receives or suffers primarily passively. In which case, a fundamental distinction must be made between the object as it is presented to us by institutions and that underlying difference or alterity which is its rightful source, that to which it must always refer. A scholarship which neglects this distinction and focuses only on the object before it, whose identity appears in its eyes to be self-evident, would be, following Takeuchi's terminology, dead. Life, conversely, would suggest an acute sensitivity to this distinction between objectivity and alterity so as to most fully allow oneself to be affected by the difference that inheres within the object.

Nevertheless, the complexity of the issue here cannot merely be reduced to a matter of decision on the part of the scholar between life and death. For it seems certain that violence is an unavoidable part of all institutional knowledge. In other words, if life is to be associated with the force of alterity of the other, then it can never be a question of a pure or absolute reception of this alterity: in the very instant of this reception by the subject, the other dies. Death would be another name for the instant of contact between the force of alterity and the surface of the subject which it strikes. Unquestionably this death is in part the subject's, and it is indeed what constantly opens the subject up to its outside, thereby disrupting what Takeuchi will call "the process of subjective formation."[2] And yet it is just as clearly the death of the other, since the subject cannot but effect a change upon or addition to this other in its desire to appropriate it unto itself, thereby re-marking the other as its own. The force of the other marks the subject as belonging to the world, to the outside, but at the same time this outside allows itself to be registered by the subject in a further instance of marking. We can perhaps describe this remarking by the subject in terms of violence: it is, precisely, a violent response to the world's violence. Now in his attack against the "dead scholarship" of sinology, Takeuchi will at a certain point appeal to a notion of life that he believes escapes the violence inherent in the relation between the subject and its other. This notion of life as somehow existing outside of violence emerges in stark contrast to other instances in Takeuchi's text, in which he very openly recognizes and attempts to theorize what may be called the generality of violence as characteristic of man's situatedness in the world and history. In this sense, the subject's violence against alterity is not so much condemned for its injustice as it is opened up to the world's own violence, that is to say, it is shown to be inscribed within the totality of relations of force. This gesture enables Takeuchi to still speak of the subject and the world without simply (or immediately) collapsing the

---

2. Ibid., p. 420.

former into the latter, such as would imply a notion of the absolute "as the night in which," as Hegel famously writes, "all cows are black."[3] And yet the critical force that the notion of life represents will be filled in and given a name by Takeuchi: against or even behind the calcified knowledge of sinology there thus appear actually living Chinese persons. Life, says Takeuchi, is equivalent to people, and in the case of sinology that life naturally refers to Chinese people.[4]

Clearly it is at this point that we would have to part ways with Takeuchi, and yet it would not be fruitless to sketch out (a necessarily rough sketch, since this problematic is elaborated in detail in the body of our work, and we intend in this Introduction to do no more than signal its importance) the logic that leads him to set forth this notion of life as opposed to death. This logic is in fact part and parcel of his notion of "resistance," which in the context of modernity and the historical emergence of the West is also referred to more specifically as "Oriental resistance."[5] Resistance is for Takeuchi necessarily resistance against death, not in the sense of biological death, of course, but rather more generally as the passage—or even fall—from the concrete to the abstract. Japanese sinology is dead because it contents itself with examining the remains of a China that is otherwise vibrant with life. It forgets that the proper origin of these remains is life itself, as embodied in actually living Chinese people. In this way, the opposition between life and death comes into focus for Takeuchi as the distinction between actual or concrete presence and the abstract doubling of such presence in the form of re-presentation. The life that is presence meets its death in the subject's representation of presence, or rather representation seems to take place by violently eliminating the presence of the other in such a way that it can be maintained henceforth in less threatening fashion, at a safe remove from itself, as it were. We can see here that the stakes of Takeuchi's argument go well beyond the institution of Japanese sinology; what he is in fact targeting is the notion of representation itself. In his view, representation succeeds only at the cost of violence to the other, a violence which takes the specific form of erasure. It is in order to preserve the integrity of the other, to protect it from the injurious appropriation by the subject, that Takeuchi sets forth the notion of resistance in the first place. In the face of

---

3. G.W.F. Hegel, *Phenomenology of Spirit*, trans. A.V. Miller (Oxford: Oxford University Press, 1977), p. 9.

4. Thus we can understand the accusation of humanism that certain critics have leveled against Takeuchi, as for example Kan Takayuki in *Takeuchi Yoshimi ron: Ajia e no hanka* (Tokyo: Sanichi Shobō, 1976), p. 251. It should be noted, however, that Takeuchi himself tirelessly criticized this same humanism throughout his works.

5. This notion is most fully worked out in the 1948 essay "Kindai towa nanika (Nihon to Chūgoku no baai)," in *TYz*, vol. 4, pp. 128-171. For this reason, as well as the fact that this essay represents in our view Takeuchi's most rigorous and sustained attempt to set forth his thought, we have accorded it a particular privilege throughout our reading.

the subject's work of objectification, the other resists. This means that the other is radically irreducible to its being as object, that it on the contrary overwhelms or overflows all attempts by the subject to thematize it within the frame of knowledge. "Oriental resistance" designates the excess of what is called the Orient vis-à-vis the subject West, just as in the case of Japanese sinology (which remains governed by an epistemological framework that belongs wholly to the West—and this as well should teach us that the West is *not* a geopolitical entity) something escapes in the acquisition of representational knowledge of China. If however Takeuchi wishes to call attention to the desire for presence that underlies such representational knowledge (and this would be an extremely strange desire, insofar as it attempts to realize itself through eliminating in an act of violence that for which it aims the better to acquire it), he at the same time seeks to locate this presence at its very heart. Sinology, in other words, desires a presence that is attenuated by its own acts of representation, with the result that it attains a China that is already dead. Resistance takes place in the refusal of concrete human life to be completely sublated in the form of abstract knowledge: this knowledge would be no more than the abandoned shell of the other, whereas its heart—the word is Takeuchi's[6]—would reside elsewhere, strictly beyond its grasp. In contrast, Takeuchi's attempt to determine the site of resistance as actually living people reveals a desire to bypass the mediation of representation altogether so as to attain life pure and simple. It is at this point that the negative force contained in the notion of resistance can be said to give way to something like the desire for immediacy.

We could perhaps have already anticipated the emergence of this desire for immediacy in Takeuchi's formulation of the relation between life and death in the context of knowledge on the basis of oppositionality. Life opposes death in such a way that resistance must always side with life. Which is to say that resistance is to be located in the refusal of representation in favor of that presence which stands opposed to it, a presence the relation to which is strictly immediate. Takeuchi's criticism of the representational knowledge that underlies Japanese sinology and reinforces the transferential relation between subject and object is a quite powerful one, and there is no question that his remarks are wholly relevant to the institution of Asian Studies as it exists today in the United States and elsewhere. Yet it would be irresponsible on our part not to call attention to what is after all a profound tendency in his thought toward romanticism. This romanticism expresses itself of course not simply in the appeal to a people's heart but instead, much more radically, in what Philippe Lacoue-Labarthe and Jean-Luc Nancy refer to when they write that "[t]he goal is to have done with parti-

---

6. "Hōhō toshite no Ajia," p. 400. For Takeuchi, this notion of heart can thus be seen to be equivalent to those of life and people.

tion and division, with the separation constitutive of history."[7] For Takeuchi, in short, there can be seen an attempt to *overcome* the division inherent in the subject-object relation so as to enter into a relation with the other that is as yet of the nature of wholeness and unity. If the relation between subject and object takes place by way of mediation, then resistance against it may it seems be legitimately erected in the name of im-mediacy. Now what we must not fail to underscore here is the importance of Takeuchi's insight into the derivativeness of objective knowledge: this knowledge has its source not in itself but in an other which both precedes and exceeds it. With this insight the very structure of Japanese sinology is potentially shaken, it can now be confronted with its own lack of foundations. Yet in order for this upheaval to take place as forcefully as possible, it seems necessary to go beyond any desire for immediate presence, thereby allowing the origin or source of knowledge to retreat from its determination in actual human life and so assume its rightful negativity. In this way, the notion of resistance would not simply gesture toward a presence that lies concealed behind a representationalism that it refuses but instead—following now a different strand of Takeuchi's text—toward a "groundlessness" that remains irrevocably other to any of its determinations.

It would not be difficult to imagine how easily an attack against sinology in favor of a notion of actual Chinese life and people could be appropriated by the institution. Conceivably the discipline of anthropology would emerge as the site in which China is most faithfully represented—or rather, since it can now no longer be a question of mere representation, anthropology would announce itself as the site in which one receives most fully and immediately the imprinting force of the other. Let us remark that such a conclusion regarding the priority of anthropology has a relatively long history in the human sciences, not only in Japan but in Europe and the United States as well. And yet it does not necessarily follow that this privileging of actual human life is best reflected in the discipline of anthropology. In the institution of Asian Studies in the United States, for example, other disciplines have produced scholars whose criticisms of this institution (criticisms which were absolutely crucial given the general antipathy toward such work, an antipathy that can be seen of course even today) were set forth on the basis of very similar concerns. For Takeuchi, interestingly enough, it is literature that is capable of expressing most profoundly the concrete life of a people.[8] But regardless of which discipline is found to capture or in some way allow itself to be informed by the life of the other, the question remains

---

7. *The Literary Absolute: The Theory of Literature in German Romanticism*, trans. Philip Barnard and Cheryl Lester (Albany: State University of New York Press, 1988), p. 11.
8. This point is argued, for instance, in the 1957 essay "Son Bun kan no mondaiten," in *TYh*, vol. 3, pp. 321 ff.

as to whether they do not accomplish precisely that which the institution itself sets out to do. In this respect, we may note that the desire for presence is fundamentally no different from the desire for the representation of presence. Even more, it can perhaps be said that the institution in its very representationalism has come to terms with the fact of death in a way that the various criticisms directed against it have not, or at least have not yet (and there would be some notable exceptions to this). In so saying, we do not by any means wish to defend the institution from its critics; rather we would like to point out a certain trap that these latter have in many cases not yet sufficiently taken into account.

In the final analysis, resistance against "dead scholarship" in the name of concrete human life can never fully succeed in escaping from oppositional logic. As we have seen in Takeuchi, this logic involves a radical distinction between the values of life, presence, immediacy and the concrete and those of death, representation, mediation and the abstract. Takeuchi's notion of resistance is of great import in thinking the ultimate impossibility of representation, and with this the overwhelming of the subject in the face of the other. What this notion fails to do, however, is take into account the necessity of the change or passage from one binary series to the next. Let us refer here to the necessity of this passage in terms of the notion of translation. With this notion, the movement from life to death need not simply be condemned out of hand, for in this case understanding is all too quickly sacrificed, with the result that a spirit of nostalgia comes increasingly to pervade one's criticism.[9] This nostalgia would be for a lost presence, one that was corrupted in an act of violence by an external force that is thus viewed as essentially improper to it. Hence the representation of China by the institution of sinology signifies an unequivocal fall from Chinese life as it is actually lived by Chinese people. In this way, death is considered to be entirely foreign to life. A thinking which grounded itself on life would likewise be forced to exclude this phenomenon of death from itself; the most it could say is that death is that which life is not, and therein of course lies its evil. And yet it is possible to think of the notion of translation as encompassing within itself both life and death: translation, indeed, would not merely align itself with either of these poles as such but rather seek to explain the *possibility of relation* between them. Paradoxically enough, this relation is by right prior to the emergence of these poles themselves. By focusing on this relation, the notion of translation is able to explain why life is in fact always penetrated by death, just as death is inescapably infused with life.

---

9. Nakagawa Ikurō refers to such a sense of nostalgia in some of Takeuchi's works in *Takeuchi Yoshimi no bungaku to shisō* (Tokyo: Orijin, 1985), pp. 27 ff.

Can there be any question that Takeuchi's appeal to actually living Chinese persons is an attempt to respect the singularity of the other, to very nobly guard it against appropriation by institutional knowledge? Yet it is necessary here to speak of something like a twofold impossibility. With his elaboration of the notion of resistance, Takeuchi astutely theorizes the ultimate impossibility of such knowledge. If representation reveals itself to be impossible, however, so too does the notion of pure or absolute respect for the other's singularity. For essential reasons, violence is done to the other in the very act of receiving it by the subject. Or rather: violence *inheres within* the space of the other in its singularity, it is what makes the other properly singular, that is, each time different from itself. Only because the other is fundamentally other to itself can translation take place, not as a fall from one entity into another but instead as an *opening up* of this entity to its "own" "internal" difference. In this respect, translation reveals itself to be nothing other than the movement of decontextualization; it is a radical departure away from a concrete site of origin to a place of abstraction, abstract because it doesn't properly belong there. (And the consequences of this insight for any rigorous thinking of history are enormous). Translation takes place as an event by concrete presence somehow dividing itself from itself, drifting away from its anchor in the singular here and now and becoming different, other and new. This alteration of the origin we have called death, but in a sense that goes beyond what Takeuchi intends by this word. If the institution in its representationalism does not hesitate to acknowledge this fact of death, however, this is actually due to its desire to hold on to its own life. The death of the other is after all what gives it life, preserves it as such. In which case, it becomes an urgent task to show how the translation that irrevocably alters the other subordinates the subject to itself as well.

1. Literature and its Dangers

The task is to change the very notions of literature and man.
—Takeuchi Yoshimi, "Bungaku ni okeru dokuritsu towa nanika"

In this opening chapter, I examine Takeuchi's understanding of literature in terms of the classical distinction between transcendence and immanence. Takeuchi's attack against the Japanese literary establishment is read here as an attempt to think literature in some sense outside of the division between a transcendent idea of literature and those particular literary instances that appear in its name. This division, it is argued, imposes a fixed directionality upon literary history: concrete works of literature are seen as entirely derivative of this transcendent idea, toward which they moreover naturally tend in their desire to emulate or imitate it, such as to become in the future that which they most originally were in the past. The result of this division is a deprivileging of the literary work in all its worldliness and immediacy. In order to think the work as belonging most properly to the world as opposed to the idea, then, it becomes necessary to show why this idea is unable to maintain itself in its transcendent perfection in the course of its translation into the world. As transcendent, the idea of literature is held to be *responsible for* those imperfect literary instances that appear in the world. This responsibility of course establishes the hierarchical relation between the idea and the work; at the same time, however, the responsibility for imperfection on the part of the otherwise perfect idea is found to corrupt this very perfection, hence endangering the unity of the idea. In other words, the relation between the literary idea and the world and work is revealed to affect not only these latter but the idea as well: just as the world receives the idea, or is imprinted by it, so too is the idea forced to take into itself the world. The consequence of this, Takeuchi realizes, is that literature must be fundamentally reconceived along the lines of its worldliness. More

9

specifically, this reconceptualization means that man's relation to the literary work is to be understood most immediately in terms of *feeling* as opposed to *knowledge*. While the quite radical effects of this rethinking of literature are carefully drawn out, attention is also paid to a certain danger in Takeuchi's notion of literature. Here I try to show how the reaction against transcendence leads, somewhat predictably, to an immanentist view of literature. This notion of literary immanence, I maintain, is necessarily of a piece with Takeuchi's very problematic notion of "national literature."

THE *BUNDAN* AND THE WORK OF LITERARY TRANSLATION

For Takeuchi, the degeneration of literature begins from the moment of its institutionalization, when literature is removed from the immediacy of its production and submitted to the rules of a discourse that is in some sense inessential, and even foreign, to it. This is why literature is not to be confused with what is called *bundan bungaku*, or the "literature of the literary establishment": taking as its initial point of departure the question "What is literature?," the *bundan* sets for itself the task of determining the universal idea of literature, which then acts as the standard against which all particular literary works are to be judged. The *bundan*, which Takeuchi describes as a "special guild-like society," in which "participation is impossible without the official recognition of fixed qualifications,"[1] operates by bringing forth those literary instances which, however imperfectly, instantiate what has been previously identified as the proper being of literature. This it does through its works of fiction as well as its literary criticism. Here we must immediately point out that Takeuchi's criticisms of the *bundan* are not motivated by a simple wish to call attention to those works and methods which are illegitimately excluded by the ideal standards employed by this "society," for he doubtless realizes that such criticism harbors within itself, more or less explicitly, the desire for recognition from—and so, in fact, appropriation by or within—the very institution against which resistance (*teikō*) is articulated. Rather than setting up another, more inclusive standard of literature which stands opposed to *bundan bungaku*, Takeuchi attempts first of all to place in question the possibility of determining the idea of literature itself. In other words, the gesture taken here cannot merely be understood as a theoretical staking out of position with the goal of overturning that determination of literature alongside of which one's own theory originally exists and asserts itself, as if in competition. Much more radically, Takeuchi tries to move behind or, in some sense, before the moment that literature is seen

---

1. "Bungaku ni okeru dokuritsu towa nanika," in *TYz*, vol. 7, p. 77. Originally published in 1954.

qua literature, thereby examining the ground upon which alone literature first gives itself to be objectively or theoretically determined.

It is in this sense that Takeuchi, when discussing the question of national literature, writes that "I did not wish to make this issue a *topic* (*topikku*) of the *bundan*."[2] For the *bundan*, in its constant concern to, literally, topicize literature, to reveal it or determinately locate it, fails to grasp what is nevertheless "the origin of literature," what Takeuchi refers to in "Seikatsu to bungaku" [Life and Literature] as "the complexity of the life of feeling."[3] At issue here is the withdrawal of literature from all determinations that implicitly presuppose an idea of literature which itself transcends the world, and which is thus fundamentally divorced or cut off from the immediacy of life—a life that, significantly, Takeuchi links to feeling. Literature, he forcefully insists, cannot be isolated from the world. And yet the *bundan*, in its conceptual determination of the literary, refers all particular or concrete works of literature away from the world back to an abstract and logically prior idea of literature that governs, in its transcendence, the literary object. Although literature, in its ideal purity, subjects all worldly literary instances to itself, it remains, by virtue of its transcendence of the world, yet more real than the literary works that we encounter everyday in all their sensual concreteness. For these works are ultimately mere appearances of the idea of literature; they are the body, changing and multiple—and for this reason not fully real—that manifests in its phenomenality the soul or spirit which itself remains inaccessible. However much the work embodies literature in its expressivity, it can in no way become one with it, since the work's very corporeality renders it imperfect. Although literature gives itself nowhere else but in the world, this world is nevertheless reduced to a medium or passageway through which literature may be glimpsed in the fullness of its reality and perfection. In this way, the relationship between the actual literary work and the transcendent idea of literature shows itself to be a relationship of reflection: the work, to the extent that it is literary, that it belongs within the proper sphere that marks itself as literature, must mimetically reflect this idea. It must strive to copy the original which, precisely, does not exist. Ideally, the goal of the work is to efface its own worldliness and express, in as transparent a fashion as possible, the purity of its literary idea. Although the work is required so that literature may give itself phenomenally, then, it also represents a danger to that idea, since the work may always, in its status as reflection, imitate the original poorly or badly. Indeed, if the propriety of the work depends upon its reflection of an ideal literature, a reflection which constrains it to remain always in view or

---

2. "Bungaku no jiritsusei nado," in *TYz*, vol. 7, p. 57. (Originally published in 1952). Emphasis ours.
3. In *TYh*, vol. 2, p. 297. Originally published in 1953.

in light of (*ni terashite*) this idea, it is nonetheless equally true that the work itself retains a certain freedom in the possibility that it may, for whatever reason, misreflect literature. This possibility of misreflection—which, let us repeat, marks the work's freedom—rests less upon any kind of willful or knowing insurrection against the idea of literature than upon the fact of the work's existence, that is to say, its fundamental status as in the world. In which case, freedom must be understood not as a subjective quality that, in this instance, points ultimately to the self-determination or volition of the work's author as an autonomous agent; rather, lifted from the sphere of subjectivity altogether, it names something like a prior moment of abandonment to the world on the part of the work, a freedom from both the idea and the authorial subject which attests to the immediacy with which the work, as a body (a "corpus," as one says), confronts the materiality of the world. It is the work's freedom, which rightly begins as the freedom of the idea to place itself anywhere in the world, hence submitting all matter to itself in the force of its imprinting or stamping, that eventually exposes the unintended dependence of the idea upon the world and the work.

This strange dependence upon the work puts literature in a very precarious position. In the first place, it seems to be entirely unnecessary: if the idea is perfect, fully real, why then risk the loss of this perfection in its translation from the noumenal world to the phenomenal world? This desire for expression reveals in fact a lack or deficiency within the otherwise perfect idea, for were the idea to remain entirely enclosed within its own self-sufficiency, that is, safely removed from the world in its transcendent being, it would at once lose the ability to govern over and essentially unify the multiple instances of literature that appear in its name. Its movement of self-expression demonstrates that the idea's identity and self-unity, which are of course intrinsic aspects of its perfection, actually require an outside with which the idea is in relation, and which allows it to originally be as idea. If this is so, however, then the idea's perfection must be recognized as in no way inherent to it but rather strangely reliant upon this outside, it is ultimately an effect of the relationality that the outside forces upon the idea. Furthermore, given that this translation from the noumenal world to the phenomenal world takes place from the very beginning, literature as idea—which lies behind the *bundan*'s objective determinations of literature, regardless of whether this be acknowledged or not—must invariably suffer the fate of its expressionism, which is none other than its contamination by the world over which it rules. As soon as literature opens itself to the world, then, it irrevocably sacrifices its own absolute purity qua idea and becomes dispersed, no longer able to simply reappropriate or refer back to itself in its ultimate oneness. The idea must remark itself in order to exist, yet we can see that what allows for this marking is at the same time what makes it impossible. This because, before its emergence as remark, during the interval (the between, the fold) of the "re-" that separates origin from its proper repetition or representation, difference has already seized upon the idea and distorted it, literally de-formed it to the point where it may henceforth always possibly not be recognized for what it truly is. In this sense, the remark is to be understood in terms of what is more commonly called literature's "loss in translation": most originally, literature does not suffer this loss in the passage from one national language to another;[4] instead it takes place in the hidden movement from the noumenal world to the phenomenal world from the very moment one asks the question, "What is literature?" For Takeuchi, it seems that this loss of essential order and hierarchy that characterizes, in the case of literature, the idea-work relation is thought under the name of "chaos."[5] It is this chaos, he implies, which through dissolving all restrictive determinations of literature helps restore it to its original immediacy.

Now the *bundan*'s role in all of this is to actively facilitate and safeguard the passage from literature as idea to the literary work as reflective instance of this idea. Its role, in other words, is that of the police. Since the work is always produced in view of the idea, a teleology is set in motion according to which the work is gradually raised up from its worldliness, becoming increasingly like that literature which it is essentially, if not yet fully in its outward appearance. Because this idea contains within itself a normative function, which thus reveals its practical and ethical force—for the goal must be recognized as a norm to be universally observed—the literary work *should be* produced in conformity with the idea of literature, which is in and of itself perfect. While this "should" is of course a prescriptive, it nevertheless authorizes itself on the basis of its putative status as descriptive. That is to say, it claims to describe an objective state of affairs

---

4. For, as has been shown in the case of the Japanese language, the notion of national language itself is produced as an effect of translation. This is why any analysis of translation as, specifically, interlingual translation must already presuppose what it sets out to explain. Interlingual translation represents but one, very derivative instance of translation in general. See on this point Naoki Sakai, *Translation and Subjectivity: On "Japan" and Cultural Nationalism* (Minneapolis: University of Minnesota Press, 1997), pp. 1-17; as well as the discussion between Sakai and Nishitani Osamu in *"Sekaishi" no kaitai: honyaku, shutai, rekishi*, pp. 101-151.

5. See, for example, Takeuchi's introductory remarks to his 1948 essay "Chūgoku no kindai to Nihon no kindai" (later renamed as "Kindai towa nanika (Nihon to Chūgoku no baai)") in the "Kaidai" section of *TYh*, vol. 3, p. 422.

Takeuchi Shigeaki, in his essay "Takeuchi Yoshimi: teikō no shisō," appropriately refers to this notion of chaos as "chaotic feeling." What is at stake here, he maintains, is a thinking that attempts to dissolve or unloosen the systematicity of conceptual thought. This is why Takeuchi's thinking "is not of the type that contains its own system, nor can its effectiveness be questioned in its interpretation of, or application to, reality. Rather the site of his thinking is located in precisely those 'obscure corners' eliminated by systems; it seeks to question the effectiveness of systematic thought itself through its obscure energy, as it were." *Sengo shisō e no shikaku: shutai to gengo* (Tokyo: Chikuma Shobō, 1972), pp. 149 and 157.

in which the idea of literature naturally governs the literary work, constrains it to be shaped or formed after the model of itself. The work of literature *should be* what it after all *is*, but not what it is actually; rather what it is in its ideal form. This work must not be what it is in its present state, for this state is an imperfect one, radically at odds with itself—and this is attested to, paradoxically enough, by the very presence of the *bundan*, which comes into being as a kind of symptom of the fact that this world, the world of the here and now, is not the ideal world but rather the fall therefrom. The "should" of the literary idea points decisively away from the present state of literature towards the future, where the gap between literature as it exists actually and ideally is teleologically reduced to the point of zero. This future is what governs from afar all works of the present, marking each as in principle superior to those of the past even as they themselves, with their eye toward the future (and their body in the world), fall immediately into the past and inferiority. And yet the future represents for the work nothing other than what it is most primordially, before even the separation between the noumenal world and the phenomenal world. In this sense, the progressive movement towards the future reveals itself to be in fact a return to, or restoration of, the past. Like a magnet, the literary idea pulls the work out of its aimless wandering in the present towards itself in the future. Yet this means, as Takeuchi will in effect argue against the *bundan*, that the idea cannot stand simply externally or extrinsically to the work, but must to some degree exist immanently within it. Otherwise it would be impossible to explain the force behind the work's obsessive attraction to and ambition for the possibility of its own self-improvement, that is to say, its own self-reduction. The work must work against itself as it is directed purposefully into the future. This activity, which is in fact the most proper to it—since it is what leads beyond itself to the source of its truth and propriety—consists in gradually eliminating from itself the non-literary. Because this latter only accrued to the work in its emergence in the world, however, the necessity arises of returning to itself in its ideal, i.e., non-worldly, being. In this way, the future represents a kind of compensation for the loss of the work's (ideal) past, a chance for it to regain itself as it once was and now should be. What is also revealed in this movement of restoration and return to origins, however, is a certain similarity between the *bundan*'s project and that of Takeuchi, a similarity that persists despite the enormous differences, in desire as well as in strategy, that characterize their respective approaches. Let us for the moment simply note this resemblance. In order to fully understand its ramifications, we must first grasp what Takeuchi intends by the notion of literature as well as examine the reasoning behind his criticisms of the *bundan*.

The governance of the work by the idea of literature takes place naturally; it operates, as it were, according to divine law, in principle without any intervention on the part of man. In this regard, belief in the ongoing advance of literature must be understood as but one aspect of modern man's general faith in the natural development of humanity and civilization, what Takeuchi refers to elsewhere as the "ideology of progress."[6] Progress is an ideology because it poses itself as natural: regardless of man's actions, literary history appears as the gradual approximation to the idea in time, such that all works of literature may be seen, if retrospectively, as increasingly emulative of this idea. While this movement of the work's growing perfection is a natural one—it is, after all, a movement of growth—it nevertheless encounters instances in the world that seem radically irreconcilable with the notion of progress. Such instances attest to the work's resistance in the face of the idea, and so as well to the considerable tenacity with which the work clings to the world in its materiality and alterity. Yet just as the modernists (who, as Takeuchi points out, dominate Japanese literature) were able to dismiss the atrocities of the Fifteen-Year War through recourse to a logic of exceptionalism—mere *"distortions* of Japan's modern society and culture," as he writes[7]—so too could this logic be effectively employed against those elements of literary production that seem to escape subjection to the idea: they are the exceptions which in fact prove the rule of progress. Nonetheless, the threat of the proliferation of non-literary works of literature, which show no attraction to the idea and the hope of their own self-improvement, remains always as a possibility that haunts the idea's governing force. This threat reveals the excess of the work, in its worldly existence, over the manner in which it should be. The challenge that it poses to the idea must not be underestimated: insofar as the idea's prescriptivity authorizes itself on the basis of its status as essential description, works of literature cannot be other than instantiations or reflections of the idea of literature; in the final analysis, they *should be* literary because they *are* literary. And yet the fact remains that many works are not, or rather are not judged to be, literature. Although ideality and actuality must in principle be unified, there nevertheless exists a *de facto* rift between them, one that testifies to a certain undeniable deficiency in the natural or divine order of things. Now it is precisely this deficiency that provides the *bundan* with its reason for being. The "should" of the literary idea gets its bearings from the "is"; confronted however by the violation of the natural order in the form of the non-literary work of literature (i.e., the fact that the "is" is somehow not itself), the *bundan* counters through appeal to a distinction between the noumenal world and the phenomenal world. But this distinction is a tenuous one given that any eidetic seeing of the former depends in the first instance upon the work, in all its opacity and concreteness, as its point of departure. The result of

---

6. "Kindaishugi to minzoku no mondai," in *TYh*, vol. 2, p. 280. Originally published in 1951.
7. Ibid. Emphasis ours.

this equivocality, or hesitation, on the part of being is that the "should" finds itself always possibly ungrounded, its authority placed in question by the fact that being, in what amounts to a reversal in reasoning, is not as it should be. Hence: the work should imitate the idea not because the idea represents the work's own intrinsic propriety, what it ultimately is at its source, but rather simply because it should, period. In this way, the idea's natural or objective being—which is nothing less than its status as truth—is reduced to the realm of mere subjective (*shukanteki*) determinations, none more valid than the next.

The idea's governing force, the "should" that attempts to provide direction to all actual works, is meaningful only insofar as works exist which are not properly literary. Without this general space of imperfect existence, the idea can have no room to operate, since it requires matter to shape in the form of itself. The idea, that is to say, acts (or translates) on the basis of a restricted economy which must ground itself upon a general terrain that itself, although doubtless participating in this idea, furnishing it with its realm of translatability, yet at the same time exceeds it, delimits it as restricted. Because there exists a gap between the noumenal world and the phenomenal world, the idea is allowed to operate. At the same time, it would not be too much to say that this translatability of the idea unwittingly reveals its ultimate untranslatability. For, as we have noted, the "should" which in its practical force effects this translation authorizes itself on the basis of its status as idea, and this authorization is possible, precisely, only insofar as no gap exists between the "should" and the idea. Were any difference to intervene between these two, the "should" would immediately lose its authority as agent of objective truth and fall into disrepute, since there would then be no last instance to which it could have recourse. This "should," in other words, would be faced with the threat of relativism. In order to be effective, the "should" must be undivided from the idea, and yet were this to be in fact the case it would paradoxically be smothered, or suffocated, by that idea; it would be rendered impotent by its own perfection. No translation between the literary work and the idea of literature is possible if the "should" remains entirely at one with the idea, since its consequent perfection would prevent it from interacting with existence. Such interaction takes place only by means of a departure from, or a renunciation of, perfection, despite the fact that this would mean that the "should" is no longer essentially grounded. Here there can be no question of a pure translation, for the idea can be translated into existence only by first giving itself up to the impurity of this latter. Being, in its double status as both noumenon and phenomenon, represents for the "should" something of the order (however "chaotic") of what Derrida refers to, in his reading of Plato, as *pharmakon*: it signifies both poison and remedy, at once the death of the "should" and its salvation.[8] In this sense, the relation between the "should" and the idea allows us to better understand the relation between the work and the idea. For the work must circle around the idea of literature in exactly the same way that moths circle around light: constantly attracted to this idea, to the light that it after all represents, the work must nevertheless avoid it at all costs if it is to preserve its own life and existence in the world. A kind of border exists between the work and the idea, one that the idea both respects and violates. This border ensures the possibility of literature's translation, the essential formation of the literary work in accordance with an otherwise transcendent literature, by means of rigorously maintaining the separation between origin (idea, the noumenal world) and destination (the work, the phenomenal world). The work, along with the world in which it finds itself, are kept outside of the idea by virtue of their imperfection. The pure light of this idea allows us to see that the work's sensuousness reflects its inferior status, for exclusion from this ideal space is ultimately determined on the basis of the values of transparency and opacity. Yet it would be wrong to attribute this exclusion simply to the idea's desire for self-purification. On the contrary, the idea actually requires such imperfection of the world as a moment of its self-constitution; it must, in other words, actively create the boundary which bars its outside so as to then gather itself within the unity of its inside. Doubtless this need for imperfection points to the idea's own imperfection, for were it fully perfect it would need nothing, its absolute self-autonomy would free it from the sphere of all need and want.

Once the idea excludes from itself this imperfect outside, however, it astonishingly begins the process of appropriating it back into itself, thereby holding existence to the ideal standards of the "should," imposing upon it a directionality which takes the form of a becoming—a becoming, moreover, whose narrative would be nothing other than the entirety of *bungakushi*, or "literary history."[9] From this double movement of exclusion and appropriation we can appreciate just how unusual this border between the work and the idea actually is. For borders do not simply separate two spaces from one another; as both these instances reveal, they also mark, and remark, points of crossing. But something even more important can be seen here as well: this is that such crossing takes place *prior to* all separation between determinate entities. Before the idea determines itself in its difference from the

---

8. Jacques Derrida, *Dissemination*, trans. Barbara Johnson (Chicago: University of Chicago Press, 1981), pp. 63-171.
9. Clearly it is the task of the *bundan* to write this literary history, but this writing, as Takeuchi's remark on the *bundan*'s desire to thematically "topicize" (*topikku ni suru*) literature suggests, is nothing more than a making explicit of what is already implicit or internal to the idea of literature itself. It is this that explains the *bundan*'s status as functionary, specifically functionary of the idea, for it writes only that which has already been written by that idea.

world and the work, that is to say, before the moment of its self-constitution qua idea, crossings—which the idea requires, but only on its own terms— will have already occurred in such a way as to render this distinction between self and other derivative, or secondary. Because of this priority, these crossings are marked by an essential anonymity: they produce effects upon the work and the idea, governing their economy of identity and difference (the economy of translation) by alternately tying and untying them together, making their relationship both possible and impossible. And yet these crossings operate only under cover of darkness, as it were, since the light of the idea has not yet come into being, but must rather await this textual groundwork. While these anonymous crossings effectively undermine the idea's monopoly over literature, the idea nevertheless cannot express itself in the world without them. For it must always relate itself to the work, and this relation cannot but take place as a violation of the border that maintains idea and work in their respective unity and self-identity. This very possibility of relation between distinct entities is necessarily grounded upon the crossings that precede their constitution as such. Hence the idea is placed in the extraordinary position of depending for its translation precisely upon that which makes it impossible in the first place.

Just as the work of literature circles around the idea, in-formed, literally, by the idea while yet forbidden to cross over into its space—which it however always already does, and never (this is the meaning of the "always already") on the idea's own terms—so too is this latter forced to make its home at the very margins of existence. The work depends upon the idea essentially: it "is" in its worldly existence only insofar as it reflects or manifests the proper being of literature, whose full reality infinitely outshines it, thereby relegating the work to its inferior status as mere copy of an otherworldly, or transcendent, origin. We have already noted that this privileging of the literary idea over the immediate, concrete work underlies Takeuchi's condemnation of the *bundan*, and, as we will try to show, his writings on literature constitute an attempt to redress this imbalance, so restoring what he understands to be literature's proper immediacy. Now the "should" derives its authority over the work on the basis of its proximity to the idea. Its governance over the work is possible only because, unlike the idea from which it derives, it does not pose itself as absolutely external to the work. Rather this "should," which *orders* the work—in the double sense here of "to command" and "to organize"—appears in the world along with it. The force of the "should" communicates with the work's permanent and unchanging core that subsists despite the differences that affect, in the course of its journey in the world, the corpus that the work *also* is in its shell-like corporeality. This "also" that both divides and unites the work has a very strange status. For it seems that the body which it introduces as part of the work appears almost as an afterthought, something incidental to literature.

Indeed, given that the idea of literature is in and of itself perfect, this body must be said to have befallen the idea, as if by accident—even if this accident opens the way for the entirety of "literary history." Here we can see that the idea, which falls into history—and so alterity, materiality—in fact conceives of this fall as a chance to gradually reduce the gap that separates it from the actual world. For if being is split from itself in its difference between actuality (the phenomenal world) and the idea (the noumenal world), it is the idea that attempts to tie these back together through the governing force of its "should." From this perspective, it is evident that the "should" more closely aligns itself with the idea than with actual, or phenomenal, being; this "should" imposes its force upon the matter of actual being in the name of the idea. Yet this "in the name of" testifies first and foremost to the fact that the idea must necessarily withhold itself, must keep itself at a distance—however slight and imperceptible this distance be—from the actual world if it is to preserve the integrity of its "should." For the "should" does not simply demand of actuality that it progressively raise itself up to the level of the idea, hence revealing the future to be less an opening onto radical difference than a process of continuous and ongoing formation. In order to pose itself to actuality at all, the idea must be essentially or structurally open to that actuality, it must have already descended from the realm of perfection in the address to its other. This essential openness between the idea and actuality is marked by the "should," which as a kind of middle-point between these two allows for the address of the idea to take place, and thus to be effective. Undivided from the idea, from which it derives its authority over the actual world, the "should" nevertheless belongs to this world, whose imperfection it paradoxically requires as its enabling condition. In the absence of the actual world the "should" would be indistinguishable from the idea, and there would consequently be no need for this "should" to come into being at all since there would only be ideal perfection. As we stated above, the "should" would then be suffocated by the omnipresence of being, a suffocation that it both desires and resists. The profound ambivalence with which the "should" views the idea takes the form, precisely, of an economy: in order to resist being swallowed up within the fullness of the idea, the "should" must postpone, or defer, itself. Grounded upon the idea, the "should" cannot but translate it into the world as that world's most proper being, that to which it must necessarily aspire. And yet were this translation to fully realize itself, were it to be immediate, the idea would then have no room to operate in the absolute coincidence (or communion) between ideal and actual being. That the "should" comes into being at all means that things are, literally, not as they should be. The idea's survival depends upon this state of imperfection even as it seeks to eliminate it. This elimination marks the desired *end* of the idea, the *telos* toward which it strives in the gradual reduction of actual being that shapes the course of its pursuit of perfection and full reality. Inescapably, however, this *end* also marks the very demise of the idea, for the purification of actuality, its translation into ideal form, is nothing other than the idea's own work or activity, that without which it ceases to be. In order for the idea to preserve itself, then, it paradoxically requires what it has initially set out to erase and appropriate within itself. Self-preservation, which appeared to operate in conjunction with the elimination of otherness, now reveals itself to be profoundly bound up with the preservation of this other. Situated between ideal and actual being, which it by definition must work to bring together, the "should" of the idea has no choice but to maintain itself by implementing a kind of infinite economy in which the translation of actuality into ideality is never fully completed but rather deferred to infinity. In this way, the "should" is able to satisfy its requirement to work in the name of the idea while however *preserving itself by preserving itself from* the idea.

Let us now return to our earlier remark that it is the deficiency in the natural or divine order that provides the *bundan* with its reason for being. This deficiency shows itself in the rift between ideality and actuality, from which the "should" emerges and makes its presence felt in all its practical and ethical force. Were actual being fully adequate to the idea, this "should" would have no reason to appear, its work would, so to speak, have already been done for it. The *bundan* comes into being as a concrete expression (an agent) of this "should": because its task is to gradually raise the literary work to the status of unblemished reflection of the idea of literature, its very existence attests, in negative fashion, to the fact of the world's imperfection and blemish. In this respect, let us emphasize that Takeuchi's criticism of the *bundan* is unconditional in the sense that he is concerned ultimately less with any specific literary movement or platform it might champion (as for example, the introduction of "democratic literature" by the *Shin Nihon Bungakkai* group in the postwar period)[10] than with the basic fact of its existence, an existence which he sees as characterized by the contradictory attempt to overcome history and the world from a position that cannot in truth be other than worldly and historical. The *bundan* regards its task as leading literature away from its fallen state back to its proper origin, which is not the material world but rather the transcendent idea that rules over it, orienting its movement. Yet the site of this activity remains the world. It is the world, Takeuchi asserts, within which the notion of the otherworldly, or transcendent, is first born; hypocritically, the *bundan* must acknowledge the importance of this world even as it attempts to negate it. Now the *bundan*, by virtue of its worldly existence, represents a radically different order than the idea. In principle, the relation between the idea and the concrete work of literature is a natural one. Because the work comes into being as a reflective

---

10. "Bungaku ni okeru dokuritsu towa nanika," pp. 75-78.

instance of the idea, its growth consists in progressively reducing the material opacity that threatens this reflection, hence imitating what it most essentially or truly is with increasingly greater success. The idea exists within the work as a kind of seed that contains latently within itself the entirety of the work's development, such that this latter is destined to *become* that which it in a sense already *is*; its growth is nothing more than the ongoing realization or expression of its nature. In this manner, the perfection of the idea of literature can be said to be mirrored, however imperfectly (because mediated by history, which imposes an economy of deferral upon the idea as the condition of its translation), by the process through which the work of literature comes to arrive at perfection. Nature empties or departs from itself only to then ultimately return to itself, its goal, in the form of a circle, albeit one in which the endpoint is richer, vastly more differentiated than its point of origin. This circle represents perfection itself. It brilliantly resolves the contradiction inherent within the *bundan*'s notion of literature as transcendent idea, for the dualism that thus emerges between the actual world and the sphere of transcendence can admit of absolutely no communication, or interchange, between them. From its position in the historical world the *bundan* conceives of the transcendent, the permanence and fullness of which attests to the perfection of ideal being. Given this perfection, however, it must be asked how the idea can possibly appear in the phenomenal world, appear, that is, while yet preserving both its own perfection and the imperfection (the fallenness) of that world? Why doesn't this translation rather immediately neutralize the division between idea and actuality, either perfecting actual existence or contaminating ideal perfection? Conversely, how is it possible that the *bundan*, from its imperfect—i.e., finite—perspective, regard the transcendent idea? In order for such interpenetration between the ideal world and the phenomenal world to take place at all, this dualism must give way to a greater unity within which alone it is allowed to operate— what Takeuchi, in an apparent reference to Hegel, refers to as the "sublation (*shiyō*) of conflict between two elements."[11] More specifically, the perfection contradictorily projected by the *bundan* onto the transcendent idea is now recognized as encompassing *both* perfection *and* imperfection. The idea does not pose itself radically outside the historical world but rather *takes place* historically. The contradictions and impossible dualities contained within the notion of transcendence are in this way resolved by an immanence that refuses to see "literary history" as ultimately distinct from the idea of literature. Rather this idea, which magnetically attracts the work, pulls it toward itself in the ordering of its future, possesses this quality of attraction only insofar as it dwells within the work itself—not at a transcendent remove from it. Hence the work's teleological movement toward the

---

11. "Kindaishugi to minzoku no mondai," p. 277.

idea is at the same time a return to its original nature or essence. This movement in which *telos* coincides with origin describes not a line stretching infinitely into the future but rather a circle in which the future reveals itself to be fundamentally no different from the past.

The circular perfection of nature, in which the idea descends from its transcendence the better to restore history—the history *of* the idea—to its proper unity and belonging, nevertheless encounters an instance of instability that threatens the project of literary translation: this is the disproportionate weight given to the *bundan*. Here it is a question of unfolding the inconsistencies of the notion of ideal transcendence without however—and this is crucial—simply resolving, or sublating, them within a unity that has already anticipated them as moments (*keiki*) of its activity. The problem of transcendence is of course the problem of the limit, it refers to an absolute exteriority that exists beyond the borders of all possible experience. Yet this limit, beyond which we as finite beings cannot go, seems to violate itself in its very posing: in order to appear qua limit, the transcendent idea must be both transcendent and historical, both perfect and imperfect (that is, both infinite and finite). Only in this way can one explain the apparently unremarkable fact that the *bundan* performs its policing of concrete works of literature in the name of the literary idea. Now the effect of this insight is to bring the idea down to earth, as it were; it is to decisively (from *caedere*, meaning "to cut") open transcendence to that history—imperfection, finitude, empiricity, etc.—over which it purports to rule. The idea wishes to rule over the world without, however, participating in it, for truth and the entire sphere of objectivity necessarily depend upon this remove. But this governance is threatened by the infinite distance thus opened up between ruler and ruled. In other words, transcendence allows for the possibility of governing the manifold things of the world while at the same time revealing—unwittingly—the impossibility of such governance, or rather the fact that the world may always possibly not conform to the idea. In order to better ensure such conformity, the idea must have recourse to that which lies properly outside of it, something that while belonging to the world is yet possessed of a translucence (*not* transparence) that enables it to bridge these otherwise radically incommensurate realms. This strange translucent entity is the *bundan*, historical guardian of the "should" of literature. Its quality of translucence is reflected, perhaps, less in the term *baikai* (mediation) than in *baitai* (medium), since it is the body (*tai, karada*) that presents in its materiality that resistance to the idea's light that the idea paradoxically requires and reduces.[12] If then the *bundan* is able to act as agent of the idea, it is

---

12. This paradox that subtends the relation between the idea and the body can best be seen in the verb *tai suru* (literally, "to body"), which means "to obey; comply with." Because of the body's density or materiality, the possibility of obedience to the idea must be said to be

primarily because it is located outside of it, excluded in advance from the idea's perfection and full reality.

The *bundan* exists outside of nature, understood here in the sense of the idea. Rather its being is in the world, which is imperfect by virtue of its status as mere copy of the idea, a representation that is invariably less real than the original. The constant preoccupation with literary *technique* on the part of the *bundan* attests to its inferiority vis-à-vis the idea, since it is only through such technique, or artifice, that the literary idea can be returned to as origin. Here again, the technique of the *bundan* represents a fall from that nature which is the pure idea of literature; at the same time, however, it remains the only possible means by which nature can once again be restored, such that world and idea—or phenomena and noumena—are returned to their proper unity or oneness. The idea's perfection is precisely what renders it ineffective, for it is incapable of joining the world to itself on the basis of its own strength alone. Instead it must appeal outside of itself to the *bundan* which, as worldly emissary of the idea, *works* (through its literary works) on behalf of it. Now this structure in which the idea, which in principle needs nothing outside of itself in its perfect autonomy, is nevertheless forced to make use of imperfection in the form of the actual *bundan*, must be carefully remarked. For it teaches us that the idea, in order to retain its value as truth, must paradoxically abandon its own natural state and take refuge in the untruthful, the unnatural. In other words, the idea requires the derivative technicity of the *bundan* so as to not only preserve but in fact institute the nature of literature—and here we see that the *bundan* does not so much *possess* literary techniques as it *is* technicity itself in its very being. This requirement on the part of the literary idea reveals that history and worldliness, which are otherwise seen merely in terms of a kind of empirical accident suffered by the idea in its fall from transcendence, are in fact essentially (or structurally) bound up with it; they form the conditions of the idea's translatability, outside of which it is nothing. In this way we may understand how the *bundan*, by virtue of its very externality and unnaturality vis-à-vis the transcendent idea, constitutes an integral part of it, for perfection, or nature, must incorporate that which is first excluded from it so as to complete itself in circular fashion. Were the idea to absolutely refuse this outside so as to maintain itself as what might literally be called "pure literature" (*junbungaku*), the result would be the emergence in the world of a perfectly impure literature which would be helpless to improve itself, and so teleologically reduce or bridge the gap between itself and its proper being,

---

grounded in its ultimate impossibility. Pure obedience, which absolutely eliminates the medium of the body, makes it fully transparent, would therefore be equivalent to pure disobedience, since the idea would then become sterile, impotent. Hence the idea is forced into compromise with the body in order to be effective, yet this compromise at once opens the possibility of its betrayal, its mistranslation.

that to which it nevertheless *should* return. That this "should" is able to appear in being at all—in the form, as we have said, of the *bundan*—means that the rift between the idea of literature and the concrete literary work is only an apparent one, and that a more profound unity must exist within which the work and the world are to be understood as in fact latently ideal. In the sphere of literature, the "should" that is here figured by the *bundan* is clearly what ties the work to the idea and the idea to the work; it furnishes the crucial point of relationality between finitude and infinity, what Hegel refers to as the "*middle* between the empirical manifold and the absolute abstract unity."[13]

If the *bundan* performs its duty of policing all actual works of literature in its privileged status as agent of the literary idea, this is possible only insofar as agency itself contains the requisite materiality that allows for practical enforcement of the otherwise transcendent idea. Yet this materiality, which reflects the light of the idea only imperfectly (hence its translucency as opposed to transparency), also threatens the work of literary translation: it provides this translation with its conditions of both possibility and impossibility. This threat can be fully eradicated only at the cost of forfeiting the work, since literature would then be banished to transcendence, removed altogether from the sphere of human activity. However, materiality in this case can no longer be conceived as simply appropriable by the idea, such as to reduce it to a latent part of the idea itself. Rather, following Takeuchi, materiality is what ultimately *resists* all idealizing operations: by its strange movement of retreat from all objective determinations, materiality simultaneously gives itself and withdraws, thereby ensuring an unpresentable or inexhaustible excess to the idea. In order to clarify this point, let us now return in what might appear to be circular fashion to Takeuchi's earlier remarks on the *bundan*, for these will effectively highlight his attempt to think this excess of that unity or oneness within which the idea of literature is invariably caught up.

For Takeuchi, as we have commented, the *bundan* translates the idea of literature into the world by thematically determining it through its work of topicization. This placing, or siting, of literature must however not be confused with what he elsewhere refers to, following the philosopher Nishida Kitarō, as "the place of action" (*kōi no ba, kōdō no ba*); rather it corresponds to the *topos* that derivatively grounds itself upon this place, what he calls the "place of contemplation" (*kansō no ba*).[14] In the sphere of literature, the "place of action" is to be understood in terms of that "place," as he writes, which somehow resists theoretical extraction even as it grounds it,

---

13. *Faith and Knowledge*, trans. and ed. Walter Cerf and H.S. Harris (Albany: State University of New York Press, 1977), p. 85. Emphasis ours.
14. See for example *Ro Jin nyūmon*, in *TYz*, vol. 2, p. 39. Originally published in 1953.

makes it possible: "Scholars for whom science consists in the extracting of concepts are merely situated within the concept of science. Writers for whom literature consists in the extracting of characters (*ningen*), and who believe that characters are ultimately extractable, are simply forcing these latter within the concept of literature. They do not think of the place (*ba*) which accommodates characters, and which allows them to move. For if they did, their scholarship and literature would no longer be realized."[15] As we elsewhere try to analyze Takeuchi's notions of place and action, let us here simply emphasize that the act of extraction, which of course is required in all concept formation—the concept being the universal that extracts or abstracts itself from all concrete particulars—is essentially bound up with that of "topic-making," which we understand in the sense of thematization (*shudaika*). For topicization or thematization proceeds by directing its focus upon the as-yet unreflected thing, only to discover that this thing cannot truly be said to exist in the world independently of consciousness—a naïve if widespread belief referred to by phenomenology as the "natural attitude." Instead the thing's actual existence must be bracketed so that it may be seen in more explicit fashion as necessarily an *object* of consciousness. In this objectification of the material thing, however, a corresponding movement takes place in which man emerges as primarily an epistemological subject (*shukan*) whose being becomes synonymous with consciousness itself. In this way, the immediacy and extraordinary fullness of what Takeuchi calls (not unproblematically) "life" (*seikatsu*)[16] is reduced to an impoverished state of narcissism (solipsism) in which the subject man sees only himself as reflected in the object world. Unlike things, objects seem unable to *affect* man since they are entirely produced by him: since all alterity reveals itself to be latently contained within consciousness, history—in which man is otherwise violently marked up, or written, by the material world, and in which he is condemned to repeat himself differentially—is now shorn of its qualities of contingency and risk, becoming instead merely the process by which the subject comes gradually to know the world as its own.

Yet Takeuchi finds literature to be the very opposite of this. Literature resists this movement in which man and world are reduced to subject and object, a movement that he sees as underlying what is merely "the concept of literature" put forth by the *bundan*. Indeed, the relation between what is referred to in the above passage as the "place" and this derivative "concept of literature" is for Takeuchi precisely the relation between feeling and topicization. For let us recall Takeuchi's earlier remark that "the complexity of

---

15. "Kindai towa nanika (Nihon to Chūgoku no baai)," in *TYz*, vol. 4, p. 146.
16. As for example in the essay, previously cited, titled "Seikatsu to bungaku." Because literature is so immediately bound up with this life, Takeuchi insists, in obvious disregard for the *bundan*, that "[t]here does not exist a specific life that one could call a literary life" (p. 296).

the life of feeling" is what in fact constitutes "the origin of literature." Just as the "place" withdraws from all conceptuality, thereby exposing this latter to the force of its other, so too does feeling resist in its immediacy and primacy those objective determinations imposed upon it by the *bundan*. As what might be called the improper source of literature, feeling points to a time prior to the subject-object relation in which man's existence is characterized by a fundamental abandonment to the world, one that can never be governed by anything other than the world's alterity and contingency. Yet it must be emphasized here that Takeuchi's recourse to feeling as that which resists subjectivity does not pose itself as a mere emotionalism; on the contrary, feeling, which attests to man's being in the world as opposed to his sovereignty over it, both gives itself to objective knowledge and withdraws from it. That is to say, whereas an emotionalism would in its simplicity be helpless to explain the *relation between* feeling and knowledge, the fact that man's being in the world includes both theory and praxis, Takeuchi is careful to insist that feeling, which inextricably binds man to the world (and this binding is precisely what is meant by the world's textuality), nevertheless allows for the possibility of its own overcoming in the emergence of knowledge. Feeling, like the "place" of literature, is strangely double. It can be said to withdraw from knowledge, to resist it, while at the same time forming a kind of continuity with knowledge such as to render it possible. The relation between feeling and knowledge is thus a relation of grounding— and, indeed, Takeuchi will speak in this connection of what he calls the "genetic ground of literature" (*bungaku no hassei jiban*).[17] Insofar as feeling essentially threatens that knowledge or conceptuality which it grounds, however, one must in the same breath refer to it as an *unground*, a kind of trapdoor through which the *bundan* always risks falling.

It seems clear to us that Takeuchi's notion of feeling owes much to Nishida, and particularly to Nishida's *Zen no kenkyū* (1911), which he at one point acknowledges as having read. (A difficult acknowledgement, let us add parenthetically, given the combination of Takeuchi's own extreme leftist leanings and Nishida's reputation in the postwar as a thinker of the right). For the (un)grounding of the mediation that is the subject-object relation vis-à-vis the immediacy of feeling is a point that Nishida reiterates in the strongest of terms. "Taking the distinction between subject (*shukan*) and object (*kyakkan*) as fundamental," he writes, "some think that objective elements are included only in knowledge and that feeling and volition (*jōi*) are entirely individual and subjective. This view is mistaken in its basic

---

17. Ibid., p. 300.

assumptions."[18] This because it would give way to a kind of rationalism in which man must overcome concrete, particular experience so as to teleologically arrive at truth, which is putatively universal and accessible to reason alone—a point of view which for Takeuchi obviously bears close connections with that of the *bundan*. In contrast to this, what Nishida refers to as "true reality" (*shin jitsuzai*) is found to exist not after but rather "*prior to* the separation of subject and object," for "[c]ontrary to popular belief, true reality is not the object (*taishō*) of dispassionate knowledge; [rather] it is established on the basis of our feeling and volition."[19] The subject-object relation is one in which the reality that I am made to feel by the world in all of my actions must necessarily be bracketed, reduced, since it is impossible to conceive of this reality as existing independently of myself. This self, however, is not a worldly or material self whose mode of existence is characterized by passivity, such that it is inescapably exposed to or inscribed by the force of alterity in the form of other selves and other things. (In which case, my actions (*kōdō, kōi*) upon these latter are possible only insofar as they *first act upon me*. And here we in fact touch upon what for Takeuchi may be described as the fundamental passivity of action, a point that we discuss elsewhere). Instead it is understood as a disembodied consciousness, a kind of solitary eye that, unquestionably modeled after the image of God, potentially sees everything without ever being affected by that which it sees. Hence the term *shukan*, for this self poses itself as a center or master (*shu*)—a word that of course also means "the Lord," as in "the Lord's prayer" (*shu no inori*)—that sees (*kan, kanzuru*), and moreover sees in such a way as to actively constitute the seen. What is however *disregarded* (although necessarily presupposed) by this sovereign "overseer" is the basic fact of existence, that is to say, the fact that man qua historical being does not simply determine the world but is irreducibly determined by it. Above all, such determination of the self by a force other to or outside of it reveals limits to the freedom with which the self constitutes objects in its intentional acts. These limits, which both precede and obstruct objective knowledge, are revealed without really being grasped: "feeling" is the name given to this unique mode of revealing, it teaches that the world can in no way be equated with the sum total of objective knowledge. The world rather exceeds such knowledge, both grounding and ungrounding it. Unlike the movement of internalization that takes place in the subject's cognition of objects, feeling points to a site of contact, a liminal threshold between man and world, at which man is ex-posed to difference and alterity. This is why

---

18. Nishida Kitarō, *Zen no kenkyū* (Tokyo: Iwanami Shoten, 1999), p. 77; *An Inquiry into the Good*, trans. Masao Abe and Christopher Ives (New Haven: Yale University Press, 1990), p. 50. The Abe and Ives translation is used here as well as throughout with slight modifications.
19. Ibid., pp. 75/49. Our emphasis.

feeling can never fully be controlled by him; it is instead more accurate to say that man suffers feeling, made to submit passively to it, regardless of whether he wishes to or not. While the *act* of knowledge emerges as the negation (or overcoming) of this passivity, feeling nevertheless haunts all such activity, draws it out of itself and towards the world in the movement of ex-positioning. As Nishida concludes: "Thus our world is constructed upon our feeling and volition. However much we talk about the objective world (*kyakkanteki sekai*) as the object (*taishō*) of pure knowledge, it cannot escape its relation to our feelings."[20]

What truly draws the *shukan*-subject out of itself and back into the world, according to Nishida, is the temporal quality that is here ascribed to feeling. This "drawing" must be understood in all of its senses, for it simultaneously pulls, cuts and writes the subject, thereby ensuring that its repetition in time is necessarily a repetition of difference. In order to see through the material world as it exists from the standpoint of the natural attitude and bring things within its proper sphere of ownness, the subject must assume the existence of an ideal space that is consciousness itself. Only in this way can the ideal objects that inhabit consciousness come into being. Now the radicality of Nishida's gesture against this understanding of subject and consciousness consists in drawing consciousness out into time. Rather than speaking of consciousness as ideal, and thus as a space of pure repetition, one must instead try to think the relation between man and world on the basis of what is called here "present consciousness" (*genzai ishiki*). (Takeuchi will elsewhere appropriate this notion as *genzaiteki ishiki*, thereby at once disguising and acknowledging the debt to Nishida). Significantly, feeling is not excluded from this consciousness but rather forms an integral part of it. In the broadest terms, a kind of continuity is opened up between the present of this "present consciousness" and the non-present that is the past and future. Yet this continuity does not function to bring the past and future back into the propriety, or the ownness, of the present—hence securing the ideality of consciousness. Directly to the contrary, it reveals the derivativeness of the present in relation to the general movement that both joins and severs this present to and from past and future, such that it now becomes impossible to speak of anything like the pure punctuality of a present instant. As a result, consciousness must be said to repeat itself necessarily differentially: "When a reappearing past consciousness has been unified within present consciousness as a single element and has obtained a new meaning, it is of course no longer identical with the original past conscious-

---

20. Ibid., pp. 76/49. Let us here simply remark what we believe to be the important resemblance between Nishida's notion of feeling and that which Heidegger calls *Befindlichkeit*, or "attunement." See *Being and Time*, trans. John Macquarrie and Edward Robinson (San Francisco: Harper and Row, 1962), pp. 172-179.

ness. Similarly, when we analyze a present consciousness, what we are left with after analysis is no longer identical with that present consciousness."[21]

Traditionally, consciousness designates a space of pure interiority that is separate from the world: once a thing is incorporated within this space and transformed into an ideal object, it becomes then *present* to consciousness. This means that consciousness can, in principle, recall it at any time as the identical object it is without any difference intervening between these distinct representations. That something is present to consciousness signifies both that it exists within the general time of the present that is proper to consciousness (such that, at the moment of recall, even the past exists as a present past) and that, relatedly, it gives or presents itself fully to consciousness in the form of re-presentation. In contrast to this, Nishida suggests that the contents of "present consciousness" can never be perfectly repeated; rather an essential loss always attends the act of representation, thus pointing to the irreducibility of the thing vis-à-vis its interiorization as object. In its opening to the world, "present consciousness" allows itself to be remarked in such a way that no single "present consciousness" can be said to be strictly identical (*dōitsu*) to another. Precisely because it takes place at the instant of the present, "present consciousness" and that feeling which is part of it can never fully present itself to itself. Constantly forced into repetition, it can only exist either ahead of or behind itself, thus eliminating the possibility of perfect self-coincidence. It is in fact this succession of distinct present instants which ensures that the *shukan*-subject's repetition is necessarily one of difference. And, indeed, it becomes impossible at this point to speak of this fundamentally temporal self in terms of *shukan*; rather one must refer to it now as *shutai* (agent of action), since what is revealed by this insight into the worldliness (or ex-positioning, ex-presence) of consciousness is the grounding of the cognitive in the practical.[22]

In this regard, we can better understand how feeling discloses the immediacy with which man relates to the world, for all efforts to grasp things in objective knowledge must presuppose, as their basic condition, the simple fact of man's worldly existence. This is why literature, according to Takeuchi, always refers back to feeling as its "origin." While it must be emphasized here that Takeuchi's discourse is not a philosophical one, we are nonetheless convinced that his linking of literature to feeling is perhaps

---

21. Ibid., pp. 15/5. What is ultimately at issue here is the notion of "continuity of discontinuity" (*hirenzoku no renzoku*) that Nishida later formulates in respect of the relation between the self and experience, as for example in *Intuition and Reflection in Self-Consciousness*, trans. Valdo H. Viglielmo et al. (Albany: State University of New York Press, 1987). Originally published in 1917.

Again, Takeuchi does not hesitate to appropriate this notion in his own work as well, although of course without the rigor and sophistication that Nishida brings to his analyses.

22. See Naoki Sakai, *Translation and Subjectivity*, p. 124.

best read in light of Nishida's formulation of this latter, for the resemblances on this point are striking. Indeed, it would not be too much to say that this linking effectively functions to bring together, or make communicate, the otherwise distinct discourses of literature and philosophy—without, however, collapsing the important differences that exist between them, as for example in the manner of Romanticism. As Takeuchi writes, "our feeling *moves*. It is shaken in accordance with things or events (*koto*). . . . Life advances incessantly, and within life feeling also advances incessantly. . . . The complexity of this life of feeling is in fact the origin of literature."[23] As goes without saying, the placidity or immobility that seems to characterize the subject's objectivization of material things can invariably be found in the field of literary activity as well. For literature has according to Takeuchi forgotten that its place is in the world, where man is by virtue of his feeling constantly affected—or "shaken"—by things or events that exist beyond his control, and that work to draw man outside of himself, outside of that presence required by all consciousness and subjective identity. As we have stated, this forgetting can be seen most clearly in the *bundan* and their project of translating the idea of literature into the world. Through its topical determination of literature, the *bundan* attempts to freeze what is inherently elusive, because bound up with the movement of feeling. This is why the "return to the genetic foundation (*konkyo*) of literature" must for Takeuchi involve what is called the "emergence outside of the frame (*waku*),"[24] for literature *resists* in its worldliness that framing which forms part of the *bundan*'s activities of topicization or thematization. Like Nishida, Takeuchi is concerned here to show the derivativeness of the subject's cognitive activities vis-à-vis feeling. Significantly enough, however, this derivativeness does not simply disable, or expose as false, that which is grounded. Rather it allows us to understand that the nature of the ground-grounded relation is such that the former at once constitutes the latter's conditions of possibility and impossibility. That is to say, literature, grounded upon feeling and thus resistant to conceptualization, nevertheless *also* gives itself to this conceptualization, allows itself to be in some sense remarked by it. Following Takeuchi, literature is to be considered in its basic structure in terms of both the (singular) instant of feeling and those (universal) conceptualizations which emerge derivatively therefrom: "If feeling merely ended as an instantaneous spasm (*ichiji no hossa*), then literature would not be born. . . . Feeling continues, and that which is bent by the repression [from "social existence"] which accompanies this continuation is *to a certain degree* universalized (*fuhenka*); literature is formed when this is fixed by expression. Thus literature can *also* be said to be that which uni-

---

23. "Seikatsu to bungaku," pp. 296-297. Our emphasis.
24. Ibid., p. 298.

versalizes and fixes man's feeling. This is the simple definition of literature when literature is understood genetically."[25]

Here, feeling's "instantaneous spasm" signals the receptivity of man to the difference of the present—or the now—which by ecstatically standing outside of itself and forming other presents, other nows, effects a kind of chain in which each link is absolutely singular. This singularity constitutes the latticework that lies at the origin of literature. And yet we must be careful not to rely too excessively upon such spatial metaphors, since what is at issue for Takeuchi is above all the "genetic" movement of literature's emergence. In order for literature to properly appear qua literature, then, it must ground itself upon this singularity while at the same time leaving it, or rather extending itself away from it in the course of the "continuation" (*jizoku*) of feeling. For without this continuation universality is impossible, precisely that universality which allows the concept (in this case, the *bundan*'s "concept of literature") to come into being as the commonality abstracted from what is at bottom the singularity of experience. In this way, literature becomes inextricably bound up with "that which universalizes and fixes man's feeling." Nevertheless, as these lines subtly reveal, the relation between literature, feeling and universality is qualified in a complex manner: the universalization of feeling that results in literature is never absolute, but rather takes place only "to a certain degree." Likewise, the "also" indicates that literature is *both* the universalization of feeling *and* that which escapes, or resists, such universalization insofar as it is grounded upon the singularity with which feeling takes place. Clearly, the ground-grounded relation as it obtains here between feeling and literature as well as singularity and universality is such that the ground must be radically heterogeneous to that which it grounds. Only in this way can one speak of the singularity of feeling, its "instantaneous spasm," as essentially capable of withdrawing, or retreating, from all those determinations which attempt to present it—as for example the *bundan*'s universal concept of literature. For this ground does not simply safeguard its grounded. On the contrary, insofar as it remains ultimately inaccessible, the ground eludes capture by that "framing" inherent to the operation of thematic "topicization," thereby threatening the very stability of this grounded. The ground is necessarily double, both grounding and ungrounding that which rests upon it. While this ground's derivative representations must be said to belong to it, they are nonetheless incapable of bringing it fully into presence. *And yet not despite but rather precisely because of this impossibility, representation becomes possible.* For the feeling that Takeuchi wishes to preserve as the source of literature remains ever open to the possibility of its betrayal—or its forgetting, from which begins the appropriation of literature as institution—at the hands of

---

25. Ibid., p. 297. Our emphasis.

the *bundan*. The singularity revealed by feeling exists in retreat (*retrait*) from all conceptualization of literature: in its elusive movement of retreat, however, it unceasingly retraces (*retrait*) itself, multiplying or disseminating instances of "itself" in such a way that none can ever fully instantiate it. This tracing movement discloses the excess and unsublatable alterity of the ground over our knowledge of it, leaving us, perhaps, only with the feeling of its unknowability.

LITERATURE AND ANXIETY

What is thus the double movement of the ground vis-à-vis its grounded can be seen to markedly distinguish itself from a simple return to the world in the form of "life" (articulated, precisely, as the "life-world" by existential phenomenology), in which the reduction of the world to sense and objectivity is rejected in the name of concrete social relations. For these social relations present themselves in their pre-theoretical immediacy on the basis of something like common sense, which while representing an everyday, "vulgar" (*tsūzokuteki*) knowledge that claims to be founded in praxis, nevertheless posits the ground as actually existing, present in its materiality. This would be more or less the position of such diverse figures as, for example, the Marxist writer Nakano Shigeharu (whom Takeuchi admired), the filmmaker Imamura Shōhei and the literary critic/cultural historian Maeda Ai. Now let us point out here that Takeuchi, despite everything, never entirely succeeds in breaking from this position either, that his overriding concern for *immediacy* as that which disturbs subjectivity (*shukansei*) and knowledge leads him, at what are in fact crucial moments of his discourse (to which we shall return later), to view this ground as finally present. As such, attention must be given to the powerful tension that, as it were, makes itself both felt (*kanzuru*) and seen (*kanzuru*) in Takeuchi's text concerning this matter. This tension expresses itself in what are unquestionably the two very different return-movements to the "origin" of literature, understood as either: (1) a simple ground, in which the immediacy of such elements as feeling, materiality and social relations presents itself as such; or (2) a double or duplicitous ground, in which retreat takes place spasmodically, instantaneously, as the always singular retracing of "itself."

Without in any way wishing to resolve this tension—it is, we believe, strictly irresolvable—let us now examine the manner in which Takeuchi attempts to articulate the relation between literature and feeling on the basis of what he calls "anxiety" (*fuan*). First of all, it must be noted that anxiety functions for Takeuchi as a synecdoche for feeling itself: while it is of course true that anxiety is but one feeling among many that man experiences in the course of his existence, here it is privileged in such a way as to represent feeling in general. With this in mind, let us read the following explicitly autobiographical passage from the 1957 essay "Son Bun kan no mondaiten" [The Central Problematic of Sun Yat-sen], in which Takeuchi recounts his first experience in China as a student in 1932: "My goal was to grasp the heart of the Chinese people, to understand it in my own fashion and enter within it even by one step. The male and female passersby as well as the porters from the boardinghouse whose faces merged together morning and night fascinated me as much as possible. I became increasingly anxious and impatient with my internal estrangement from them. While I felt that a common rule must be operating between them and myself, I was unable to extract it. I was convinced from experience that this rule could only be extracted by literature."[26] What is so striking in these lines is that Takeuchi appears to be equating literature with the mere "concept of literature" that he earlier links with the *bundan*. For in both cases focus is directed to the act of "extraction" (*toridasu*), in which, literally, something is "produced" as a "taking out," as for example one says of an object that is produced (extracted, taken out) from a pocket or box. The difference is that whereas in the previous instance literature is extracted from a ground-like "place" by means of a concept that remains necessarily derivative of that place, here literature itself performs the extracting of what is felt to be a common rule operating between Takeuchi and those Chinese whom he encounters. But just as both literature and the concept of literature take their bearings on the basis of that place, to which they must return as their point of origin, so too does literature and this common rule depend entirely upon a ground which precedes them, makes them possible. All extracting refers by necessity back to this ground, since in order for something to be produced or taken out there must first be a place (not unlike a kind of pocket) *from which* it is taken, or from which it emerges—and here we may note that the produced object does not preexist in readymade form the instant of its emergence, that its grounding is rather such that it comes into being only in that singular instant. Regardless of the particular content of the extraction, it must in principle follow this twofold movement of grounding. That is to say, first, it must derive from a ground from which it is originally "taken out" and, secondly, the extraction that is its coming into being represents but the retreat/retracing of this ground in which, as we have said, the ground retreats from itself in the very movement by which it retraces itself.

Now what is here being extracted by literature is the "common rule" (*kyōtsū no rūru*) that putatively holds between Takeuchi and those Chinese

---

26. In *TYh*, vol. 3, p. 322. These lines are also quoted and discussed by Yoshimoto Takaaki in his essay "Takeuchi Yoshimi." *Yoshimoto Takaaki zenchosakushū* (Tokyo: Keisō Shobō, 1968), vol. 7, p. 381.

he encounters. This rule is a universal one: while it is considered extractable by literature, it too exists as the extraction or abstraction of properties that are shared in common by diverse instances of experience. Indeed, all rules by definition must possess this quality of universality: a rule which could be applied only once would no longer be a rule, since it would be impossible to even *arrive at* the formulation of such a rule given the difference of experience. This "arriving at" points to the process of the rule's emergence by which it must first traverse difference so as to finally come to the sameness that is its proper universality. In this way, we see that the rule must paradoxically found itself upon difference while at the same time, in its status as rule, negate that difference in its claim to universality. The moment of this transition from differential experience—where the rule exists only inchoately, as it were, not yet fully born—to universal sameness is precisely the moment in which, having achieved its formulation, or literally *come into its own*, it becomes applicable. The rule's universal applicability thus derives from experience only to then, in a kind of somersault, fold itself back upon it from a position that now appears to be entirely transcendent to experience. And yet the actual application of this rule takes place necessarily in experience, that is, it requires to speak itself at an instant of enunciation that in no way belongs to it, and that is rather irrevocably caught up in the movement of difference. So it is that both the formulation and application of the rule presupposes as its condition the singularity of the instant of experience. When Takeuchi tells us, then, "I was convinced from experience that this rule could only be extracted by literature," we can conclude that experience both allows the rule and disallows it, since the instant of its formulation (extraction) involves a multiplicity of other instants which differ, and so detract, from it. Likewise, even were one to assume that this rule could ever come into being as self-identical, it would find itself to be radically inapplicable, since the enunciative instant of its application would necessarily take place at a different time than those other applications required for its universality.

Takeuchi is clearly interested in thinking the relation between rule and experience in these lines, for this relation has an important bearing upon his notion of literature; and yet this problematic vanishes as soon as it appears, leaving the reader to fill in the spaces left vacant in the text. In this regard, it is significant that the recourse to literature is made only after an admission of failure on Takeuchi's part: "While I felt that a common rule must be operating between them and myself, I was unable to extract it." This common rule is "felt," as he writes, and this feeling serves as the departure point for the subsequent extraction of what is felt—an extraction of which, however, Takeuchi proves to be incapable: *sono rūru wo toridasu koto ga dekinai.* Now this incapacity is very quickly passed over here, as the rule is believed ultimately accessible through literature. Were one to stop and explore this incapacity, however, it would become apparent that it is not at all caused by merely individual, or empirical, reasons; rather it is an essential incapacity, and as such intrinsically bound together with the rule itself. With Takeuchi and against him, we can say that the rule, in order to rule, must be both universal and singular, both "common" and uncommon. The rule of course poses itself solely as universal, applicable in diverse instances as unfailingly the *same* rule, as if existing outside of time. In this way it seeks to conceal what is in fact the violence of its application, an application that is nothing more than its instantiation in time. For the violence of the rule consists ultimately in its taking place: regardless of its specific content, and likewise irrespective of the nobility of Takeuchi's intentions in introducing it so as to better understand the relations between himself and those Chinese to whom he feels drawn, the rule must be understood as perpetrating an originary violence against the difference of time, or against time "itself" understood qua difference. Here it would not be difficult to show how this "common rule" that putatively holds between the Chinese and Takeuchi (as Japanese)—and it must be emphasized that Takeuchi never sufficiently questions these notions of national-cultural identity, despite sketching out a movement whose effects work to radically unground them—presupposes the ideality, or perfect repeatability, of not only itself as a whole, but also of each of its elements. Taking for example the term "the Chinese people" as used in this passage, we could argue that it is utterly senseless, since no such entity (whether real or ideal) could possibly maintain itself *as such* given the difference of time. If this term does have sense, however, it is only because violence has been done to time in such a way that the difference that is the term's taking place has been effaced, thus giving the appearance of pure repetition, or what may be described as the emergence of the enunciated (*énoncé*) on the forgotten site of its enunciation (*énonciation*). In order for this notion of "the Chinese people" to be grasped by Takeuchi, it must first have a history; yet this history, which provides the minimal basis for intelligibility, is precisely what exposes the notion to difference, surrenders it to a movement that goes infinitely beyond its control. This difference surreptitiously inhabits the notion, or term, and so by extension the "common rule" of which it is a part, even before it comes down to Takeuchi, and his subsequent use of it constitutes in the end but an additional link in what we earlier saw Nishida refer to as the "continuity of discontinuity."

In this respect, both the rule and those linguistic elements that comprise it must be said to follow another, more general rule, one that sets forth the conditions of (im)possibility for this and indeed all rules: this general rule[27] formulates the relation between rule and experience in such a way as to reveal their point of imbrication in something like the *cut of decision*. Decision marks the contingent origin of the rule, which, although claiming in its universality to exist outside of time, in fact begins as a decision that takes place necessarily in experience, and that moreover attempts to make sense out of experience. In this way, the rule seeks to overcome experience by rendering it intelligible. Nevertheless, we must be extremely careful here to avoid the empiricist-historicist trap of simply reducing the rule to history. Decision rather introduces a *twofold necessity*, and this is precisely what allows it to account for both singularity and universality, both experience and the rule. For if the universal rule can be shown to take place by necessity within experience at the singular instant of decision (movement from universality to singularity), it is at the same time also true that this decision-rule must necessarily always take place, that at every instant I am forced to decide, regardless of the content of this decision (movement from singularity to universality). The structure of the decision essentially ties universality to singularity just as it does singularity to universality without, however, ever uniting these two together in the fashion of Hegel—or rather, more accurately still, it *unties* the one from the other in opening up a kind of middle space between them from which alone these activities of tying-untying are then allowed to proceed. This constant movement between singularity and universality corresponds to a double violence. As we have already noted, the universality of the rule does violence to the singular difference of time, a violence that we now understand to be unavoidable since the decision-rule cannot but take place. And yet the violence of the universal vis-à-vis singularity is in fact possible only insofar as it is grounded upon a more originary violence, which would be that of singularity "itself" in the destructive (yet generative, productive: *hasseiteki*) movement of its taking place. It is this originary violence that, literally, *intervenes* within universality, ensures that its repetition occurs via difference, thus releasing the wholly new—new experience, new rules—into the world.

Now Takeuchi tells us that the rule he discovers originates in feeling, just as the extraction of it by literature refers back to experience. At this stage relation takes place prior to all determinations thereof, in the simple immediacy of its happening: there is an encounter between Takeuchi and another, an encounter that produces anxiety, but this interaction is not yet marked by the symmetry or oppositionality that exists between a "Japanese" and a "Chinese." In this context, anxiety names something like the singular

---

27. Or what Derrida in several places calls "the law of law," as in "Force of Law: The 'Mystical Foundation of Authority,' " in *Deconstruction and the Possibility of Justice*, ed. Drucilla Cornell et al. (New York: Routledge, 1992), pp. 3-67.

instant of contact with an outside from which (universal) determinations then emerge. Let us point out here that, throughout his writings, Takeuchi will consistently associate the feeling of anxiety with such contact, and particularly with contact with others, and that he will moreover do so within the general scope of literature. So for example in his 1948 essay "Seiji to bungaku no mondai (Nihon bungaku to Chūgoku bungaku I)" [The Question of Politics and Literature (Japanese Literature and Chinese Literature I)], Takeuchi describes a round-table discussion devoted to the topic of Chinese literature whose participants included, among others, the Chinese poet Li Shou, various scholars of Chinese literature from Japan, and such writers from the journal *Shin Nihon bungaku* [New Japanese Literature] as Miyamoto Yuriko, author of the 1946 novel *Banshū heiya* [The Banshū Plain]. Written only three years after the war, criticism is leveled at many of the Japanese participants for what Takeuchi perceives to be their profound lack of anxiety in relation to their interlocutor, Li Shou: "It appeared that the Japanese writers had no desire to understand Chinese literature from the outset, and that their professions of interest in the subject were merely expressions of courtesy. They turned away from things and neglected the remarks of their interlocutor. Having fixed preconceptions of Chinese literature, they sought out only those responses which fit within that framework (*waku*). Not one of these writers felt any anxiety in the face of their interlocutor, and indeed it seemed that they lacked the simplicity of heart required to feel anxiety in the first place. How is it possible for writers to gather together and discuss literature without there appearing even the slightest flash of contact or communication with one another?"[28] Nearly the same sentiment is expressed in another essay of the same year, titled "Bunka inyū no hōhō (Nihon bungaku to Chūgoku bungaku II)" [Ways of Introducing Culture (Japanese Literature and Chinese Literature II)], although here Takeuchi chooses to focus upon the encounter between Lu Xun and those Japanese writers who traveled to China to speak with him: "Generally speaking, the Japanese writers who met with Lu Xun had not seriously read his works, and were attracted solely by his reputation. In other words, their meetings were strictly political. They met with Lu Xun not as writers but rather as 'China *rōnin*'. . . . These writers met with Lu without feeling any anxiety, and thus were not influenced by him. Such a spirit in which things are handled matter-of-factly without the least self-questioning once existed within Japanese literature, and indeed can be said to still exist even now. This is a debilitated spirit which makes literature *decadent*."[29]

---

28. In *TYz*, vol. 4, p. 103. Honda Shūgo provides a very helpful background reading of this essay in his *Monogatari sengo bungakushi* (Tokyo: Shinchōsha, 1975), pp. 510 ff.
29. In *TYz*, vol. 4, pp. 115-116. The term "China *rōnin*" refers to the considerable number of Japanese who traveled to China at the beginning of the twentieth century for such diverse

The encounter with the other is before all else an encounter with that other's alterity, an alterity that however in no way belongs to him, and even less to myself. Because of this impropriety, in which I am exposed to an outside that exceeds all of my attempts to determine it, to locate it, I feel anxiety. In this regard, Takeuchi introduces once again that strange word or concept that we came across earlier in his discussion of the *bundan*: *waku*, meaning "frame, framework." Just as literature originates in feeling, according to Takeuchi, so too does framing originate in anxiety: the Japanese writers who meet with Li Shou in fact do experience anxiety in this meeting, since some contact does take place; this anxiety is not allowed to come forth and fully affect them, however, but is rather immediately subdued by or upon the emergence of the frame. Given this frame, any real understanding of Chinese literature as presented by Li Shou becomes impossible. In so saying, however, we must not imagine that understanding can ever occur outside of all framing, in what would amount to an act of immediate, noninferential intuition—something of the order of what Takeuchi elsewhere refers to as "literary intuition" (*bungakuteki chokkan*).[30] On the contrary, if framing is required for understanding to be effected, anxiety indicates that such understanding might always be imperfect, defective, which in turn points to the essential incapacity on the part of the frame to contain entirely within itself what is very profoundly called its "subject matter" (*shudai*). Were the framing operation to be faultless, it is suggested, anxiety would then disappear, since no traces of this subject matter would remain to haunt the subject, or make its presence felt in such a way as to impress upon him the fact that matter somehow escapes or exceeds the boundaries of the frame. Anxiety reveals the porosity of solipsism by introducing an irreducible difference between the world as it affects us and our objective knowledge of it, which knowledge may be regarded as man's proper response to the world's initial giving or donation of itself. Secure in the conviction that the objectified world may be "handled matter-of-factly without the least self-questioning," however, these Japanese writers remain effectively closed off to the "influence" from other things and other persons, thus giving the lie to the notion that, as Takeuchi remarks, "a profound level of consciousness is to be shaken (*yusuburareru*) by literature."[31]

What Takeuchi is criticizing here is a form of relationality in which subjects interact with one another on the basis of a system of exchange, such that what is given to me by the interlocutor in the act of communication is received, consciously processed, and returned back in inverse form.

---

purposes as that of personal adventure, furthering the expansion of Japanese imperialism, and participation in Chinese revolutionary politics.

30. "Kindai towa nanika (Nihon to Chūgoku no baai)," p. 138.

31. "Bungaku ni okeru dokuritsu towa nanika," p. 79.

In this way, the alterity of the other can be successfully domesticated—and my own anxiety reduced—since I am able to see this other now strictly in terms of myself, that is, as contained within my field of consciousness. For I know, even prior to my reception of it, that the content of what he gives to me necessarily *reflects* that which I give to him: in the final analysis, what ties us together in this intersubjectivity is the mirror, in whose light we are both presented as symmetrical images of the other. Clearly what is at issue here is the notion of transference, for the other, having lost all transcendence in relation to my determinations of him, becomes a kind of blank screen upon which I project images whose point of reference is myself alone. The Japanese writers who meet with Li Shou or Lu Xun, for example, experience nothing new in these meetings, but rather merely confirm themselves and that which they already know. Everything takes place entirely within the "frame" that is the subject's field of consciousness, and this because, to use a term from Hegel, the recognition (*Anerkennung, shōnin*) of the other presupposes as its condition the reduction of alterity (transcendence) to propriety or ownness (immanence). That is to say, it is important but ultimately insufficient to realize that my being as subject requires an outside which, standing opposite me as my ob-ject, takes the form of the interlocutor, the other subject. For in truth this other subject can in no way be other to me, his presentation to my gaze means that what I initially felt to be his transcendence vis-à-vis myself is an appearance only, nothing more than an illusion that I am able to restore to truth. And this I do, precisely—if paradoxically—by restoring myself to myself, as I gradually come to recognize myself in the guise of the objectified other. If this other were purely transcendent, it would be impossible for recognition to take place at all. The most I could do is contemplate this other in his ineffable absence, an absence that would be strictly *unremarkable*. That the other comes to me in such a way that I am able to remark this coming, present him as entering within my sphere of ownness, means then that he exists in latent or incipient form as part of my consciousness. For this reason, the "shaking" of consciousness that is the instant of anxiety and of contact with the other qua other dissolves (or, as Takeuchi writes, "decays, degenerates" (*daraku suru*)) into a scene of repetition whereby the subject comes in all security to claim the world as his home.

Intersubjective exchange proceeds so smoothly only because it erases what is in fact the violence of the other's coming: regardless of whether I wish it or not, I am irrevocably "shaken" by my contact with the other. This other disturbs the home that I attempt to make not simply *in* but rather, much more fundamentally, *of* the world, thereby forcing me to come to grips with other things and other persons in an entirely new way, a way for which I am unprepared. The violence that the other does to me in my capacity as subject, however, engenders another violence, one that attempts to negate the earlier violence by appropriating it as part within the universal whole that I posit myself as. Yet unlike the manner in which two negatives are said to cancel one another out, so restoring an original state of affairs, these two forms of violence work to incessantly mark and remark the subject, determining him as a being that is both passive and active. As active, the subject spontaneously constitutes the world and brings it within his sphere of ownness, as we have witnessed for example in the case of those Japanese writers singled out by Takeuchi who refuse to understand Lu Xun and Li Shou except on their own terms. Nonetheless, the subject's activity comes into being necessarily after the fact (*après coup*), only upon first passively receiving the shock or blow (*coup*) that takes place in the experience of the world and of others. These shocks are instantaneous, and they are registered not by cognition but by *feeling*, as Takeuchi never tires of repeating. But for Takeuchi feeling has a privileged relation with literature. The conceptual chain that binds together feeling, experience and anxiety also includes within it literature as well. Given that his criticisms are directed at writers who he believes remain stolidly unaffected by the coming of the other, too well-protected from this latter's blows (its violence), how then does he envision the disruption of intersubjectivity and the concomitant opening or exposure to the other's alterity?

As with so much else, Takeuchi responds to this violence against violence by way of Lu Xun. This response is of course a strategic one, and must be understood on both a "philosophical" and "political" level: wishing to gesture toward an outside of the "framing" that encapsulates and presents the other to the objectifying subject, Takeuchi focuses here upon a parable that reveals in explicit fashion the impossibility of interiority; in addition, this movement of excess or overflow beyond the borders of the frame is placed in the institutional context of Japanese literature, in relation to which Lu Xun can only be understood as an outsider. Significantly enough, however, Takeuchi seems in this instance to avoid the temptation of locating the outside as a simple beyond.[32] For, among other problems, this would in-

---

32. It must be noted that Takeuchi was extremely inconsistent on this point. As many scholars have pointed out, Takeuchi all too often tended to *figure* resistance and exteriority—in, for example, the figure of China, of Asia (the "Orient" (*Tōyō*)), the nation/folk (*minzoku*), as well as of Lu Xun himself—thus falling into a simplistic binary logic which effectively hypostatized the terms being employed. For such criticism, see e.g. Lawrence Olson, *Ambivalent Moderns: Portraits of Japanese Cultural Identity*, pp. 43-77; and Kitagawa Tōru, "Takeuchi Yoshimi to sengo nashonarizumu," in *Sengo shisō no genzai* (Tokyo: Dentō to Gendaisha, 1981).

In so saying, however, we must also emphasize that Takeuchi was not entirely unaware of this problem, that he at times saw that the active figuring of resistance was necessarily resisted by the movement of resistance "itself." Thus can be read the closing lines of "Bunka inyū no hōhō (Nihon bungaku to Chūgoku bungaku II)" (p. 127): "It seems to me that Lu Xun is necessary for Japanese literature, but this necessity is such as to in fact finally make him unnecessary. Without this latter aspect, it becomes meaningless to read him. What I fear is that

variably lead to a thinking of the outside in a manner that is at once empiricist and theological (in the sense of mystical). Empiricism is ultimately unable to explain the possibility of its own discourse, and any discourse on the alterity of the other as resistant to intersubjective exchange and symmetry must in some way account for itself if it wishes to be rigorous. If one were to assert simply that the other refuses all discourse and so all framing, then the charge can be made that even this statement is self-contradictory, since the other is still being represented, however minimally. To posit an absolute break between the experience of the other and the concept abstracted therefrom would render such conceptual discourse absurd, as it would be impossible to respond (or: re-spond) to the other at all. (And doubtless a similar argument could be made against Takeuchi's notion of "chaos" that we referred to earlier, since what truly demands to be thought is the *relation between* chaos, understood here as the impossibility of conceptuality, and the concept of chaos, which somehow comes to emerge from this latter, and so owes its possibility to it). Relatedly, insofar as the other is understood as a pure outside that resists the framing of the concept and of discourse, one could claim to acknowledge its being by observing a solemn and respectful silence, a silence that would in fact bear a strong resemblance to worship. This other would then conceivably be referred to in a language that mystics have traditionally reserved for God, as can be seen for example in negative theology: in his transcendence he infinitely exceeds all human understanding, such that knowledge of him can only be negative, for we can only know that which he is not. In this way, the attack against knowledge seems to lapse into something like faith, which for Takeuchi would constitute an easy escape from the anxiety that we must feel in the coming of the other. While it is doubtless necessary to receive, or welcome, this coming, it is equally necessary to give expression to it—yet in such a manner that the other is allowed to freely haunt our discourse, inhabit it without entirely overwhelming it.

Now if Takeuchi's thinking of the other avoids these traps of empiricism and mysticism in its refusal to equate this other with a simple or pure outside, it is because he is focusing here specifically upon Lu Xun. In relation to Japanese literature, Lu Xun occupies the strange position of outsider who nevertheless at least partially inhabits this inside. As Takeuchi recalls, not only did Lu Xun first begin his literary activity in Japan—as is well-known—but he also co-authored a 1923 text on modern Japanese fiction[33]

Japanese literature will make Lu Xun into an authority, that it will transform this poet of the people into an icon or idol of bureaucratic culture. This danger is a real one. Indeed, have I not myself considered Lu Xun simply in terms of a 'Lu Xun type'?"

33. Takeuchi has high praise for Akutagawa Ryūnosuke in his role of introducing this text into Japan, as can be read in "Bunka inyū no hōhō (Nihon bungaku to Chūgoku bungaku II)," p. 121.

in addition to composing several essays in Japanese. Let us emphasize that the point of this interweaving between inside and outside has little to do with Lu Xun's biographical information as such. Rather Takeuchi wishes to show why he turns to him in order to articulate the general relation between literature and anxiety, for this relation reveals that the other must come *both from within and from without* if it is to effectively disturb intersubjectivity. Thus we are given to read Lu Xun's 1925 parable entitled "Congmingren he shazi he nucai" [The Wise Man, the Fool and the Slave], the plot of which Takeuchi sketches out as follows: "The slave's work is hard and he constantly complains. The wise man consoles him: 'Your fate will certainly turn for the better before long.' But the slave's life is hard, and he next complains to the fool: 'The room given me doesn't even have a window.' 'Tell your master to have a window made,' says the fool. 'What an absurd idea,' answers the slave. The fool at once departs for the slave's house and begins destroying the walls. 'What are you doing, sir?' 'I am opening a window for you.' The slave tries to stop him but the fool does not listen. The slave then shouts for help, and other slaves appear and drive the fool off. Finally the master appears and the slave informs him what has happened: 'A bandit began destroying the walls of my house. I was the first to discover this and together we drove him off.' 'Well done!,' the master praises him. The wise man visits the master after this incident and the slave thanks him: 'Indeed, sir, you are very prescient. My master praised me. My fate *has* turned for the better.' The wise man seems pleased. 'I'm sure of that,' he replies."[34]

Here, the anxiety inherent in relationality can very literally be described in terms of the uncanniness of *Unheimlichkeit*, since what is at issue is the destruction of home and property, such that one runs the risk of being displaced from that which is most familiar to one. For both Takeuchi and Lu Xun, the familiarity that is the home obviously extends beyond the slave's actual home to include his relations with the master and the wise man, for these provide him with the security in his own self-identity that he so desperately craves, in other words, they teach the slave what is to be his proper place in the world. The slave requires the master in order to assume his identity as slave, and he is willing to endure various physical deprivations— hard work, poor conditions, etc.—so as to maintain the relationship in the stability of its terms. Although the wise man does not appear to stand opposite the slave in the clear-cut fashion of the master, he is nonetheless determined by a similar positioning. For the slave manifestly posits the wise man in relation to himself, just as the wise man in turn posits the slave vis-à-vis himself, as if the two were locked in a continual dance. This dance unfolds seamlessly, without a break, since it is choreographed by the give-and-take

---

34. "Kindai towa nanika (Nihon to Chūgoku no baai)," pp. 154-155.

of subjective desire. The slave complains of his hardships, to which the wise man (who, let us note, Takeuchi associates with the standpoint of humanism, and thus also with the "West") offers consolation, holding out to him the hope of improvement, or progress. When the slave's lot does improve with the desired recognition from the master ("My master praised me. My fate *has* turned for the better"), the wise man is himself recognized for his wisdom ("Indeed, sir, you are very prescient"), thus receiving back in circular form the gift of self-identity that he first gave the slave at the beginning of the tale. Indeed, it would not be too much to say that this parable describes, in both its form and content, the circularity of intersubjective exchange. Regarding content, the exchange between the slave and the wise man repeats itself in the dialogue between the slave and the master. Upon driving away the fool, the slave promptly seeks recognition from the master for his actions, for these have resulted in the preservation of the home: "A bandit began destroying the walls of my house. I was the first to discover this." In this manner he asks for confirmation of his identity as slave, and all that is required on the part of the master—his symmetrical other—is simply to acknowledge his efforts: "Well done!" Communicative exchange is here organized in such a way that what is sent out from the slave is immediately returned to him in inverse form, without the slightest loss or misdirection. For really it is unimportant what the slave actually says. All that matters is that he be recognized by his interlocutor, and in this sense the response from the master ("Well done!") is virtually identical to that of the wise man ("I'm sure of that.").

And yet by participating in this game of recognition, both the master and the wise man reveal themselves to be slaves as well. At the moment when they confirm the slave's identity as slave they simultaneously confirm their own identities, since, as Hegel teaches—and of course this parable is but a variation of the famous dialectic—self-recognition never takes place in isolation but is rather necessarily mediated by (or via) recognition of the other. The circularity that ensues in this movement of sending and return of the self is, as we have suggested, mirrored by the very form or structure of the parable as related by Takeuchi. The first words that the wise man offers to the slave ("Your fate will certainly turn for the better before long") are, as it were, *given back to him* at the end of the narrative ("My fate *has* turned for the better"). That is to say, these first words, in their status as prediction or forecast, do nothing less than open the future of the narrative. Now this opening must not simply be understood along the lines of a traditional literary criticism which would be content to link it together with the narrative's conclusion, thereby extracting a kind of invariant pattern or form whose function it is to structure the text as a whole. For such criticism could only emerge by forgetting what we have seen Takeuchi refer to as the "genetic ground of literature," a ground that, precisely, ex-frames the text, sets it in motion. (And in this connection let us recall Takeuchi's explicit linking of feeling with movement). Rather, by opening the future of the narrative, these words in effect open the narrative to the future, they expose it to a movement that, once released, goes infinitely beyond its control.[35] And this is what the term "fate" (*un*: meaning also "destiny," "luck") of course tells us: in the barest way possible, it says only that the future will come, and that it will be absolutely other to all that we have known and all that we believe. In this sense, fate is merely another word for what we earlier spoke of as "violence," for what is announced in it is the radical disruption—or "shaking"—of the subject in face of alterity, which for Takeuchi means above all the alterity of other persons. Yet this is something that must be rejected by the wise man and the slave, for, seemingly incapable of anxiety, fate presents itself to them strictly in the form of a circle, whereby what leaves the subject will always find its way back, it will literally *home in* on the subject, since that is its proper origin. With the words "Your fate will certainly turn for the better before long," then, the narrative takes leave of itself only to ultimately return back to its point of departure at the end; and all that changes is the tense of the verb, from *un ga muitekuru* to *un ga muitekimashita*, for this passage of time signifies solely that the return journey has been a successful one. In this parable which treats of the mirroring of intersubjective exchange, it seems entirely fitting that this content will itself be mirrored by the circularity of the parable's form. The form plays out in a highly suggestive manner the refusal of anxiety that attends the encounter with the other. This anxiety may be understood as a response to the utter unpredictability of the future, the new, in which others will come to me in such a way that I will always be "shaken" by them. From the viewpoint of the wise man and the slave, however, this exposure to the future that is here called "fate" is reduced to a kind of calculable process in which any risk I incur is nothing more than a self-investment whose eventual return is assured me in advance.

What then of the fool? For it seems that Takeuchi, following here Lu Xun, points to the figure of the fool as somehow expressing the truth of

---

35. At issue here is the Derridean notion of grafting: as soon as something appears, it submits itself to a future that can never strictly belong to it, since it may always possibly be grafted onto something else. For us, the importance of this notion in this specific context lies in its effects of disturbing the boundaries between national literatures—a point that, as we will try to show, must ultimately be brought to bear against Takeuchi himself. Based on the decision we have made to treat the text in its Japanese translation as opposed to its original Chinese, can it any longer be said to simply belong to the genus "Chinese literature," or does it now belong in some sense to the genus of "Japanese literature" as well? Although the grafting that is translation is generally used to confirm such boundaries (as they function, for example, in what is called "Area Studies"), nevertheless grafting "itself" reveals that the text in its opening or exposure to the future betrays all belonging, it teaches that the genus can never entirely contain its species, or parts.

relationality. In his violence, the fool reveals the fragility of intersubjective transference not only as it takes place between the slave, the wise man and the master, but also, outside the narrative, as it so clearly informs the desire of those Japanese writers who encounter Li Shou and Lu Xun while seeing only themselves, as if gazing in a mirror.[36] In this respect, it is unquestionably significant that the fool's violence takes the specific form of destroying the walls of the slave's home. "I am opening a window for you," the fool cries in response to the slave's question, for what the slave takes to be reckless destruction is from the fool's point of view merely an "opening," an effraction or breaching of an enclosure that was most originally not present. Indeed, just as for Lu Xun "the earth had no roads (or "ways": *lu, michi*) to begin with," as he writes in the short story "Guxiang" [My Old Home] (1921)—which in turn is cited repeatedly by Takeuchi throughout his works—so too were there no homes to begin with, since the distinction between inside and outside that the notion of home implies is a derivative one, necessarily secondary in relation to violence (which, understood here in the sense of *polemos*, alone is originary). The violence perpetrated by the fool seeks to disturb the boundaries of the home, as these boundaries represent a violence against violence. This latter violence attempts to ward off originary violence by, precisely, erecting walls against it, in the vain hope that it can be effectively contained. So we find that the slave, who desires above all to maintain the walls that organize his relations with others, ordering them properly as relations between subjects on the basis of the logic of identity (such that I can only stand *opposite* you, and you me), has no choice but to drive away the fool, hence excluding violence by an act of violence. In this violent exclusion of violence, however, we see that violence is in fact ineradicable, that it possesses a kind of generality which enables it to threaten all boundaries or homes even as it paradoxically allows for them.

In concluding this section, let us call attention to what we believe to be a danger in Takeuchi's understanding of the relation between literature, anxiety and relationality, a danger out of which, however, he himself may be said to point the way. This would be the trap of thinking anxiety on the basis of an oppositional logic according to which various "types" (*kata*) are presented as either possessing or lacking anxiety. Clearly Takeuchi's treatment of the encounter between the writers from Japan and China could easily be read along these lines, and let us add that certain passages in various other texts (for example, the 1961 "Hōhō toshite no Ajia" [Asia as Method]) do little to discourage such a reading. What this notion of "type" suggests is a kind of philosophical anthropology that merely characterizes man, who is

---

36. Cf. "Bungaku ni okeru dokuritsu towa nanika," p. 79: "As if leaning on a companion, one reads the works of authors whose identity (*sujō*) is known in order to avoid anxiety by confirming the values one already holds."

given empirically, as opposed to the much more fundamental task of inquiring into what man essentially is. As we have earlier remarked, anxiety is what is felt by man in his abandonment to the world and to others, it exposes him to the radical alterity of the outside, forcing him to repeat himself as different. Because of this, anxiety troubles at its root the possibility of all determinations of man, which a typology or characterology must obviously presuppose. In order to better understand what is most truly at stake in this notion, then, let us go beyond its reduction to "types" and concentrate instead upon what Takeuchi refers to as "despair" (*zetsubō*), which we believe articulates in his thought essentially the same logic as that of anxiety, and which moreover seems to function interchangeably with it. "While 'despair' is a state of consciousness," he writes, "this state is one of disturbance (*fuantei*). A settled despair is not a true despair. . . . Despair is like the nothing (*mu*) that is able to express itself only by way of being (*yū*)."[37]

Focusing here solely on this final line—"the nothing that is able to express itself only by way of being"—how might we more rigorously approach a thinking of anxiety on the basis of what Takeuchi has already told us? In the parable we have been following, the slave discovers that the walls which have previously housed him are on the verge of being destroyed, and that nothing will shelter him from the dangers of the outside. Although this outside seems to refer most immediately to other persons, or rather, more accurately, to other persons *qua other*, let us remember that the fool's violence takes place as a moment within the circularity of "fate," a circularity that it threatens to "open" in much the same way as it does the slave's window, thereby restoring fate to its proper futurity, or effectivity. For it is only because of the future that others can appear to me in all their difference, such that even those who share my "home" are in the final analysis strangers to me as well. What this means is that the other necessarily exists in time, and specifically in the time of the future. In this respect, it is the movement of "fate" that releases the fool, and his violence is nothing other than the *effects* of this movement.

Now the future, understood here as the time of the coming of the other, is what ensures that the slave never truly encounters the master and the wise man as other subjects who exist simply opposite himself. (Such intersubjectivity takes place only in the present, in the timelessness that is the presence of the present). In its coming, the future rather introduces into the subject something of the nature of what Takeuchi refers to as "nothing." For the encounter between the subject and the other is never simply a dialogue between two present entities. What strikes or shocks the subject is on the contrary a nothingness within the other, and it is this that allows it to continue coming back to the subject, drawing it outside of itself and towards the fu-

---

37. *Ro Jin nyūmon*, p. 38.

ture. In the encounter, the subject desires to locate the other as another subject, in which the difference between the two is based ultimately upon their generic sameness as subjects. This is achieved by incorporating the other within its sphere of ownness where it is recognized at the level of "being," understood here as present being. As present being, the other comes to the subject always in the same way, since future encounters can be understood on the basis of the past, which is nonetheless present to the subject in memory. (This of course would be the very opposite of Nishida's "present consciousness"). Here, recognition takes place precisely as repetition in which no difference (or violence) intervenes in the recurrent comings of the other such as to effect a "shaking" of the subject, a "disturbance" of the walls of its home. It is at this level, clearly enough, that the slave conducts his relations of exchange with the master and the wise man. In Takeuchi's language, such relationality as founded strictly on "being" must be regarded with profound suspicion in the seeming absence of any "anxiety," or "despair," which he insists is characteristic of relationality as such. Anxiety arises when the subject is faced with something in the other that steadfastly *resists* its recognition, something that, as Heidegger writes, involves "no mere lack of determination but rather the essential impossibility of determining it."[38] Yet this "something," by remarking itself outside of the subject's space of interiority, is in fact "nothing." Or rather, what is not quite the same thing: it is "like the nothing that expresses itself only by way of being." For Takeuchi is extremely wary here of falling into a theological discourse in which "nothing" becomes essentially synonymous with God, such as to allow one to speak in terms of, say, "religion and nothingness." If the other qua other radically transcends the subject, it nevertheless does not exist outside of the world, as the notion of "nothingness" might easily suggest. As we have stated, the other exists in time, and this is what of course renders it phenomenal. And yet this other cannot be understood as *simply* phenomenal, as it invariably retreats in its appearance, such as to resist ever fully presenting itself as such. In this sense, the other must be described as both being and nothing, both within the subject's sphere of propriety and without. Only by existing within this between, this no-man's-land, as it were, is the subject able to be struck with the feeling of anxiety at all.

Ceaselessly retreating or retracing itself, the other withdraws in its presentation, which is to say that it gives itself in the very movement by which it absents itself. For this reason, Takeuchi is forced to speak of relationality, and the anxiety that is an integral part of it, in terms of both "being" and "nothing." Relationality between present beings describes merely the regulated give-and-take of intersubjective exchange, whereas, on the

---

38. "What is Metaphysics?," in *Basic Writings*, ed. David Farrell Krell (New York: Harper and Row, 1977), p. 103.

other hand, to speak too quickly of the subject's destruction at the hands of "nothingness" runs the risk of depoliticizing or dehistoricizing what is necessarily the other's marked intervention in time. Rejecting both of these alternatives, the violent coming of the fool represents instead a kind of middle space between nothing and being, from out of which alone these terms can be understood to emerge in their distinctness. This middle space effectively works to "open" the subject (the slave), that is, it opens him to *possibilities* that infinitely exceed or overflow the bounded relations of recognition, thus allowing for something like an encounter with the new to take place.

REFUGE: THE TURN TO *KOKUMIN BUNGAKU*

If Takeuchi has been considered in postwar Japanese intellectual history as an important thinker of resistance, it is necessary that we attempt to trace out this notion in his works while at the same time giving full attention to his nationalism. For Takeuchi is *also* widely known as a thinker of *minzoku*, which can be translated here alternatively as "nation," "*Volk*," "race," or "ethnos," but which at least in Takeuchi's usage—which is, however, not always consistent—encompasses to some degree all of these meanings in a complex, overlapping fashion. Indeed, in a recent text on *Kojiki* and *Nihon shoki* scholarship, Takeuchi is briefly referred to solely in respect of his notion of *minzoku*.[39] In literary circles, Takeuchi's writings on the nation (*minzoku*) are generally treated on the basis of his work on "national literature" (*kokumin bungaku*) as set forth most centrally in the 1954 collection titled *Kokumin bungaku ron* [On National Literature]. Yet it would be incorrect to understand Takeuchi's notions of resistance and nation as ultimately separable from one another. Were one to do so, it would become quite impossible to analyze the political difficulties inherent in Takeuchi's articulation of resistance, just as it would be impossible to appreciate—however critically, and without in any way acting as an apologist—the reasoning that leads him to regard the nation as a privileged *figure* of resistance, as for example is perceptively noted by Nakagawa Ikurō in his study of Takeuchi.[40] For what is required here is not simply an untying of the

---

39. Isomae Junichi, *Kiki shinwa no metahisutorī* (Tokyo: Yoshikawa Kōbunkan, 1998), p. 127.
40. *Takeuchi Yoshimi no bungaku to shisō* (Tokyo: Orijin, 1985). For Nakagawa, Takeuchi is to be understood in the light of modern Romanticism, and particularly in its desire for "figuration" (*keishōka*), which he defines as the giving shape to the "concrete form of 'the eternal.'" "Significantly enough, this desire that constitutes modern Romanticism emerges only upon the widespread "sense of loss of absolute values," that is to say, the onset of relativism, which is however characteristic of modernity as such. Hence Takeuchi's project as a modern Romanti-

various threads that constitute Takeuchi's text, such as would sever the relations between resistance and nationalism. Of equal importance is the tying together of threads—or the making of connections—without which any rigorous understanding of a thinker is impossible. But let us resist the temptation to take up a position that would see itself as in any way outside this text (i.e., the position of the *shukan*-subject), thereby enabling us to treat it merely as an object (*taishō*) existing opposite ourselves. As Takeuchi himself writes (in the context of a debate with Japanese Marxist scholars), one must at all costs avoid the "mistake of attempting to grasp in history only moments of rupture (*danzetsu*) without grasping moments of continuity (*renzoku*)."[41] While we of course recognize in these words Takeuchi's continued thinking of Nishida's notion of "continuity of discontinuity," as was discussed earlier, we must also endeavor to take heed of them in our own reading of Takeuchi's text. And nowhere is this more urgently required than when we encounter two strands of thought that seem to be so fundamentally incompatible with one another, as is the case here. Those concepts in Takeuchi's text that can be grouped together under the general heading of resistance—as, for example, those of feeling, anxiety and nothing—obey a kind of logic that, precisely, "opens" or breaches the "home" that is represented by the nation. The question therefore is this: how can Takeuchi, on the one hand, articulate such a forceful logic of unbelonging and displacement while, on the other, still seek refuge within the boundaries of the nation? Here it would be extremely easy to explain this phenomenon by recourse to a (theological) logic of the fall, such as to set forth a "good" Takeuchi, the thinker of resistance, who is subsequently corrupted by a "bad" Takeuchi, the thinker of the nation. Given the ease with which such an argument could be formulated, however, it should immediately arouse our suspicion of it, for in a text as complex as that of Takeuchi's such facility would point only to the hubris or naïveté of the researcher himself. Instead, let us try to avoid this trap and focus for at least the time being on the "continuity" between textual threads, hoping in this way to disrupt any simple political judgments on Takeuchi's thought, whether these be favorable or unfavorable. This strategy of reading will force us to reexamine certain notions already discussed in our earlier sections, to which we now turn.

It would not be too much to say that Takeuchi's concept of the nation relates directly to his thinking of literature, and as such can be situated in part within the context of his criticisms of the *bundan*. In this connection,

---

cist may be described, following the language of one of his own essays, as an "overcoming of modernity" (pp. 27-38).

While we confess to having certain reservations concerning Nakagawa's work, it must be said that his reading of the notion of figurality in Takeuchi is an important one, and helps us better think the complex relation between resistance and the nation as it appears here.

41. "Nihonjin no Chūgokukan," in *TYh*, vol. 3, p. 58. Originally published in 1949.

let us recall that Takeuchi's resistance to the *bundan*'s notion of literature focuses on what he finds to be the excessively abstract nature of this latter. For the *bundan* conceives of literature strictly on the basis of a dichotomy that functions to divide literature from itself, a dichotomy which is subsequently overcome only in the most artificial or external manner possible, through the *bundan*'s own coercion. Here, abstraction takes the form of an idea of literature that governs, in its transcendence of the world, all concrete literary works. In this way, the materiality of the work becomes subordinated to an idea that it can never fully reach, but which constantly attracts it to itself. This force of attraction sets loose a movement whose proper *telos* can be described only as the *end* of literature, in the double sense here of "completion" and "death," for the attainment of ideal perfection on the part of the work necessarily coincides with its own annihilation, since materiality or corporeality is of course a condition for the work's existence. As we have tried to show, the *bundan*'s manner of thinking of literature gives rise to a series of oppositions (e.g., immediate vs. mediated, concrete vs. abstract, worldly vs. transcendent, etc.) the relation between the terms of which it is unable to satisfactorily work out. For Takeuchi, these oppositions are evidence of a profoundly intellectualist approach to literature, one that views and judges it primarily in light of a conceptual knowledge that he finds to be symptomatic of literature's growing professionalization, and so decadence.

Reacting against this trend, Takeuchi attempts to conceive of literature in some sense outside of these oppositions. This leads him to articulate a notion of literature that cannot be so easily appropriated by the *bundan*'s conceptual activities, a literature that escapes what we have previously seen him refer to as the operation of "framing." This he calls *kokumin bungaku*. Now if we decide to translate this term as "national literature," it must be understood that it could with equal fidelity be rendered as "people's literature," as indeed has been done in the small body of English-language scholarship that has appeared on Takeuchi.[42] What is in any case imperative is that we hear in the word *kokumin*—and as well in the word *minzoku*, since for Takeuchi (unlike, for example, the political scientist Maruyama Masao) these two are virtually synonymous—reverberations of an immediate and original form of being that precedes, and hence potentially disturbs, all oppositionality. For Takeuchi's move against the *bundan* is to return to a moment prior to the determination of literature qua literature, which itself becomes possible only by way of positing a transcendent literary idea to which all concrete works must at once return and aspire. But here we see

---

42. J. Victor Koschmann gives this term as "national literature" in *Revolution and Subjectivity in Postwar Japan* (Chicago: The University of Chicago Press, 1996), p. 9; whereas Lawrence Olson translates it as "people's literature" in *Ambivalent Moderns*, p. 59.

that Takeuchi is actually forced to repeat the logic of the *bundan* in the step back to origin: the difference between them lies solely in the manner in which that origin is to be conceived, not in the return move itself. This is of course no mere coincidence, but rather points to the fact that all discourse necessarily presupposes for itself a ground from which inquiry is allowed to proceed. From the viewpoint of the *bundan*, the recognition of particular literary works qua literature is possible by virtue of their participation in a universal literary idea, of which they are imperfect copies. This idea precedes the work, that is, it can never be arrived at empirically by abstracting from existing works since it shapes all experience of literature to begin with. Now the origin to which Takeuchi makes appeal will be referred to as the "essence" of literature, an essence which he identifies at a certain point as the "nation" or "people." These of course do not occupy a position of transcendence vis-à-vis the work but are instead believed to be immediately present to it. In this sense, what Takeuchi says here of "national literature" holds true for literature as a whole: "Because national literature is the issue that has been originally brought forth, it must not stray in the direction of debates within the *bundan* hegemony. It must always be treated according to its essential (*honshitsu*) aspects. It is necessary to discuss [national literature] by grasping it as a thought that has matured among the masses. . . . The discourse of national literature must develop along three directions. The first of these may be called something like the discourse on essence, and would proceed through conceiving of the relation between nation formation (*kokumin no keisei*) and the establishment of national literature."[43]

Before considering the very different notions of literary origin as formulated by Takeuchi and the *bundan*, let us first try to explain what doubtless appears to be a glaring inconsistency in Takeuchi's understanding of literature. Previously we saw that criticism of the *bundan*'s project of theoretically topicizing literature became necessary insofar as this topic making served to erase what Takeuchi set forth as "the origin of literature," namely, "the complexity of the life of feeling." Feeling, we observed, refers to the immediacy of man's practical being in the world, an immediacy that by right precedes all oppositionality, and particularly that between the subject and object of epistemology. Feeling designates for Takeuchi a primary opening or exposure to alterity on the part of the actant (*shutai*), which we tried to show both grounds and ungrounds all subsequent knowledge. Here it was demonstrated that Takeuchi's conception of feeling on the basis of "movement" bore significant traces of what Nishida (and Takeuchi after him) calls "present consciousness," in which consciousness, and the feeling that is part of it, is revealed to repeat itself necessarily differentially by virtue of the fact that it takes place in time. Now the negative force of this no-

---

43. "Bungaku no jiritsusei nado," pp. 59–60.

tion of feeling in relation to the *bundan*'s determination of literature is considerable, and we have tried to draw out its effects as they appear in Takeuchi's text. Nevertheless, in his articulation of feeling qua resistance Takeuchi will very explicitly come to link this feeling with the nation (or people). For Takeuchi, in other words, the conceptual chain that ties together feeling, immediacy and difference also contains within it, astonishingly enough, the nation as well. Let us hasten to add that there are important historical and political reasons for this linking, to which we shall return momentarily. In any event, if one were to reconstruct from his texts the course of this linking between feeling and nation, attention would at some point have to be given to the word *kokujō* as it appears in Takeuchi's treatment of Lu Xun. Although this word carries a strict dictionary meaning of "national conditions" or the "state of affairs in a country," its significance here lies in the fact that it combines in compound form the characters for "nation" (*koku, kuni*) and "feeling" (*jō*), such that the term may literally be read as "national feeling." In the passage within which this word appears, Takeuchi refers to Lu Xun's attribution of misunderstanding between himself and certain Japanese writers to what he calls "differences in national conditions."[44] While no connection is overtly established at this point between the notions of "feeling" and "nation," it is nonetheless worthy of mention that this word occurs in the context of a discussion of such important concepts as those of feeling, anxiety, corporeality and action, all of which are for Takeuchi directly associated with the thinking of resistance. Given that these concepts point to what is understood to be the ultimate impossibility of subjective interiority, they would seem to threaten or do violence to the notion of the nation, as opposed to merely supporting it. For Takeuchi, however, precisely the opposite is true.

Much less ambiguous as regards this connection between feeling and nation is a passage to be found in the essay "Kindaishugi to minzoku no mondai," in which Takeuchi condemns the leftwing for its rejection of the nation in the postwar period: "Although it is true that there existed [within the left] the slogan of 'national independence' (*minzoku no dokuritsu*), the nation was here conceived in an a priori fashion (*senkenteki ni*); hence it belongs in the category of a certain type of modernist ideology. [This concept of the nation] did not emerge from natural life and feeling (*shizen no seikatsu kanjō*). It represents an attempt to take Asian, and especially Chinese, nationalism as a model and apply it to Japan."[45] Several pages later, Takeuchi will emphasize this intimate relation between nation and feeling in speaking of what is for him the "simple feeling of nationalism" (*sobokuna nashonarizumu no shinjō*) (p. 279), a phrase which is then repeated as

44. "Bunka inyū no hōhō (Nihon bungaku to Chūgoku bungaku II)," pp. 115-116.
45. "Kindaishugi to minzoku no mondai," p. 275.

the "feeling of the nation that is simple at its origin" (*hassei ni oite sobo-kuna minzoku no shinjō*) (p. 280). In point of fact, much the same idea is expressed in "Nihonjin no Chūgokukan," in which the notion of "national feeling" (*kokumin kanjō*) is now explicitly brought forth in the course of a discussion on the Chinese Revolution. Given that "the opposition between the Chinese Communist Party and the Nationalist Party is [merely] an intellectual [or "ideological"] opposition," as he maintains, it is nothing more than "a Japanese prejudice to conceive of ideological opposition as directly equivalent to an opposition in national feeling."[46] Indeed, in contrast to what Takeuchi finds to be the immediate unity of Chinese nationalism, the various divisions within Japanese society are attributed to the seeming lack of underlying feeling, what he goes so far as to call "the frigidity (*fukanshō*) of the Japanese people" (p. 56). This theme of a Japan in some way impoverished in its capacity for national feeling is repeated in the essay "Seikatsu to bungaku": what we have just seen Takeuchi refer to as "natural life and feeling" is here associated negatively with Japan, which is once again denounced by reason of the many (unnatural, derivative) oppositions, or divisions, existing therein: "The nation (*kokumin*) of Japan is [in its parts] mutually divided by class, region and profession. It possesses a common feeling and yet is unable to express this through a common language. These divisions are reflected on a conscious level where they become the divisions between ideologies. They are also reflected in the individual, where they become the divisions between flesh and spirit, thought and feeling, and aesthetics and values."[47]

Although, as this last passage makes perfectly clear, Takeuchi opposes the oppositions that he associates with the *bundan* and, more generally still, with modernity itself, it is not difficult to see that this stance invariably replicates the very oppositional logic that he is criticizing. In the final analysis, it must be said that Takeuchi's notion of resistance never entirely succeeds in overcoming this trap: an underlying tension pervades it through and through, such that it becomes virtually impossible to determine the precise moment either when oppositional logic collapses upon itself, thus opening a window upon alterity, so to speak (the moment of violence), or when alterity suddenly gives way to the regulated exchange of oppositionality (the moment of violence to violence). No doubt this very problematic must be radically rethought, since it is impossible to inquire into the opposition between oppositionality and alterity without thereby committing violence to this latter. In so saying, however, it is not entirely useless to attempt to untie

---

46. "Nihonjin no Chūgokukan," p. 54. The passage continues: "It is truly Japanese to problematize ideology in and of itself apart from its base (*kiso*) in national feeling, thus making it an index of transcendent (*chōetsuteki na*) values" (pp. 54-55). Once again, transcendence is opposed by Takeuchi to the ground or base that is feeling and the nation.
47. "Seikatsu to bungaku," p. 306.

these threads one from the other, since without so doing one becomes incapable of making any sort of intervention in regard to the political stakes of Takeuchi's text from a viewpoint that is not simply external to it, but is indeed that of Takeuchi's. This of course requires on the part of the reader a sensitivity to the various relations between the terms being opposed. In the above quotations, for example, the link between feeling and the nation is forged in opposition to oppositionality itself. The nation is not to be conceived transcendentally as an *a priori*;[48] because it emerges most properly on the basis of "natural life and feeling," it must be grasped in all its immediacy as "natural," "simple" and "original," to use the language favored by Takeuchi. Existing prior to the outbreak of oppositions that work to divide it from itself, the nation is understood most essentially as a totality or whole (*zentai*) that is immediately bound together by "common feeling."

Let us point out here that this concept of the nation is by no means unique to Takeuchi, and may in fact be traced back to the Romantic reaction against the universal rationality of the Enlightenment in eighteenth century Europe. Opposing the Enlightenment tendency to view man in the explicitly universalistic terms of mankind and civilization, the Romantics turned instead to the particularism embodied in different nations and cultures. Since the move to negate particular difference was effected above all by *reason*, which was thus identified with universal mankind (as exemplified, of course, by Europe itself), Romanticism came in reactive fashion to conceive of national and cultural difference on the basis of *feeling*. Feeling, then, was what truly distinguished particular nations and peoples (*minzoku*, *kokumin*) from one another. Having established this point, it is of course an easy jump to conceive of the immediacy of national feeling as that which "resists" the universalizing movement of progress and civilization. In this respect, Takeuchi can be seen to have faithfully repeated the Romantic gesture. We may read this in the direct criticisms of Enlightenment thought (*keimōshugi*) so prevalent in his works, thought which he associates with the modernity—that is, Eurocentricity, "universality"—of modern Japanese literature, as symbolized for instance in the figure of Mori Ōgai. We may read it also in his attacks (however justified) against "world history" (*sekaishi*) and what is referred to as the "monistic view of civilization" (*bunmei ichigen kan*), and along with this his rejection of such figures as Fukuzawa Yukichi in favor of, say, Kita Ikki and Ōkawa Shūmei.[49] (Up to a certain point, more-

---

48. It should be noted here that Takeuchi appears to be completely indifferent to the Kantian distinction between the transcendental and the transcendent. For him, the term *senken* functions as an equivalent to *chōetsu*.

49. H.D. Harootunian aptly notes this apparent contradiction in which Takeuchi, "whose sympathies were often with the left, devoted so much energy to resuscitating the tarnished careers of prewar right-wing activists" such as Kita and Ōkawa. In "Visible Discourses/Invisible Ide-

over, this binary logic informs even Takeuchi's interpretation of the May Fourth movement in China, in which Lu Xun plays the Romantic to Hu Shi's classicist). So too may we understand his move against the left's conception of the nation as an *a priori*, which essentially repeats his earlier move against the *bundan* and its positing of a transcendent idea of literature. These formal abstractions must, he insists, be brought down to earth in the concrete form of a literature that immediately expresses a nation's (or people's) "natural life and feeling," namely, "national literature."

In order to comprehend what for Takeuchi was most centrally at stake in this appeal to national literature, it is imperative that we remember the sociopolitical context within which it emerged. As the literary scholar Izumi Aki points out, however, this is not to suggest that it be seen solely in the wake of the Japan Communist Party's policy of national independence as set forth in the late 1940s.[50] Let us recall that Japan was during this period fully under the regime of the American Occupation, which lasted from 1945 up until 1952. What Takeuchi calls "independence in literature" in his essay "What is Independence in Literature?" represents at the same time political independence from the Occupation and its aftermath, as a reading of this text makes clear from its opening lines: "Japan has today lost its independence. Other than a few exceptions, there is perhaps no one who does not recognize the fact that Japan has been placed under the control of another nation. And other than a few exceptions, there is perhaps no one who does not despise such subordination and wish for independence."[51] Although this passage was written after the Occupation had formally ended, it seems clear that Takeuchi wishes to call attention to the effective continuity of American rule in Japan. Particularly in light of the defeat of the Chinese Nationalist forces and the establishment of Mao Zedong's People's Republic of China in 1949, the United States attempted to severely restrict the spread of Communism in Asia, with the result that Japan was, as Takeuchi writes, "forced in the direction of becoming an anti-Soviet military base": "Because Occupation policy sprang from the Potsdam Declaration, it forced Japan in the direction of becoming an anti-Soviet military base. Signs of suppression of free speech again became noticeable. Even since the Occupation formally ended, the Japanese government, which substantially inherited Occupation policy, has passed a series of legislation aimed at the suppression of free speech, beginning with the Anti-Subversive Activities Law. Also, the government has in some quarters forcibly initiated a practice that is practically equivalent to censorship" (p. 74). According to Takeuchi, this

---

ologies," collected in *Postmodernism and Japan*, ed. Masao Miyoshi and H.D. Harootunian (Durham, NC: Duke University Press, 1989), p. 74.
50. *Nihon rōman-ha hihan* (Tokyo: Shinseisha, 1969), p. 211.
51. "Bungaku ni okeru dokuritsu towa nanika," p. 66.

imposition of power by a foreign nation violates something like a people's right to self-rule. Yet this right does not represent here an abstract and legalistic notion, one that could be simply opposed to morality. Rather it reflects what for Takeuchi is the people's most proper desire: the desire to freely express itself in its essential being. If the Japanese as a *minzoku* "despise [American] subordination and wish for independence," if in other words they "unconditionally desire emancipation from American domination" (p. 67), this is due first of all to the fact that the Japanese are *essentially* Japanese. This national-cultural identity is, as we have seen, "natural," "simple" and "original," it has existed throughout history as the force that actively shapes the Japanese in their development or becoming. Indeed, just as a plant only expresses in the course of its growth that which it innately is in its original seed form, so too does freedom on the part of the Japanese *minzoku* consist in being allowed to become that which it in a sense already is, however inchoately. Hence the call for "emancipation from American domination," for this domination functions to unnaturally impede that self-growth of the Japanese. Following the examples given by Takeuchi above, this unnaturality can be seen in the suppression of free speech and censorship practices as instituted by a government which no longer represents the direct will of the people, but instead the political demands of a foreign power.

Given these conditions of American domination, we can now better situate Takeuchi's appeal to national literature. This appeal emerges primarily as a *reaction against* foreign presence, a desire to preserve the integrity of the Japanese nation from American imperialism in the context of the Cold War. For Takeuchi, the articulation of a national literature that is absolutely unique or particular (*tokushu*) to Japan must be seen in terms of "resistance" against the West, that is to say, against the universalism that in modernity is exemplified in the privileged figure of the West. Nevertheless, insofar as it attempts to effect a return to Japan, this resistance remains profoundly reactive, less resistance than straightforward opposition. In this sense, it is important to note that the principal distinction here between self (Japan) and other (the United States, the West) is intimately bound up in Takeuchi's argument with such oppositions as particular-universal and essence-accident. Now on the one hand, there can really be no question of the political import of Takeuchi's gesture of resisting western hegemony, and especially in the form of American domination over Japan during the Cold War. On the other hand, however, the recourse to Japanese (or, more broadly, Asian) particularism as instrument against western universalism cannot but replicate the very logic or structure of this latter even as it opposes it. For the *minzoku* represents for Takeuchi a "whole," a unity whose subsumptive relation to its parts is precisely that of the universal West to the various regions throughout the globe. The *minzoku* is an essence that putatively exists unchanged throughout Japanese history, it defines the Japanese people as Japanese regardless of differences between them, differences which are thus reduced to the form of specific difference as contained within the genus "Japan." As such, the American Occupation and its effective continuation after 1952 is ultimately to be considered an artificial and accidental incursion upon an essential Japanese *minzoku*. Regardless of its impact, it can do nothing to harm the core of Japanese identity, which remains essentially intact, unbroken. Japanese identity, which derives from this essence, can in principle always be restored to its original propriety. And this restoration is the central task of national literature.

We can see that, for Takeuchi, the loss of Japan's independence is inextricably bound up with the decadence or degeneration of its literature. For the Japanese *minzoku* is a whole whose parts are necessarily affected by the general state of this former: the unnatural suppression of the *minzoku* in the form of American domination is reflected in the artificiality of modern Japanese literature. Nevertheless, Japan's domination by a foreign power—what Takeuchi will refer to as its "coloniality" (*shokuminchisei*)—is shown to actually predate the wartime defeat in 1945 and the subsequent Occupation. As the following lines reveal, the origin of this status can be traced back to the early part of the twentieth century when Japanese literature attempted to divorce itself from its *minzoku* essence and participate in the creation of a universal "world literature." Let us quote here at length a passage taken from the "Bungaku ni okeru dokuritsu towa nanika" essay we have been following (in which Takeuchi quotes himself from a previous essay, "Kokumin bungaku no mondaiten" [The Central Problem of National Literature]): "So, in order to illuminate the question of 'What is independence in literature?' it would behoove us to think the opposite concept: coloniality in literature. I believe that Japanese literature is at present colonial. Yet this is not to say that it suddenly became colonial because of the Occupation; resistance against colonization had already been abandoned quite early. In terms of approximate periodization, this [abandonment of resistance] began from the time of the *Shirakaba* group and became conspicuous with the New Sensationalist school [*Shinkankaku-ha*]. By exhibiting a perfect slave nature during the war, [Japanese literature] became completely colonial in the postwar. It is said that Japanese literature made great strides during the war, but this is an inevitable result of its coloniality. For its abandonment of the struggle against colonialism intensified at this time. Its literary coloniality can be measured by its representations of a world literature unmediated by the nation (*minzoku ni baikai sarenai sekai bungaku no hyōshō*). The fact that there has today appeared the projection of a perfect representation [of world literature] reveals that [Japan] has today become a perfect colony. I am not speaking of individual phenomena. [Rather] I am referring to the general situation in which both writers and critics, if they do not make use of methods from the I-novel, must borrow methods and even images from abroad. That is to say, they have lost their creativity. Independence in literature must struggle for and achieve the recovery of that creativity. And since it is generally self-evident that the source of creativity lies in the very lives of the masses, efforts to recover this creativity coincide in practice with the goal of the national (*kokuminteki*) emancipation of literature" (pp. 89-90).

The recovery or restoration (*kaifuku*) of literary creativity is here conceptualized as a return to a Japanese *minzoku* essence, for the *minzoku* is understood as the uniquely creative force that has shaped the Japanese throughout history. Now if Takeuchi writes that "the source of creativity lies in the very lives of the masses," this is because these lives are in turn expressions of *minzoku* essence. That is to say, the "masses" (or the "people," "populace": *minshū*) are for Takeuchi first of all Japanese masses, and their lives embody in concrete form what Japan essentially is. Hence a reciprocal relation exists between literary creativity and the actual lives of the masses: while the former originates in the latter, so too does the latter derive its being from that essence which Takeuchi identifies as the creative force of the Japanese *minzoku*. Similarly, we see that this reciprocity is what binds the Japanese writer to the *minzoku* community that is Japan, it is what determines his identity as a specifically Japanese writer. For these writers owe their identity to this community, in which they participate as members, and they acknowledge and requite this debt by the return-gift of their literary work, which serves to embody the community as its proper corpus:[52] the work of Japanese literature, then, is necessarily a work *of* Japan. Indeed, it seems clear that Japanese literature can only survive as such through this movement of give-and-take between the Japanese writer and the *minzoku* community of which he is part. The community that endows the writer with his essential creativity yet requires that this creativity be expressed, and this expression in turn helps sustain the community. In this way, Takeuchi signals that literary creativity is ultimately not to be attributed to something like the genius of the individual writer. Rather it must be understood on the level of the community, understood here as national community. The increasing professionalization of writers takes place as a misguided departure from this community—which is concretely particular—and concomitant entry within the abstract or artificial universality of "world literature." The result of this is an ever-widening gap in the modern era between universality and the individual. According to Takeuchi, this gap is most properly bridged by what he refers to as the "mediation" of the nation. If, as he writes, "literary coloniality can be measured by its representations of a

---

52. See here Charles Taylor, *Hegel and Modern Society* (Cambridge: Cambridge University Press, 1979), pp. 84-95.

world literature unmediated by the nation," then "independence in litera-ture" would on the contrary involve not simply a rejection of universality in the form of world literature, but rather (in Hegelian terms) the introduction of a *concrete universality* which embraces the mediation of its self-differentiation in the form of particular determinations. These particular determinations of world literature would be, precisely, the *kokumin bungaku* of all nations. What is at issue here is a thinking of the universal that is not merely opposed to its determinations, and that is thus supremely, if impo-tently, undifferentiated; the true universal instead allows for its own self-othering, for only in this way can it concretely express itself in the world. The concrete universality that Takeuchi conceives of is one in which world literature determines itself through the mediation of the nation while at the same time sublating these determinations. Lacking this, modern Japanese literature in its coloniality can only "borrow methods and even images from abroad," since its own *part* within this universal is not recognized, either by itself or by other like parts (i.e., other national literatures). From Takeuchi's standpoint, Japanese literature is unable to resolve the contradiction that subtends the relationship between itself and world literature. Although Japanese writers feel themselves forced to obey this universal of world lit-erature, they fail to understand that this injunction can in no way be given externally, that they themselves rather exist as an expressive part within the universal whole. What binds them as individual writers to world literature is the nation: only through the prior mediation of their own nation Japan can they take their place as writers of world literature. In direct contrast to the writers of the *Shirakaba* group and the New Sensationalist school, writers of *kokumin bungaku* must therefore acknowledge before all else their proper identity as members of the Japanese *minzoku* community.[53] Their writings must reflect this *minzoku* essence.

The "opposite concepts" (*hantai gainen*) of literary coloniality and lit-erary independence are of course grounded in the opposition between out-side and inside. The coloniality of Japanese literature derives from its de-pendence upon, or domination by, foreign literatures: in their exteriority to Japanese literature, these literatures are to be understood as inessential. While it is true that Takeuchi writes in the final lines of "Bungaku ni okeru dokuritsu towa nanika" that "[n]ourishment from foreign literatures must be massively absorbed. There must be no exclusionism or ultra-nationalism" (p. 101), nevertheless these literatures can never encroach upon the essential space of Japanese literature proper. In contrast to this coloniality, literary

---

53. In this connection, Takeuchi approvingly refers to Natsume Sōseki's attempt, as expressed in such works as *Kokoro* (1914) and *Sanshirō* (1908), to "internalize" the process of Japan's modernization, such that it be not simply what he calls an "external affectation." In "Hōhō toshite no Ajia," *TYh*, vol. 3, p. 404. Originally published in 1961.

independence would designate something like the free reflection in Japanese literature of its core *minzoku* essence. If, as Takeuchi believes, Japanese literature is in the midst of crisis, this is primarily due to the fact that its *minzoku* essence has been unnaturally obscured, prevented from expressing itself as it truly is. A Japanese literature is consequently produced which is Japanese in name only; its inauthenticity can clearly be seen in its reflection of "methods and even images from abroad," thus revealing a marked disunity between its inner and outer self. This disunity is overcome only in *kokumin bungaku*, which returns literature to its rightful status as a more or less transparent reflection of an underlying *minzoku* essence. For Takeuchi, Japanese literature—which is as yet the literature of the *bundan*—is divided most centrally by its inability to conceive of its own *Japanese* being as actually one with its *literary* being. Literature must refer back to the integrity and immediacy of *minzoku* life if it is to be a true literature, at home in its independence. As opposed to this, the modern Japanese literature of the *bundan* remains fundamentally at odds with itself, since it refuses to see literature as innately related to the *minzoku*. Literature is here thought on the basis of an opposition between inside and outside, but one that far exceeds the determinate division between Japanese literature and foreign literatures: this opposition is of course that between the worldly (or historical) and the transcendent. In this way, the idea of literature not only loses its direct link to the *minzoku*; it is divorced from the entire realm of empiricity itself. As we have previously discussed, literature for the *bundan* represents a transcendent beyond which all actual works of literature can imitate only imperfectly. Literature, that is to say, governs the work while being radically removed from it. Takeuchi finds this separation to be responsible for the excessively abstract nature of both the universal of literature and the individual literary work. He insists that the proper concreteness of literature rather derives from the fact that this universal *inheres within* the work, such that the work exists as a natural outgrowth or expression of it. Furthermore, he suggests that the impossibility of transcendence allows us to recognize that the *bundan*'s appeal to literary universality in fact conceals its reliance upon a notion of literature that is western through and through. For if the *bundan*'s understanding of literature is abstractly universal, it goes without saying that this understanding did not simply arise out of thin air, produced spontaneously by an autonomous subject. Rather it can be traced in its emergence to specific historical reasons. And the reasons that Takeuchi identifies all relate in some way or another to the fact of the West's colonial domination of Asia. In this respect, western colonialism is seen as an attempt on the part of the West to attain to universality. That the *bundan* believes its understanding of literature represents a pure universal essence that transcends the historical world—and so as well this opposition between East and West—signals for Takeuchi a profound naïveté, one that is not unrelated to the *bundan*'s political irresponsibility. This naïveté is at once philosophical and historical, since the *bundan*'s refusal to come to terms with the impossibility of a transcendent positionality (which for Takeuchi represents the position of the *shukan*, and hence the position of human-ism),[54] blinds it to the fact that in modernity it is the West that presents itself as universal. Western colonialism does not appear in the form of simple power relations in which one (or a group of several) particular *minzoku* comes to gain power over another *minzoku*, which is likewise particular. On the contrary, the extreme force of this colonialism derives from the West's self-representation as universal. This universality putatively expresses itself in the fact of the West's technological superiority—its advance (*zenshin*) or progress (*shinpo*), as Takeuchi will write—over the "Orient." Such superi-ority was conceived of teleologically, and thus believed to indicate greater proximity to a universal idea that was nevertheless transcendent, always in excess of worldly determinations. When for example Takeuchi writes, in the above quotation from "Bungaku ni okeru dokuritsu towa nanika," that "[t]he fact that there has today appeared the projection of a perfect represen-tation [of world literature] reveals that [Japan] has today become a perfect colony," he is referring to the historical process by which the West has gradually come to be identified as a universal entity. This process has unfor-tunately been erased or forgotten in Japan, and nowhere is this more evident than in the *bundan*'s understanding of what was originally a strictly western notion of literature as now a transcendent universal.

Once again, Takeuchi is to be admired for his acumen in having drawn attention to the paradoxes that inhere in the historical emergence of the West as in some way representative of a transcendent universality. Pre-dictably enough, however, resistance against this universality takes the reac-tive form of a particularism (*tokushushugi*) centered on the Japanese *min-zoku*. This can be seen in a cursory examination of Takeuchi's language throughout several of his works. Among the many like passages which could be brought forth here, let us note simply that in "Seikatsu to bungaku" Takeuchi attempts to determine what he calls alternatively "the conditions particular (*tokushu*) to Japan alone" and "the circumstances particular to Japan alone," while in the 1953 essay "Nihon no minshū" [The Japanese Masses], reference is made to "the particularity (*tokushusei*) of the forma-tion of Japanese capitalism."[55] And yet the point of these remarks is cer-

---

54. "Kindai towa nanika (Nihon to Chūgoku no baai)," pp. 154-161.
55. "Seikatsu to bungaku," p. 304; "Nihon no minshū," in *TYh*, vol. 2, p. 57.
    Cf. also "Kindaishugi to minzoku no mondai": "What Mr. Takami [Jun] calls the correct part of the 'Japanese Romantic Faction' refers to their search within Japanese literature for a 'healthy ethical consciousness.' Yet I believe that this could also be understood as national (*minzoku*) consciousness. To that extent, I think Takami's words were appropriate. This is what is meant to be the *antithesis* (*anchitēze*) of the ideology of modernity" (p. 277; italics ours).

tainly not limited to an examination of Takeuchi's language. At the deepest levels of his thought, we can see that resistance to (western) "universality" remains all too often informed by an oppositional logic that privileges instead Japanese—and, in a larger sense, Asian—particularity. This resistance fails inasmuch as it neglects to call into question the meaning of these terms themselves. No matter how forcefully articulated, Japanese particularism, qua particularism, finds that its efforts ultimately do nothing more than reinforce the comprehensive hold of the West. For this particularism assumes as its underlying presupposition the West's universalism—and in this respect one can see virtually no difference between it and the colonial logic of the West itself. Any effective challenge to this universalism must necessarily begin by examining the nature of the whole-part relation upon which it is founded. Sensitive to the massive historical injustices wrought by western colonialism, Takeuchi desires to, precisely, *overturn* the hierarchical relations between whole and part, the West and its Asian colonies. This overturning is to be accomplished by a strengthening of *minzoku* consciousness, such that, for instance, national literature comes to perfectly reflect one's immediate belonging to a concrete and determinate part (i.e., the national community) as opposed to an abstract universal whole. What is thus ignored by Takeuchi is the fact that this colonial logic of the West is entirely capable of appropriating such a gesture of particularist resistance, that the whole-part relation remains essentially unchanged by the mere expansion or fortification of the part. This for two reasons: 1. Since the part itself is internally differentiated, the relation between itself and its sub-parts invariably replicates the relation it maintains as part with the whole. That is, as Hegel of course knew, the part is always both particular and universal, depending upon the term with which it is being contrasted. The Japanese *minzoku* is particular when compared with the universal West as well as with other particular *minzoku*, and yet at the same time it must be understood as a universal whole insofar as it contains within itself individual Japanese citizens. (This duality can very clearly be seen in the term *kokumin*, which means both "nation" or "people" and "citizen," "member of a nation." In this regard, Takeuchi's notion of *kokumin bungaku* assumes even greater significance). The obvious danger here is that, in order to be effective, particular resistance against the whole would conceivably proceed through a mobilization of its own parts, such as to render itself finally indistinguishable from that whole; and 2. The overturning of the whole by the part ends not in an overcoming of the whole-part relation itself, but rather in the mere reorganization of the terms contained therein. Upon the realization of this

---

Without question, this very problematic notion of "antithesis" as represented by the figure of the Japanese *minzoku* vis-à-vis the ideology of modernity (*kindaishugi*) is for Takeuchi the antithesis of the particular in relation to universalism.

overturning, the part comes into being as a whole and the whole as part. Regardless of the changing identity of these terms, the formal structure of the relation remains entirely in place, as dominant and inflexible as before. This is of course the problem of the reversal (*tentō*), which Takeuchi, who is otherwise extraordinarily sensitive to this trap, conceives of in terms of the master-slave relation. Although he fully recognizes that "the slave reveals his perfect slave nature [only] when he becomes the slave's master,"[56] nevertheless he insists on conceptualizing Asian resistance against the West as leading necessarily to Asia's own universalization, that is to say, its own (slavish) mastery of the West. Nowhere is this idea more unambiguously expressed than in the final lines of "Hōhō toshite no Ajia." "The Orient must re-embrace (*tsutsuminaosu*: literally, "rewrap") the West," Takeuchi writes, "it must change the West itself in order to realize this latter's outstanding cultural values on a greater scale. Such a rollback (*makikaeshi*) of culture or values would create universality (*fuhensei*). The Orient must change the West in order to further elevate those universal values that the West itself produced. This is the main problem facing East-West relations today."[57]

Given that the West has identified itself in modernity as a universal entity, however, doesn't this reversal result ultimately in Asia's (the Orient's) own westernization? For if the terms of part and whole are strictly formal, so too must one understand the terms of Asia and the West. This can easily be illustrated by the case of Japan, whose "traditional" identity as Asian and so particularistic has given way to its more recent economic and political emergence as a nation of the West. In any event, it seems evident that Takeuchi's failure to rigorously examine the limits of the whole-part relation condemns his resistance against the West and the notion of universality to unwittingly repeat the same logic. The paradox here is that it is Takeuchi who above all alerts us to this colonial logic, teaches us to be vigilant against it, while at the same time he astonishingly incorporates it into his own discourse. In this regard, the two aspects of this logic to which we have just called attention have been carefully addressed by Naoki Sakai in his reading of Takeuchi. Concerning the replication, or restaging, of the whole-part relation in the bond between the part and its elemental sub-parts, Sakai writes tellingly of "Takeuchi's conviction that, in order to counteract the West's aggression, the non-West must form nations. Then what is heteroge-

---

56. "Kindai towa nanika (Nihon to Chūgoku no baai)," p. 158. Recall also in this connection the lines earlier quoted from "Bungaku ni okeru dokuritsu towa nanika": "By exhibiting a perfect slave nature during the war, [Japanese literature] became completely colonial in the postwar. It is said that Japanese literature made great strides during the war, but this is an inevitable result of its coloniality. For its abandonment of the struggle against colonialism intensified at this time."

57. "Hōhō toshite no Ajia," p. 420.

neous to the West can be organized into a kind of monolithic *resistance* against the West, but within the nation homogeneity must predominate. . . . Exactly the same type of relationship as that between the West and the non-West will be reproduced between the nation as a whole and heterogeneous elements in it."[58] Certainly it must be said in Takeuchi's defense that he in no way intended for his notion of resistance to become complicit with the colonial logic of the West, against which it was of course explicitly formulated in the first place. And yet the fact remains that in his thought resistance is intimately bound together with the work of nation formation, at least in the context of Asia. Here we may begin to understand in what sense Takeuchi's text remains vulnerable to a rightist or conservative reading in which the various excesses of nationalism within the nation come to be seen as justified in relation to the overall project of resistance against the West. While such a reading represents in our view a blatant misunderstanding of this text, nevertheless Takeuchi's failure to radically question the whole-part relation results in a serious confusion on his part between the notion of particularity (which ultimately confirms the universal) and that of singularity (which infinitely exceeds or escapes it). This confusion leads us to Sakai's second point, in which Takeuchi's reversal of the West is found to end, predictably enough, in the accomplishment of Asia's own universality: "Insofar as he never loses faith in the universal emancipation of mankind, Takeuchi is certainly a modernist. Therefore, he believes that monistic world history is, after all things are considered, an inevitability and that, consequently, the universal emancipation will be realized not by the West but by the Orient. In history, he says, the true subject is the Orient."[59] As we have suggested, the particularism that Takeuchi identifies with Japan and Asia necessarily contains within it a moment of universality, however silent or implicit. In a strange way, Takeuchi both knows this and does not know it: meaning that while he unquestionably views Asian resistance against the West in terms of resistance against universalism and the monolithic exclusion of difference, he will at the same time conceive of the West's overcoming (its "rollback," as he describes it) as the moment in which Asia arrives at its own proper universality. Indeed, it strongly appears here that Takeuchi's notion of resistance is at a certain point unable to rid itself of what Nietzsche called *ressentiment*, that is to say, a kind of reactivity in which the slave endures the master's dominance only the better to triumph over him in the end, thus confirming his own slave values as superior. And yet even without reference to the passage from "Hōhō toshite no Ajia" quoted above, in which Takeuchi states in quite straightforward terms that genuine

---

58. "Modernity and its Critique: The Problem of Universalism and Particularism," in *Translation and Subjectivity*, p. 174.
59. Ibid.

universality can emerge only through Asia's historical contribution to the universal values already created by the West—thereby confirming Asia's status as the "true subject" of history, as Sakai writes—we can see that the collapse or conflation between the notions of particularity and singularity establishes in advance the fate of his thinking of resistance. For the universal-particular (or whole-part) relation is through and through a relation of identity, and in this sense Takeuchi's project of *kokumin bungaku* reveals itself to be ultimately an attempt at forming a unique part whose unity and internal homogeneity will allow it to effectively counterpose the hegemony of the West. In this work of Japan's self-formation (*jiko keisei*), Takeuchi loses sight of the fact that the exteriority or difference that is rejected by western universalism is for essential reasons also excluded in his own thinking, insofar as this thinking resists going beyond the principle of identity which informs the whole-part relation. What must be borne in mind here is that exteriority can never be located, claimed as one's own; rather it violently disturbs and displaces all such determinations, even as it allows for them. As a result, resistance against the West necessarily sacrifices its status as resistance the moment it is localized, determinately identified as, following Takeuchi's language, "Oriental resistance." Whatever the political or strategic importance of this gesture by which resistance is identified with Asia, it must nonetheless be recognized that resistance finally resists Asia just as surely as it resists the West.

THE MOVEMENT OF WRITING: COMMUNITY, LITERATURE, ADDRESS

Understood as *kokumin bungaku*, literature should reflect what is believed to be one's immediate belonging to the nation. Consistent with the logic of the whole-part relation, the nation is conceptualized by Takeuchi as a whole whose parts include not only its citizens (the *kokumin* of the *kokumin*, as it were) but also literature itself. Hence the proper reflection of the nation in or through *kokumin bungaku* is in fact a reflection of the whole in its parts. The part derives its identity strictly by virtue of its participation in the whole, whose essence it naturally expresses. As Takeuchi writes in "Son Bun kan no mondaiten": "The proposition that literature represents the sum total (*sōwa*) of a nation's (*minzoku*) life and feeling has always existed as a self-evident premise at the root of my notion of literature. . . . An author and work cannot be conceived as isolated. They can only be considered in terms of their harmony or disharmony with the whole (*zentai*). The whole means the whole of social life. When I think about literature, therefore, a downward-looking consciousness is always at work, and I wish to arrive at the actual conditions of life. Ideally, an understanding of individual literary [phenomena] coincides with a grasp of the whole."[60] Here the whole seems to refer most generally to the notion of "life" (*seikatsu*), and yet a series of slippages will allow Takeuchi to very quickly equate life first with "social life" and then with "national life," as if these terms were all perfectly synonymous with one another. No doubt Takeuchi wishes to designate by this notion of life something like the immediacy and materiality of man's existence in the world. This existence is first of all characterized by man's interaction with both things and other people, an existence in which, as we saw earlier, man is primarily made to *feel* the force of alterity in precognitive or pre-reflective fashion. In this regard, life must be understood as that which furnishes the material conditions for the possibility of man's objective knowledge of the world, for knowledge is possible only insofar as man exists as a corporeal being (as opposed to the disembodied subject of subjective idealism). At the same time, this corporeality establishes important limits or restrictions upon man's objective knowledge, and in this sense life presents itself *also* as a condition for the impossibility of knowledge. A similar logic informs the more delimited whole which Takeuchi calls "social life," the major contours of which are very clearly sketched out in his reading of Lu Xun's parable, "Congmingren he shazi he nucai." To briefly recall, social existence is there determined by Takeuchi on the basis of one's encounter with the other, or rather, with the elusive otherness of that other. This otherness can never fully be apprehended by man; instead man suffers this otherness inasmuch as its force constantly writes or inscribes itself upon him, thereby disturbing the home that constitutes his being as subject. Through the privileged figure of the fool, Takeuchi attempts to show how the regulated exchange of intersubjectivity (the measured reciprocity of its give-and-take, the symmetry of the transference) as demonstrated by the slave's dealings with both the master and the wise man necessarily gives way before the violence of the social relation, which precisely puts in jeopardy the possibility of any neat or simple division between entities as marked by the term "inter-." That the fool destroys the walls of the slave's home in his attempt to "open up a window," as he says, is for Takeuchi emblematic of the unforeseen coming of the other, who in his approach incessantly breaches the enclosure of my interiority and exposes me

---

60. "Son Bun kan no mondaiten," p. 323. Cf. also "Kokumin bungaku no mondaiten": "National literature refers not to a specific literary mode or genre but [rather] to literature's ontological form (*sonzai keitai*) as the whole of the nation." In *TYh*, vol. 2, p. 288.

   This point is summarized by Nakagawa Ikurō as follows: "According to Takeuchi, literature is that which expresses the sum total of a nation's life, and the study of a foreign literature is nothing other than the study of the total life of that foreign nation. As such, Japanese literature should also be the expression of the total life of the Japanese nation." In *Takeuchi Yoshimi no bungaku to shisō*, p. 52.

to the outside. In this respect, we can see how potentially threatening these notions of "life" and "social life" are to the "national life" that Takeuchi nevertheless insists on thinking alongside them. The intimate belonging to the *minzoku* that literature is supposed to reflect—and as well, as we shall argue, actively effect or produce—appears to derive entirely from the slave's desire for refuge, is in other words something that would present itself as an obvious target for the fool's violence. And yet we must remember that the feeling Takeuchi finds to be characteristic of life in general, which is in turn akin to the receptivity or openness associated with social life, profoundly informs his notion of national life as well. Indeed, it is no coincidence that national life is explicitly referred to in this passage as "national life and feeling." In this way, we are better able to understand that the apparent slippage between the notions of life, social life and national life is in fact motivated by the underlying presence of feeling as a common trait which helps link these together.

So we are faced with the argument that the literature that is properly *kokumin bungaku* represents, as Takeuchi writes, "the sum total of a nation's life and feeling." Let us here proceed in our examination of Takeuchi's understanding of the whole-part relation by turning to Takeuchi's own self-representations of *minzoku* identity, in which he addresses the reader from the enunciative position of a specifically Japanese writer. From this we will better appreciate the unique responsibility with which literature is charged in the work of forming the national community, of cementing the ties between individual *kokumin* in their co-belonging to the whole that is the *kokumin* Japan. To begin with, it must be noted that Takeuchi occasionally makes use in his writing of a certain inflection of the first-person plural: whether consciously or otherwise, this form serves to call attention to the putative identity shared by the writer and reader. Now this identity is extremely important for Takeuchi, and may in fact be understood as an essential aspect of the *kokumin bungaku* project itself. In the opening lines of "Seikatsu to bungaku," for example, he declares that "[t]he total aim of this section is to consider from various perspectives the literary life that *we Japanese* are leading today."[61] Once again, we find that the notion of life is associated with the nation in the context of a discussion of literature. Yet whereas in the earlier passage from "Son Bun kan no mondaiten" national life is introduced in very general terms, that is, abstracted from any specific nation or people, here it is presented in reference to Japan alone. In any event, this same form of address (*watashi tachi Nihonjin*) is repeated in "Bungaku ni okeru dokuritsu towa nanika," where it again appears at the opening of the essay. Speaking of the widespread indifference among the

---

61. "Seikatsu to bungaku," p. 296. Emphasis ours. (The word *nerai* ("aim") appears here in *katakana*).

Japanese in regard to their nation's loss of independence (for this loss is not "sensed (*jikkan sareru*) to the degree that it penetrates the flesh," as he writes), Takeuchi now alludes to "a psychological inertia among *us Japanese*, one that has been formed historically."[62] Here we strongly suspect that these appeals to a common Japanese identity shared by writer and reader alike are situated strategically, that they appear at the very opening of Takeuchi's *discourse* so as to at once remind the reader of the immediacy of the ethnic-national bond that ties them together, locates them in one and the same home, as it were. In this case, the word "discourse" must really be used to describe what is taking place, for everything transpires as if this were a scene of speech, one in which the interlocutors were physically present to one another. Otherwise how is it possible for Takeuchi to identify the reader with the same self-assurance (or lack of anxiety) with which he identifies himself, as "we Japanese"? Doubtless the point will be made that these essays were originally written in Japanese, and as such it is perfectly natural for Takeuchi to assume a Japanese readership. Such an appeal to common sense, however, in fact harbors an implicit and entirely uncritical assumption of a natural or immediate unity existing between ethnicity/nationality (*minzokusei*) and national language. As goes without saying, not all "Japanese" speak or read the Japanese language, just as accessibility to this language is in no way restricted to those who identify themselves as Japanese. (And even more: this essential openness of language, the fact that it can be more or less inhabited by anyone regardless of personal identity, is what ultimately disables its status as *national* language. In this respect, the unity or interiority of national language reveals itself to be every bit as fragile as the slave's home in Lu Xun). Following Etienne Balibar, this conflation between a people and a common language can only be understood in terms of what he calls "fictive ethnicity."[63] In all rigor, strict distinctions must be made and maintained between the notions of ethnos, nation and language, and this is something that Takeuchi does not do. Actually, such appeal to a Japanese "we" or "us" may be said to reveal a powerful desire for immediacy on Takeuchi's part, one to which he all too easily surrenders in his reaction against idealism. For even assuming that his intended readership at the time of writing unproblematically identified themselves as Japanese, Takeuchi nevertheless fails to take into account the possibility of errancy, or the essential non-presence between writer (origin) and reader (destination), that structures the very movement of the address. What is at issue here, we believe, is precisely that "movement" (*ugoki*) which we earlier saw linked to what Takeuchi conceives of as the "genetic ground of literature."

---

62. "Bungaku ni okeru dokuritsu towa nanika," p. 66. Emphasis ours.
63. Etienne Balibar and Immanuel Wallerstein, *Race, Nation, Class: Ambiguous Identities*, trans. Chris Turner (London: Verso, 1992), pp. 96-100.

Significantly enough, this notion of movement is introduced in the same passage in "Seikatsu to bungaku" where Takeuchi addresses the reader as "we Japanese." It would not be too much to say that this movement entirely gets away from Takeuchi, and that this is nowhere better exemplified than in the (impossible) recourse to "we Japanese."

Let us explain what we mean by this. At the instant of the address, Takeuchi believes himself to be in the immediate presence of a Japanese community, for only in such presence can one regard the other as identical to oneself, as in other words part of a communal "we." This shared intimacy is one in which, as he puts it elsewhere, "the writer simply sings together with the people (minshū)."[64] As this image suggests, the ideal of communicative transparency between writer and reader seems to be understood by Takeuchi in terms of the voice, as speech or song. Through the medium of the voice, the writer appears able to overcome that opposition which otherwise separates him from the reader, which restricts his writing to the level of mere representation, and achieve a unity with the whole of which he is most originally part: in this way he not only sings for the reader (the people), or derivatively on their behalf, but instead "together with" (tomo ni) them. This is why song, which Takeuchi determines as the most original form of literature, comes to be associated with a pure or as yet uncorrupted communality, as represented by the twin figures of the child and primitive man: "Children sing when they are overcome with feeling, and often these songs are of their own making, composed in impromptu fashion. No doubt the same was true of primitive man."[65] The community of children is identical to the primitive community in that in each case the members' sense of co-belonging to one another as well as to the group as a whole is expressed, in all its innocence, by the voice. For the voice appears as a natural medium: it transparently reflects the immediacy of this belonging, or togetherness, and in this sense it serves as an apt model for the writing of kokumin bungaku, which in similar fashion must directly reveal "the sum total of a nation's life and feeling." Indeed, the feeling that Takeuchi situates at the level of national life, and which naturally comes forth to seek expression in national literature, is essentially no different from the feeling that motivates, or literally animates (from the Latin anima, meaning "breath," "soul"), song. If feeling is that which breathes life into song, then that life is inherently a communal or holistic one, at some point marked by attachment to the minzoku. The externalization that nature and life are forced to endure in the movement of self-expression (i.e., the coming into being of literature

---

64. "Bōkoku no uta," in TYz, vol. 7, p. 27. (Originally published in 1951). Izumi Aki discusses this passage in the context of Takeuchi's nationalism in Nihon rōman-ha hihan, p. 209 ff.

65. "Seikatsu to bungaku," p. 302. We can clearly see in this passage how the immediacy of "feeling" slides imperceptibly into that of the voice, since song is as it were spontaneously or naturally (sokkyō: impromptu, extemporaneous) produced by an excitation of feeling.

and song) signals a transition from the immediacy of feeling to a necessarily mediated articulation in the world. But this mediation in a substance foreign to itself, which otherwise suggests death and unnaturality—and is of course the beginning of culture, of technicity—yet remains for Takeuchi part of life insofar as it emerges in the voice. The voice, then, must be understood here as somehow both spirit and matter, both feeling and articulation, and so as well both inner and outer: it allows for the exteriority of ex-pression without, however, truly exposing this natural life to alterity or corruption.

In vocal song, moreover, the communities of children and of primitives are not ever rent by the opposition between activity and passivity, singer and listener. Rather each member of the community is able to freely partici-pate in what might be called the chorus (*gasshō*) of the community's self-expression. Relatedly, the writer must at all costs avoid alienating himself from the community in his writing, since ultimately it is *the community which writes itself* through the writer. (At bottom, this is what is meant when Takeuchi, in the lines from "Son Bun kan no mondaiten" quoted above, states that "[a]n author and work cannot be conceived as isolated. They can only be considered in terms of their harmony or disharmony with the whole." The writer's essential belonging to the whole means that this latter differentiates or articulates itself in such a way as to produce itself through its parts, thereby appropriating in advance the writer's writing as its own. And yet this articulation of the national community in the form of writing is itself possible only insofar as articulation has already taken place in the form of the writer: *kokumin bungaku*, in other words, is produced by the particular *kokumin* who is himself produced by the *kokumin* as a whole). Because the writer most originally comes from the people, he must in circu-lar fashion attempt to return to them through his writing, thereby reestab-lishing the fundamental integrity of the "we." Without this return there can be no chance of forging a true *kokumin bungaku*, and indeed one would run the risk of falling into the abstract oppositions so characteristic of the litera-ture of the *bundan*. In order to insure that *bungaku* (literature) does not be-come unanchored from its proper base in the *kokumin* (the nation)—where, according to Takeuchi, its drift would invariably be towards the West and its false universalism—it must remain close to communal song, prior to all "social divisions." Once separated from the *kokumin*, *bungaku* loses its pri-mal energy, that is to say, its life; and to be sure, this is the overriding mes-sage of the essay titled, appropriately enough, "Seikatsu to bungaku" [Life and Literature]. The *animation* that literature finds in the nation is equiva-lent to that force which ties all worldly articulation back to immediate feel-ing, since for Takeuchi the nation is in its essence nothing other than "na-tional life and feeling." In other words, just as feeling is seen as the proper origin of articulation, so too must the nation, or the national community of "we Japanese," be understood as the source to which all literature may be ultimately reduced. Concluding this comparison between the national-literary community of writer and reader and the communities of children and of primitives, Takeuchi draws attention to what he terms the "continuity" (*renzoku*) between artistic production and reception, which might otherwise seem to be disparate processes. Again, what is basically at stake here is the underlying oneness of the community: "It appears today that professional writers are clearly separated from the recipients [of their writing], i.e., the general public. Upon close observation, however, we can see that a moment of creation is necessarily contained in the act of reception, just as reception is interwoven by professional writers within the process of their creation. Literary creation requires the continuity of this process, which involves writer and recipient in equal part. This form [of creation] is identical to that of children and primitive man."[66]

What must be borne in mind is that the distance which the writer (or the addresser) takes from the reader (the addressee) in the very act of writing seems to be radically minimalized through the medium of the voice, or through a writing which stays close to the voice by virtue of its resemblance to speech or song. The writer of course writes, he does not sing; and yet Takeuchi envisions a community of Japanese writers and readers who communicate with one another through a song-like writing. In such a community, the words "we Japanese" are immediately comprehensible, indeed much more so than any other words in circulation within that enclosed and familiar social space. Like a song in which readers join their voices to that of the writer—as in the fashion of children or primitives—these words seem to admit of no separation between the enunciating subject and his intended readership. On the contrary, they reflect (and actively produce) the profound "continuity" which exists between them. Following Derrida's now well-known analyses of the notions of *phonē* and *gram*,[67] we can see that the voice has traditionally been associated with the selfsameness of subjective identity (whether the subject be identified as an individual person or as a collective people) in which one appears to immediately receive, or interiorize, that which has been emitted or exteriorized, such that the subject is considered to be entirely autonomous and auto-poietic, radically independent of the material world. In contrast to this seemingly natural state, although of course very much alongside it, writing has most often been condemned on account of its distance and artificiality (that is to say, its technicity). Writing threatens always to escape the circle of the subject's auto-

---

66. Ibid. In the first line, the word "clearly" (*hakkiri*) is emphasized in *katakana*.
67. It should be evident that our understanding of the notion of voice here owes much to Derrida's early works, not only of course to his writings on Husserl but also, and especially where it is a question of the relation between voice and community, to his commentary on Rousseau and the *Essay on the Origin of Languages*, as set forth in *Of Grammatology*, trans. Gayatri Chakravorty Spivak (Baltimore: Johns Hopkins University Press, 1976), pp. 165-268.

affection in its exteriority to the subject: once produced, or fallen into the world, it can in its movement be interjected into a plurality of contexts in such a way that its meaning may come to irrevocably differ from "itself," from the manner in which it was originally intended. Just as writing would in this case bring about a kind of dissonance within the unity of the authorial I, so too does the written articulation of the words "we Japanese" seem, in comparison with their voiced expression, at infinitely greater risk of misunderstanding, for they can now freely be exposed to difference, beyond the immediate reach of hearing/understanding (*entendement*). More specifically, these words can, once written down, always be read by non-Japanese, to whom they are in a certain sense nevertheless addressed, or destined for, in their status as writing. This uncontrollability of the address, which is nothing other than its movement towards the future, forms part of what we earlier referred to as the essential openness of language. Indeed, it is precisely at this point that we are confronted with the "movement" which Takeuchi links with literature—albeit in a way that is still far too insufficiently developed—and which we understand as the very basis for the structure of the address. (Ultimately, of course, both literature and the address are to be considered as instances of writing, taken here in its most general sense). Let us remember that the words "we Japanese" which Takeuchi addresses to the reader are exemplary in that they appear to be transparent, if not to say redundant. No cognitive reflection is required on the part of the reader to grasp what is being said, or rather what is being meant (*vouloir-dire*: the "wanting to say"), since they directly refer back to the interiority that is one's immediate feeling as a Japanese—an interiority that is communal as opposed to individual. Clearly, articulation supposes here a prior moment in which the whole (*zentai*) is yet preserved, left intact. As we have already seen, this moment of pre-articulation is described by Takeuchi in terms of life, feeling and *minzoku*, all of which notions designate for him a kind of primal state of nature.

In this connection, it will be remarked that feeling is now no longer associated with what can be called the general process of receptivity, by which man is repeatedly exposed to the world's exteriority and difference, which literally inscribe themselves upon him, producing anxiety. To be sure, feeling must still be understood as immediate insofar as it is situated at the very border between man and the world. (And this is why, let us note, Takeuchi insists on linking feeling with the body). And yet this immediacy is strictly inaccessible: it is characterized—if indeed it can truly be characterized at all—only by a kind of negativity, as that which radically exceeds or is in surplus to all attempts at appropriation, such as would be the translation of feeling into knowledge. If however feeling is nothing, properly untranslatable, it nevertheless *also* allows for an infinite number of (mis)translations of "itself," since this is its inescapable fate as origin—and an origin would be unthinkable without derivatives, or representations, in relation to which alone it may give itself qua origin. Immediate feeling, then, finds itself subject to a double logic according to which it is somehow *both* exorbitantly silent *and* exorbitantly prolix, that is to say, it *both* retreats from articulation *and* repeats or remarks itself in such a way as to be nothing but articulation. This re-treat of feeling must be understood as a movement: as Takeuchi writes (and which we have already quoted), "our feeling moves. It is shaken in accordance with things or events." What this means is that feeling, to use Takeuchi's own language, *resists* ever presenting itself as such; it ceaselessly moves away from anything that would claim direct lineage or ancestry from itself, as for example the *kokumin bungaku* which he yet wishes to trace back to "national life and feeling." Hence we see, astonishingly enough, that *movement takes place even prior to articulation*, that the articulation of feeling which we commonly recognize as its setting in motion, its release and subsequent passage in the world, in fact communicates with or is merely an extension of that movement of feeling which precedes it. Now when it is a question of attacking the *bundan* (and the political importance of this gesture, we believe, must not be underestimated), Takeuchi attempts to think feeling as that which escapes, and thus disturbs, all appropriations of literature. On the other hand, however, there can plainly be discerned a competing strand of Takeuchi's thought in which he very much desires to preserve the integrity or wholeness of this pre-articulated origin of articulation. Here, feeling is regarded as a kind of substance, one which ultimately gives itself to be identified as such. As substance, feeling literally supports all translations of itself, and can in principle always be returned to by way of these derivative translations or articulations on the basis of what is after all a very traditional notion of "expression" (*hyōgen*)—the logic of which, let us remark, Takeuchi himself explicitly dismantles in the essay "Kindai towa nanika (Nihon to Chūgoku no baai)." This substantialist notion of feeling allows him to say that just as song originates in, and so is the reflective expression of, the pure feeling of children and primitives, so too must one understand the ground of *kokumin bungaku* as situated in "national life and feeling." In other words, whereas feeling was previously seen in terms of movement, that is, as an origin that nevertheless resists (or ungrounds) its own representations, interrupts (*danzetsu suru*) the continuity which it otherwise maintains with them, it now comes to be determined as a self-identical substance whose articulations emerge in the act of its self-expression. Feeling becomes a final resting place for thought, that to which thought must destine itself if it is to lay bare the hidden force or energy which produces representations of the world. Paradoxically enough, the materialism which so profoundly informs Takeuchi's thought in his recourse to such notions as those of feeling and life comes in this way to merge with the most classic of idealisms.[68]

If, as Takeuchi wishes us to believe, literature can successfully be returned to its proper sphere of feeling, how then can we, in response to this thesis, attempt to think feeling on the basis of movement in such a way as to show that this simple relation of expression and return can always possibly be disrupted, unachieved? In so saying, it should be made clear that we do not believe the expressivistic relation which putatively holds between feeling and literature to be merely false, nothing more than a product, as some would say, of ideological consciousness. For this would all too easily release one from examining the underlying logic of this notion of expression, when it is precisely this logic which is most threatening to expression itself. Once again, it is a question here of refusing to adopt a positionality which would claim for itself—whether consciously or otherwise—the space of a simple outside, a pure exteriority. Just as Takeuchi's text demands to be read on its "own" terms, as it were, so too does this difficult notion of expression, which in fact grounds the entire project of *kokumin bungaku*, demand to be treated "internally." Indeed, this notion can be seen to govern not only the relation between feeling and literature, but as well Takeuchi's implicit understanding of literature and the address on the basis of song and voice as opposed to writing. For let us remember that—at least up to a certain point—literature for Takeuchi is most properly an address to one's own national community: the writer (addresser), who is himself a concrete expression of this community, expresses this expression to the reader (addressee) through the return-gift of his writing. In this way, writing shows itself to be close to the voice, that is to say, close to that circularity of the subject's auto-affection which has traditionally been associated with the voice. *Kokumin bungaku* never leaves the *kokumin*, the subject of its enunciation, for it is by definition *of* the *kokumin*, an expressive part which cannot but belong to the whole that is its origin. But this origin is at the same time a point of departure, for the national community must necessarily express itself as it is, it in other words must, as Hegel writes of Spirit, "bring into existence the unity of its self and substance *as its own work*, and thus as an *actual existence.*"[69] This necessity of expression, we believe, essentially communicates with what Takeuchi tries to think—if inadequately—under the heading of movement. It would be possible here to reformulate this notion of movement in such a way that it is not simply opposed to expression, but instead comes to comprehend, or inscribe, this latter entirely within "it-

68. But here we are only repeating a lesson learned from Takeuchi himself, who draws attention to this complicity of materialism with idealism in "Kindai towa nanika (Nihon to Chūgoku no baai)," p. 149.

69. G.W.F. Hegel, *Phenomenology of Spirit*, trans. A.V. Miller (Oxford: Oxford University Press, 1977), p. 266. Emphasis ours.

self." Nevertheless, this inscription would no longer reproduce in itself the logic of the whole-part relation (i.e., the logic of universalism), since the whole would now correspond only to movement, which of course in and of itself is nothing, or nothing, in any event, which could possibly present itself as such. (And yet it will be recalled in this connection that, for Hegel, Spirit is spoken of primarily in terms of movement as well). The step back from literature to feeling, which itself presupposes a further step back from feeling to movement, can be conceived in terms of what we have seen Takeuchi refer to as the "genetic ground of literature." While this ground naturally inscribes within itself its grounded, as for example the structure of expression, it nevertheless does so along the lines of movement, which in this case establishes both the conditions of possibility and of impossibility for something like expression to take place. Expression is possible only because there is movement, or, stated slightly differently, only by virtue of its own status as movement. And yet we could equally put forth the opposite proposition: precisely because movement takes place, expression must be said to be ultimately impossible. In any case, it seems clear that the notion of expression first emerges in response to the need to think relationality, or difference: given the existence in the world of manifold beings, how might one conceive of the nature of the bond between them? If however this notion of expression obviously presupposes difference, it would not be too much to say that it attempts at all costs to domesticate it, order it, such that difference may be shown to derive from an origin that is in and of itself beyond difference. Difference, then, according to the structure of expression, is to be regarded as merely secondary, something that befalls a prior instance of identity.

Generally speaking, expression requires the prior existence of an expressive substance, which Takeuchi, in very classical fashion, identifies as feeling. (That art emerges as the expression of feeling is, once again, a symptom of Takeuchi's deeply entrenched Romanticism. His particular inflection of this Romanticism can be seen in the fact that he wishes to develop this expressivity in the direction of a specifically national art—*kokumin bungaku*—which emerges from the immediacy of a specifically national feeling. Nevertheless, as we have tried to emphasize throughout, this thinking cannot in all fairness be understood without historical reference to Takeuchi's efforts of resistance against the West, and especially against the American colonization of Japan in the postwar). Feeling is the source to which all literature properly returns, as to its home. The expression of feeling allows for the appearance in the world of a multiplicity of literary works, whose considerable differences vis-à-vis one another in terms of, say—to name only the most obvious criteria—period, author, genre, readership, etc. may in principle be negated (or: sublated) by their common foundation in feeling. In order for the movement of expression to take place, this foundation must be a homogeneous one, strictly unified within itself. Paradoxically enough, it is expression—the expression *of* feeling—which ruptures what is in effect this initial plenitude of feeling, since feeling comes to find itself incapable of maintaining this state of pure equilibrium or immobility; it is in other words helpless to resist the exteriorizing force of expression. As in the passage from Hegel just quoted, there seems to suddenly emerge within this pre-expressive unity the desire for autopoiesis, which decisively interrupts or even cuts the whole, violently sweeps it up into the labor of making itself "as its own work, and thus as an actual existence." In Takeuchi's own language, this setting into motion of labor gives itself to be thought as the "process of subjective formation" (*shutai keisei no katei*).[70] Here, the *movement* of expression reveals itself most clearly: expression is literally a force or energy which seeks the outside as its rightful *telos*, it is a "pressing outward" beyond itself, ecstatically. In this sense, expression must be grasped as that activity which is most threatening to all structures or systems—from which it however comes—for these necessarily require the presence of borders whose function it is to ensure containment and interiority, whether this interiority be immediate, as with feeling, or more complex and mediated, as for instance in the case of the nation-state. At the same time, however, feeling has ultimately no choice but to allow for expression if it is to avoid condemning itself to silence, which in this context would mean the absence of literature. Feeling is in this way caught between the proverbial rock and hard place: perfect self-presence and interiority can be preserved only at the cost of suffocation, or at least entropy; whereas absolute exteriorization (ex-pression) would be equivalent to death, a kind of self-diffusion whose parts may always not be recovered.

Now it must be remarked that this inherent difficulty of the notion of expression as it informs the relation between feeling and literature is for Takeuchi the greatest obstacle to *realizing* (*jitsugen suru*) the project of *kokumin bungaku*, allowing it to come forth "as an actual existence." But even more than this, the problem of expression finally reveals itself to him as the problem of modernity itself, and above all when it is a question of Asian (and more specifically, Japanese) resistance against the West. For, in the context of Takeuchi's determination of modernization in terms of westernization, the central problematic emerges roughly as follows: in order for Japan to establish itself on the international stage as a modern nation, it must, in the double sense of the word, *subject* itself to the process of westernization—exactly as the subject of the "process of subjective formation" is forced to subject itself to difference or alterity (everything that Hegel, and more recently Slavoj Žižek after him, famously link with the "tarrying with the negative") so that it may in time come to be formed as an actual, as opposed to merely a potential, subject. This transition (or translation) from potentiality to actuality is nothing other than the movement of expression, in which the self gradually fills out the contours of its destiny by becoming that which it in a sense already is. The obvious danger here lies in this crossing (the "trans-"), which although endured or suffered in full view of the self-realization that is its *telos*, nevertheless may always possibly fail, literally come up short. This failure of expression would be equivalent to a loss of self. The journey from an immediate self to an articulated, internally differentiated self is after all a circular one, in which the self initially loses itself so as to finally gain itself back in the end, precisely in the manner of Odysseus. In the case of Japan's expressive development into a modern nation, the risk of losing itself to the West is powerfully felt by Takeuchi. Indeed, we may even say that Takeuchi understands this loss to have already taken place. For proof of this, one need look no further than the state of modern Japanese literature. "Japanese literature is in crisis," he declares. "Or rather, it would perhaps be more accurate to say that a state has emerged in which literature is lost (*bungaku no sōshitsu jōtai*)."[71]

Just as literature is said to be an expression of feeling, so too may we understand this loss of literature as expressive of a loss of feeling among the Japanese. And we would recall in this connection the strange word of criticism Takeuchi uses in reference to the Japanese: *fukanshō*, which is the common medical term for frigidity or sexual apathy, the component characters of which may be literally translated as "an illness characterized by the absence of feeling." If literature is for Takeuchi inseparably bound up with the notions of nation, life and feeling, and moreover if, as we have seen, the relation between these notions is to a considerable extent determined on the basis of expression, it should come as no surprise that the disease or even death that haunts feeling afflicts in its turn literature and the national community as well. Given Takeuchi's appeal to the figures of the child and primitive to designate a pure community of voiced song, one which could be characterized—if indeed it can truly be characterized at all—only as natural and spontaneous, an originary "in itself" that is as yet untouched by any "for itself," does it come as a surprise to find that the transition from community (*Gemeinschaft*) to society (*Gesellschaft*) is at a certain point linked with writing? In keeping with the traditional historical-anthropological identification of writing as that which marks the boundary or limit between the realms of nature and culture, Takeuchi suggests that it is in effect the unnatural separation inherent in the structure of writing which is primarily to blame for the rupture of community, as represented here by the estranged relations between writer and reader. In this passage, the writer is, so to speak, artificially written by another writing, one which

---

71. "Seikatsu to bungaku," p. 298.

must be understood as strictly foreign to the original writer-reader relation. This writing is the journalism that appears in all modern societies: "Another thing to be considered is the mechanics of creation and reception, and above all the specialization of creation. What has spurred on this specialization is the development of mass communication. Today the strong impersonal will of journalism stands between the writer and the recipients [of his writing]. Journalism commands writers, and through submission to its will they have come to be severed from the immediate link with readers (*chokusetsu no tsunagari wo tatareteiru*). This will of journalism not only controls writers, it is so powerful that it even artificially (*jiniteki ni*) produces readers. The process of exchange between creation and reception which used to take place long ago in that communication (*komyunikēshon*) between writers and readers in such places as the salon, the workplace and the farmhouse fireside, has now virtually disappeared."[72] The series of oppositions that structures these lines and lends them their cogency should be quite familiar to us by now: creation vs. reception, writer vs. reader, active vs. passive, writing vs. speech, distance vs. proximity, artifice (*technē*) vs. nature, mediation vs. immediacy, severance vs. unity, miscommunication vs. communication, present vs. past. Solely on the basis of these oppositions, a *chronology* (for it is in fact a question here of a subordination of time to logic, of "movement" or "genesis," to borrow Takeuchi's words, to form and structure) could be developed which corresponds in large part to Takeuchi's narrative of community, one which however is in no way restricted to him alone. (But again, as if in demonstration of this very point, such a chronology would have to take into account the historical singularity of Takeuchi's text, and this is of course what would differentiate it from other like chronologies). In its most basic outline, this chronology would trace the movement from Oneness to multiplicity, a movement that Takeuchi describes in unequivocally theological terms as a fall, a lapse. It is, to reproduce his own language, a "crisis," "decadence," "sterility" and "disease," and this catastrophe naturally sets into motion—what is really a counter-motion, since it goes against the very grain of movement—a curative logic of recovery or restoration (*kaifuku*) (the "restoration of energy that has been lost in literary creation," as he writes some pages later, or again, "today's urgent task of restoring the creative force of literature in [this] period of transition").[73] This catastrophe represents a departure from what is claimed to be an originary plenitude, in which the community harmoniously created itself and received itself in one and the same gesture, or rather one and the same

---

72. Ibid., p. 304.
73. Ibid., pp. 307 and 308. As Takeuchi comments, this restoration proceeds by "an analysis of the disease" so as to arrive at a "diagnosis," whereupon one then commences "basic treatment" (p. 300).

breath, as it were. No separation (*bungyō, zure*) existed between writer and reader at this time since both derived their identity strictly in terms of the community, of which they are in the end merely parts, or members (in the sense of limbs attached to a body). This communal whole, it must be emphasized, is a space of synchronicity: the time of creation coincides exactly with the time of reception, for only in this way can perfect understanding be ensured. This understanding is for Takeuchi "communication" in its most authentic and proper sense.

All too typically, such communication is projected onto a distant past, a *mukashi* that is, if now vanished from our modern day society, yet not entirely dead, for it may once again be recovered, and this of course through the work of *kokumin bungaku*. But what is perhaps no less typical is that this sacred space of the past is *figured* (*keishōka suru*—this word, significantly enough, appears in the very same pages we are here examining)[74] by sites of nostalgia, of immediate proximity and belonging, as for example the literary salon, the workplace and the farmhouse fireside. Above all, these sites seem to be characterized by Takeuchi as privileged instances of speech or orality, very much in the same manner that children and primitives are determined as exemplars of communal song. Whereas the time of the present is marked by an acute discontinuity (*hirenzoku*) in social relations, in which an external and contingent force has somehow come to "stand between (*hasamatteite*) the writer and the recipients" of his writing, such that the "immediate link" between them is now "severed,"[75] as Takeuchi claims,

---

74. "When the social function of literature is working effectively, writers can observe both their own lives and those of others, and absorb the nourishment from the roots of those lives. In this way, literature blossoms forth. Writers are thus able to express through artistic figuration (*geijutsuteki na keishōka ni yotte hyōgen suru*) the smallest details in feeling of the people's lives" (p. 303).

75. As concerns this extremely important notion of the cut or severance in Takeuchi, cf. his criticism of the writers of proletarian literature in "Kindaishugi to minzoku no mondai": "Although it is at a certain stage necessary to define man as abstractly free or as [belonging to] classes, proletarian literature, like all the schools of modern Japanese literature, did not escape the precipitate sense of its own self-importance when *its relation with the concrete and whole image of man became severed* (*gutaitekina mattaki ningenzō to no kanren wo tatarete*), thus allowing it to regard [its own notion of man as abstractly free and as belonging to classes] as complete" (p. 278; emphasis ours). (These lines are discussed in the broader scope of Takeuchi's nationalism in Koschmann, *Revolution and Subjectivity in Postwar Japan*, pp. 203-205).

Without any exaggeration whatsoever, we can say that everything that is at stake here comes down to the relation between these notions of relation (*tsunagari, kanren*) and the cut. For Takeuchi, relation is all too often conceived as a cut from an originary whole, within which "relations" were not yet of the nature of the cut, for they were still "immediate," as he writes, meaning absolutely intimate. Hence, following the chronology we have detected in his text, there exist two types of relation, of radically different orders from one another. On the one hand, a relation within the whole that in no way divides it from itself, but rather simply opens up the space of its "communication"; and on the other, the relation which represents the fall of this as yet unmarked or pure space of the community. Clearly, this second type of relation is

the literary salon, workplace and farmhouse fireside of the past are on the contrary characterized by the pure continuity of "exchange" that is determined as communication. Once again, in this privileging of the notion of exchange we witness the supplanting of the fool by the slave, what might be called the *presentation* of the social relation. The literary salon, workplace and farmhouse fireside were sites in which reader and writer could discuss literary writing face to face, interchangeably, just as writers would doubtless on occasion read their writing aloud to their readers. Moreover, this literary activity had the added advantage of taking place all under one roof, such that writers and readers were, at least theoretically, always within earshot of one another. In any case, these communal spaces, which are determined by Takeuchi in direct contrast to, or as the simple negative of, modern society—and we may read in this a profound (if implicit) admission that presence can as a rule never be conceived of directly, but rather only in roundabout fashion as the negation of a negative—were free from the artifice of journalism. Here in these immediately familiar settings peopled only by writers and readers, there were no "commands," no "control" and no "submission," nothing that imposed its "will" upon this natural relation. As goes without saying, these particular locales named by Takeuchi are nothing more than the symbols of that perfect interiority which is the writer-reader relation. This interiority is temporally one with itself, utterly synchronous, since, as in the fashion of song, what is being presented here is a scene of speech. The literary community communicates with itself in such a way as to self-reflexively hear itself speak, and there is no possibility of misunderstanding (*malentendu*) since expression exteriorizes only that which is most immediately felt by the community, which is of course the sense of its own communality, the certainty of co-belonging that binds the parts to one another as well as to the overall whole. The expression of feeling by the writer's writing never truly comes to threaten this feeling insofar as writing is believed to be absolutely reducible to speech: in the literary salon, the workplace and the farmhouse fireside, writing is safely brought back to that voiced interiority of the community from which it first emerges. In this way, expression is followed by complete comprehension in accordance with

---

what destroys the natural beauty and truth of the original community. And yet it is not difficult to see that the incisiveness of this second relation already marks the first relation; that is to say, the community in order to "communicate," to be in relation with itself, and thus indeed to be a community at all, must already have experienced its own self-severing. Which means then that no pure whole in fact preceded the cut, that this whole could only have been conceived of retroactively, and so nostalgically. Understood in its most general sense—and yet with regard to Takeuchi's specific example of journalism—we may say that the community is from its inception necessarily a community *of writing*, and no community of song, such as that of children and primitives, could possibly have escaped this writing.

the circular structure of auto-affection, what we have seen to be the subject communing with itself in isolation from the historical world.

Upon the advent of modernity, however, the community is suddenly forced to reckon with the threat of distance, or overflow, for now social stratification has advanced to such a degree that it is impossible to any longer keep the parts entirely under the same roof, which is to say, as with Lu Xun, within the walls of the same home. This distance or overflow, which irrevocably fractures the community, opens it up to the violence of its self-differentiation, is represented by Takeuchi as the destruction of speech, as figured in this instance by the supersession of the salon, the workplace and the farmhouse fireside, and the concomitant emergence of writing in the form of journalism. Significantly, this opposition between journalistic writing and these delimited, bounded spaces which house literary writing ultimately comes down to the question of whether writing can in fact be housed at all. For we suspect here that Takeuchi's condemnation of journalism actually stems from his desire to properly situate writing, to arrest what is quite literally the uncanniness (*Unheimlichkeit*) of its movement. Unlike more traditional communities in which literature involved an active *gathering* of communal members around sites which were clearly marked out in advance, journalism seems characterized not only by the absence of such places—for this would still be but an empirical fact—but even more by the essential dissolution of place itself. This dissolution of place could be defined most generally as an untying, or unloosening, of the relation between writing and determination, but only on the condition that we understand that the movement of writing is such as to simultaneously determine and undetermine itself, that it is somehow binding and unbinding at one and the same time. Journalism is, as Takeuchi recalls, an instance of "mass communication," but this communication (*dentatsu*) reveals itself to be profoundly inauthentic, hardly worthy of the name when compared to the established places of true communication (*komyunikēshon*), or true community, the borders of which journalism nevertheless dissolves. And yet this dissolution is in no way to be confused with a total annihilation of place, such that everything simply collapses into utter nothingness. Rather, as journalism plainly demonstrates, the dissolution of place opens up the possibility for new and different places to be created, places which are no longer purely continuous with those of the past. (But isn't this movement precisely what Takeuchi tries to think, following Nishida, under the distinct if related headings of *ba* or *basho* (place) and *hirenzoku no renzoku* (the continuity of discontinuity)? The question then would be what prevents Takeuchi from thinking this movement in relation to journalism, and so by extension to the destruction of community). In this way, journalism calls attention to the fact that the dissolution of place is for writing most truly an *affirmation* of place, that, indeed, the unsettling movement of writing not only seeks but in some sense actively creates the places which in turn come to determine it. There seems to be here a certain uncontrollable drift inherent to writing, in the face of which Takeuchi experiences a great deal of anxiety, for he regards such writing as a clear threat to the survival of community.

Now if it is true that writing signals the death of community, this is above all because of its dehumanizing effects. For this transition from natural community to modern society, or from voice to writing, is necessarily also a transition from man (or at least man as he has traditionally been defined) to that which exceeds man. The discourse of dehumanization is of course an extremely common one, and can be seen to inform the most diverse of political projects, on both the right and the left, in Japan as well as elsewhere. In Takeuchi's text, the threat of dehumanization reveals itself most forcefully in his understanding of journalism in terms of what he calls its "impersonality" (*mujinkaku*). For if the community is most properly a human community, as Takeuchi believes to be the case, its destruction would be equivalent to a kind of effacement of man, such that the writing which was previously produced and received by man must now be regarded as vastly beyond his control, it has somehow taken on its own life independently of him. Just as the privileged sites of the salon, the workplace and the farmhouse fireside have been superseded by the movement of writing, so too does man come to find himself superseded. This is why Takeuchi must call attention to what he considers to be the unnatural violence of journalism. In the form of literature, writing was nothing more than the product of the community essentially expressing itself to itself,[76] it belonged solely to the circuit of communication. Journalistic writing, however, violently shatters the community, and this it does by externally "commanding writers, submitting them to its will," as Takeuchi asserts. That is to say, in modernity the hierarchical relation between man and writing has undergone an astonishing and decisive reversal, with the result that man is now no longer the sovereign subject of writing—he is indeed no longer man, but rather something anonymous, nameless, without any substantial identity. Because the impersonal force of journalism has proven itself to be more powerful than man, its anonymity effectively sweeps up man in its grasp, requiring that he be determined henceforth strictly in terms of writing.

Now if writing in this way ultimately destroys the community and man along with it, if it dissolves in its movement all that would seek to determine it, how then does Takeuchi respond to this writing? As we have seen, his response is one of the most thoroughgoing nostalgia, shaped by the desire for the restoration or recovery of a lost presence. More specifically, he conceives of the project of *kokumin bungaku*, which takes as its goal the

---

76. What Jean-Luc Nancy has named "immanentism," in *The Inoperative Community*, ed. Peter Connor (Minneapolis: University of Minnesota Press, 1991), p. 3.

cessation of such movement and the proper return of writing to its immediate site of origin, in "national life and feeling." Given the decline or, in some cases, total disappearance of the traditional literary-communal places of the past (the salon, the workplace, the farmhouse fireside), the home of writing must necessarily be figured anew by the nation. It is the nation that is believed capable of restoring that unity and wholeness which supposedly preceded the cut of journalistic writing, thus allowing for authentic communication between writer and reader to again take place.

For Takeuchi, the threat posed by writing lies in its essential opening to the outside: if writing enacts a movement, as is certainly the case here, this movement is a profoundly centrifugal one, tending always away from the otherwise circular and self-enclosed system, however this latter may be defined. The movement of writing is a distancing, an overflow. Now the system that Takeuchi so ardently wishes to preserve is that of the community, represented here by the literary community of writer and reader. In its foreignness, journalistic writing is said to violate the natural immediacy and integrity of this community. Prior to journalism, it appears, the writer and reader enjoyed relations of transparency, and this because writing was read (or heard) as a reflective expression of a preexisting communal feeling that bound the community together in its parts. In a strange sense, the original writing that took place within the community was redundant, since it only revealed to the community the fact of its own communality, which it in any event already felt. (And we must not fail to recognize this same redundancy in Takeuchi's spoken-written address of "we Japanese"). If one were to inquire a little into this redundancy, however, certain questions would very quickly arise. Given that there was originally no distinction between the actually existing community and its essential communality, for example, why does it then become necessary to articulate this communality in the first place? That is to say, if we are to believe that the community is, prior to writing, immediately communal, how can one possibly begin to explain its desire to exteriorize itself, to sacrifice this pure and unmarked interiority, so as to effectively reveal itself to itself in its writing? Insofar as the problematic of writing is framed in these terms, however, Takeuchi has no choice but to conceive of community along the lines of the most traditional (and theological) of narratives, as in other words a simple paradise lost. Hence: interiority is destroyed by exteriority, essence is betrayed by contingent existence, or the One is superseded by the multiple. In all cases, the violence that ruptures community is situated on the outside, it is what befalls an original goodness. This may be formalized as follows: spatially violence is exterior, while temporally it is secondary, derivative upon a prior instance. And we should perhaps see here a sign that the most laborious and thorough of historical thinking, as was Takeuchi's, is in no way exempt from the most nostalgic of ideals, insofar as such notions as those of man, writing, and community remain unexamined, complacently taken for granted.

Invariably, the question comes down to thinking the origin beyond nostalgia as in some sense already divided from itself, already multiple. We can better grasp this by generalizing Takeuchi's thinking of feeling *on the basis of* movement in such a way as to allow this movement more play, more freedom of movement, as it were. For it can never be a case of simply ignoring the question of origin—and Takeuchi understood this perfectly. If thought obeys a law, this law demands that thought return to the ground, or the place, from which all things first come into being. In Takeuchi's text, this ground is determined primarily in terms of feeling and life. Writing is what then befalls this ground, even if it is considered in some instances as expressive thereof. Upon closer examination, however, we can see that, in the context of feeling, the articulatory movement from feeling to writing is in fact preceded by another movement, one which already moves feeling away from itself. Here, feeling undergoes a kind of shift in status such that it is no longer merely an expressive substance, an interiority waiting to actualize itself, but instead, even before this, a receptivity that is constantly marked over by the world's writing. Prior to man's active *expression* of feeling, then, there takes place a fundamental suffering on his part, a passive *impressionability* that signals his exposure to the alterity of history, the world, and others. In this respect, we see that the movement from inside to outside is possible only insofar as it is grounded upon a more powerful movement, one which travels from outside to inside. Expression no longer can be traced back to the departure point of feeling since feeling itself originates in the world; in other words, writing returns us in the end not to an author but rather to a surface that is itself written. Nevertheless—and this is crucial—this writing before writing does not simply disable all projects of expressive writing, as for example that of *kokumin bungaku*. Such projects still take place, but they take place, significantly, only on the basis of a more original place (*basho*) (thus a place before place, a writing before writing, a movement before movement) which furnishes them with their conditions of possibility and impossibility. Naturally enough, this place of origin can be seen in the community which Takeuchi wishes to protect from writing in the form of journalism. This community can never be restored in its immediate integrity since it is, in principle, already written, and thus already divided from itself. The cut of journalistic writing really does nothing more than repeat the cut from which the community already suffers. For, as Takeuchi tells us, the community is peopled by writers (creators) and readers (recipients), who in their distinction from one another represent the community's self-differentiation, the disappearance of its essential oneness and communality. The return movement from journalistic writing back to the community reveals this latter to be in fact already articulated by the writing of literature, and from this we are forced to conclude that the origin of writing is necessarily writing. If for Takeuchi journalistic writing marks the end of authentic community and communication, then it seems clear that this writing is not to be opposed to the writing of literature; instead it helps us think the originary violence that the community must suffer if it is to appear qua community. Just as feeling reveals itself to be essentially open to the world's inscriptions, so too does the community teach us that its most original or natural state is paradoxically one of writing.

2. The Instant of Experience

This second chapter may be read as an extended dwelling on the following words: "Surprise, however, *is* experience, and any empiricism without surprise, any empiricism devoted entirely to the customary and the everyday, fails to do justice to empiricity."[1] In order to "do justice to empiricity," there is a need to think the notion of experience anew, not merely as something that can be grounded in the final instance on a selfsame subject, but rather as that which, precisely, over-takes the subject, exposes it to the alterity of the world. This exposure lies at the very heart of Takeuchi's thinking of experience as articulated through such notions as those of corporeality, feeling and the instant. What this thought calls attention to is the recognition of a kind of border that rigorously separates experience from knowledge: because of this border, experience emerges as the proper limit of knowledge, that which knowledge cannot or must not cross over into and fully appropriate for itself. And yet if knowledge is forced in this way to respect the difference that is experience, this in no way implies that experience can now simply be privileged in opposition to knowledge. Let us suggest that Takeuchi is extremely ambiguous on this point. While he forcefully demonstrates the precarious position of knowledge, which in his view is always the knowledge *of* experience, there can nevertheless be seen in his work a tendency to ontologize experience, as if the border which separates experience from knowledge did not at the same time put these two into relation, thereby opening experience up to the possibility of its betrayal, or violation, by knowledge. This tendency remains in tension with another understanding of experience that he introduces, one which is explained through recourse to

---

1. Peter Fenves, "Foreword: From Empiricism to the Experience of Freedom" to Jean-Luc Nancy, *The Experience of Freedom*, trans. Bridget McDonald (Stanford: Stanford University Press, 1993), p. xxx.

the elusive "here" and "now." Certainly Takeuchi's efforts to articulate a more originary notion of experience represent an attack against empiricisms which do not take sufficiently seriously the division between experience and knowledge, for only on the basis of this division is something like "surprise" possible. It is in this connection that I examine the pragmatism of the Chinese thinker Hu Shi, which Takeuchi judges to be ultimately a subjectivization of experience, a failure to think the practical agent in all its bareness and alterity. Following Takeuchi, I attempt to show that the nature of experience is such as to render impossible the formation of a subject which could in any way represent the unity of experience and knowledge.

"SENSUALITY": IMPRESSIONS OF THE BODY

In his 1966 article "Jissenteki mujun ni tsuite" [On Practical Contradiction], the poet and literary critic Yoshimoto Takaaki appears to criticize what he refers to as Takeuchi Yoshimi's "sensual" reading of China: "As concerns my reading of [Takeuchi's] work, no matter how theoretically dense [that work may be], I can always feel that he interprets China on the basis of something like sensuality (*nikkan no yō na mono*)."[2] It would not be too much to say that, for us, this remark singularly grasps what is at issue in Takeuchi's writings: not only does it reflect what we understand to be Yoshimoto's deep ambivalence regarding Takeuchi's position vis-à-vis China and Chinese literature; in addition, it in a strange way performs the insight that so forcefully informs that position. Within Takeuchi's writings on China, that aspect of "sensuality" which coexists alongside of his "theoretical density" can be isolated, perhaps, without undue difficulty. In "Wasurerarenai kotoba" [Unforgettable Words], for example, Takeuchi alludes to a certain bodily reaction in his discussion of the notion of ways, or paths, in Lu Xun: "It is easy to walk in those places where ways [already] exist. When one is about to step forth into a place where there are no ways, however, the entire body tenses up, the heart pounds and one breaks out in a cold sweat."[3] This same emphasis on the body can be found in "Seiji to bungaku no mondai (Nihon bungaku to Chūgoku bungaku I" [The Question of Politics and Literature (Japanese Literature and Chinese Literature I)], where we read of what are literally Takeuchi's "impressions" (*inshō*) of the Chinese poet Li Shou in the course of his description of the latter's roundtable discussion with a group of Japanese writers from the leftist journal *Shin Nihon bungaku* [New Japanese Literature]: "Of course the record of a

---

2. This essay is organized under the heading "Takeuchi Yoshimi," in *Yoshimoto Takaaki zenchosakushū* (Tokyo: Keisō Shobō, 1968), vol. 7, p. 389.

3. In *TYz*, vol. 2, p. 361. Originally published in 1958.

round-table discussion differs from its actual atmosphere at the time, and so my impressions might well be mistaken. But even in that incomplete record or transcription, there was something in Li Shou's remarks that pressed in upon me with an intensity that struck to the bone. I understand what Li felt in the very pores of his body. He felt this strongly; and it is through this feeling that I understand him, though I have not read his works. . . . [For he] spoke in a language whose profundity emerged from experience (*taiken*)."[4] In both these passages, Takeuchi's "sensuality"—the term in Japanese combines the characters for "flesh" and "feeling"—reveals itself through a peculiar concern with the corporeal. This concern is motivated by a desire to inquire into the conditions of both knowledge and meaning, the very possibilities of which are for him inextricably bound up with the question of corporeality, or materiality. For, as Yoshimoto's remark seems to suggest, the "theory" (*riron*) whose density or rigor Takeuchi's work admirably displays can never be found in isolation. The concept of theory is in and of itself senseless; by right, it derives its meaning strictly in relation to that other which it is not, in this case "sensuality." Yet in order for theory to safeguard its own theoreticality, whose purity of thought and speculation stands entirely opposite from what we understand as the sensual, it must deny that relation and claim some type of conceptual autonomy or integrity for itself. The intelligibility of the concept of theory depends upon its *difference* from the concept of sensuality; but insofar as that difference is necessarily also a relatedness, "theory" is unable to fully divorce itself from "sensuality." In this respect, Yoshimoto's express linking of the two together functions as a valuable corrective to that tendency which insists upon their separation. Here we can perhaps make out something of an effect, or an echo, of Takeuchi's own discourse.

Hence in his discussion of the notion of "ways" in Lu Xun, which Takeuchi reads as expressive of the simultaneous grounding and ungrounding of knowledge in concrete experience, the body is seen as the immediate departure point from which emerge all representations of the world. In order for these representations to accurately reflect the world, however— "accurately like a camera, 'accurately' in showing time and space reduced to two dimensions," as Takeuchi will write elsewhere[5]—the body must be made transparent, its opaqueness attenuated in such a way as to allow it to function as a vehicle connecting world to mind in a fluid, uninterrupted

4. In *TYz*, vol. 4, pp. 103-104. Originally published in 1948. Donald Keene devotes several pages to the journal *Shin Nihon bungaku* as well as to the organization and activities of the "Shin Nihon bungakkai" in *Dawn to the West: Japanese Literature in the Modern Era* (New York: Henry Holt and Co., 1984), vol. 1, pp. 972 ff.
5. "Kindai towa nanika (Nihon to Chūgoku no baai)," in *TYz*, vol. 4, pp. 159-160. Originally published in 1948.

fashion. The body, that is to say, is to be recognized as that unique passageway through which world becomes word (*kotoba*), through which, in other words, that being which is otherwise utterly senseless is raised to the status of reason, or *logos*. Now it is against this very problematic notion of translation that Takeuchi is forced to inquire into what actually happens to the body in its experience of the world. In the walking along ways that are at each instant new, such that one is always overtaken, or literally surprised, by that newness, the body reacts unexpectedly, it becomes, so to speak, caught up in the outside: "the entire body tenses up, the heart pounds and one breaks out in a cold sweat." The experience that Takeuchi is here describing is in no way delimitable; it is not something that takes place only in determinate, given contexts, as for example the "limit situations" (*Grenzsituationen*) of which the philosophy of existence speaks. Rather, as he seems to suggest, it represents the generality of experience itself. This is why, ultimately, there can be no places in which ways are already marked out in advance: insofar as each "step" of experience breaches a new and entirely unprecedented way, the physical reaction sketched out by Takeuchi (which he represents, significantly, as the singular reaction of *anxiety* (*fuan*))[6] occurs constantly, regardless of whether one is conscious of this reaction or not. Although the body must first experience the world so as to subsequently give birth to knowledge, the immediate instant of that experience works to disrupt this process by marking the body in ways that consciousness is unable to fully take into account. The body shows itself here to be both active and passive: while it traces ways upon the world in all of its actions, thereby poietically making the world over, imprinting difference upon it, it is also at the same time forced to submit to its own marking, or way-making, in the face of experience. What we see in this relation between body and world is a kind of reciprocal tracing of surfaces in which man's activity of way-making becomes just one instance of a more general tracing (or waying, writing) between things. From this, in fact, we can understand that man in the first instance necessarily receives or suffers tracing in his experience of the world just as he himself actively traces upon it. While this relation is indeed a reciprocal one, it should nevertheless be clear that it is not at all symmetrical, and that there is rather a serious imbalance between man and world. For inasmuch as we define the world, after Takeuchi, as "a place where there are no ways," all of man's way-making occurs unavoidably as part of the general activity of tracing within which is utilized man's body as a receptive and impressionable surface.

---

6. Among the numerous places where Takeuchi discusses this notion, see "Seiji to bungaku no mondai (Nihon bungaku to Chūgoku bungaku I)" and the 1948 "Bunka inyū no hōhō (Nihon bungaku to Chūgoku bungaku II)," in *TYz*, vol. 4, pp. 115-127.

We can begin to see that, for Takeuchi, the body's importance lies in its functioning as a material surface which receives in its experience constant impressions from the world of things. It is this notion of "impressions" that deserves particular emphasis in this regard, for without understanding the logic which so intimately ties this notion to the body and its experience of the world, one is bound to underestimate or even disparage the strange presence of "sensuality" in Takeuchi's writing. In the passage taken from "Seiji to bungaku no mondai (Nihon bungaku to Chūgoku bungaku I)" above, the "impressions" of which he speaks should for this reason be treated with a certain weight. Read too quickly, the word is reduced to its most commonplace meaning as to suggest simply an "understanding" or "idea" that Takeuchi receives on the basis of his study of the record of the round-table discussion held between the Chinese poet Li Shou and members of the Japanese *bundan* at the time. The proof of this misreading can be found in the lines which immediately follow Takeuchi's use of this word: "But even in that incomplete record or transcription, there was something in Li Shou's remarks that *pressed in upon me with an intensity that struck to the bone. I understand what Li felt in the very pores of his body.*" Far from implying merely an initial grasp of the discussion that is as yet uncertain and tentative, we can see on the contrary that these "impressions" contain a meaning that is unfolded only in the description which succeeds the appearance of this term. In this context, the notion of "impressions" communicates with that "intensity" with which, as he writes, the poet's remarks "pressed in upon me" (*sematte kuru*). While this linking between "impressions" and "press" in the English is of course fortuitous, and in no way reflects a parallel connection in the original Japanese, what is nevertheless of central importance is that more general conceptuality that joins together the notion of inscription upon a surface (*inshō*) with that of pressure, or force (*semaru*). At issue here is the alterity of the world that in the course of experience inexorably forces itself upon the body in the form of writing, such that the pressure I feel from this outside can be identified only in terms of the "impressions" that it produces and leaves behind. These "impressions," however, do not exist simply *between* the self and its outside, for the body that they mark up is not yet an "I" whose existence is one of independence from, or opposition to, the world.[7] Indeed, the effect of these "impressions" is

---

7. Understood in this sense, the body would be nothing more than what Jean-Luc Nancy refers to as the site of *opening* (or exposure). Bodies, he writes, "are the *open* space, that is to say in a sense the properly *spacious* rather than spatial space, or that which one can still name the *place*. Bodies are the places of existence, and there is no existence without place, without *there*, without a 'here' for the *this*. The body-place is neither full nor empty, it has neither outside nor inside." And again, several lines later: "All its life, the body is also a dead body, the body of a death, of this death that I am living. Dead or alive, neither dead nor alive, I *am* the opening, the tomb or the mouth, the one within the other." *Corpus* (Paris: Éditions Métailié,

precisely to disturb and call into question the imagined fixity of this border. At this point the body exists on equal par with all things in the world, which likewise are continuously exposed to the imprinting force of "impressions." Takeuchi underscores this fact in his text by the attention he gives to the corporeal: he admits to finding himself in his reading of the record of the round-table discussion "struck to the bone," and this by something that Li Shou "felt in the very pores of his body." In the immediacy of these bodily impressions consciousness has not yet come to the fore; instead Takeuchi's emphasis is on the register of "feeling" (*kanji*), a term which is to be understood as synonymous with "impressions." Hence the poet "feels" through his body, "he felt this strongly," and this feeling somehow communicates itself to Takeuchi (it makes itself felt, as one says) despite the fact that he has never read the works of this writer. Unlike consciousness, which operates on the basis of the absolutely fundamental distinction between identity and difference, or self and other—such that that which is thought in its oneness and unity must necessarily differ from something else—"feeling" is capable of registering only the "intensities" that derive from the outside world, intensities which in their exteriority, or alterity, are in no way governed by that law of contradiction which divides identity from difference. In this sense, "feeling" refers to man's unmediated exposure or opening to the world, that is to say, it refers to the notion of *experience*. And this is what Takeuchi calls attention to in his account of Li Shou, who he finds speaks "in a language whose profundity emerged from experience." The conceptual chain that Takeuchi is here implicitly constructing is one that includes the notions of impressions, corporeality, feeling, and experience. Each of these notions links up with the others in designating what are for him the essential limits of consciousness: since there can be no (active) knowing or awareness (*jikaku*) of the world without the prior (passive) receptivity to its givenness—wherein receptivity, as we have discussed, takes the singular form of impressions traced out upon a feeling body—consciousness has no choice but to ground itself upon these more fundamental notions. And yet insofar as this very relation of grounding threatens the possibility of consciousness and knowledge, that it in other words establishes their conditions *both* of possibility *and* of impossibility, consciousness must, to borrow a term from Freud, "disavow" that relation. That is to say, just as for Freud the male is forced to disavow (or deny) the fact of the absence of the penis in the female out of fear "of the possibility of his being castrated himself,"[8] as he writes, so too must consciousness insist on acknowledging in that (un)ground only that which enables it, which insures its survival and proper

---

1992), pp. 16-17. Emphasis in the original.
8. *An Outline of Psycho-Analysis*, trans. James Strachey (New York: W.W. Norton and Company, 1949), pp. 59-60.

functioning. Therefore it is in seeing its limits that it must, paradoxically, disavow the fact that it is seeing them. Or rather: what it recognizes in those limits is precisely that which cannot be seen, something which in retreating from sight yet opens up the precarious space of its possibility—a precariousness which consciousness cannot see but only *feel*. (And this is exactly what Takeuchi means by his use of the word "anxiety"). For this reason, the body's imprinting of experience constitutes for seeing consciousness what in "Seiji to bungaku no mondai (Nihon bungaku to Chūgoku bungaku I)" is appropriately referred to as a "blindspot" (*mōten*).[9] In its obsession with seeing, consciousness is fundamentally unable to "see" that which resists and exceeds visuality: its "blindspot," in other words, lies nowhere else but in its activity of seeing. Because it sees, it blinds itself to that which underlies, and ultimately undermines, all seeing. This unseen ground of consciousness is what guarantees that there will always be a surplus of meaning, a remainder or *restance* that escapes the system of thought and intelligibility even as it allows for it. In its status as the immediate departure point of consciousness, i.e., the "stuff" upon which consciousness raises itself and makes use of, this remainder forms an essential part of the unity and totality of this system. But because it also marks itself outside the system, it effectively opens the system up to its Other, thus disturbing its very systematicity. The paradox here is that this disturbance does not in any way *en*croach or *in*trude upon consciousness from a space that would be simply exterior to it; rather, in a very strange fashion, conscious interiority discovers that it has from its beginning (its outset) always already betrayed itself, that the outside from which it desires to safeguard itself in fact forms part and parcel of its inside.

With this in mind, let us now turn back to what we understood to be Yoshimoto's criticism of Takeuchi's "sensuality," a sensuality whose presence in the latter's text we have been trying to unfold. As we have seen, Takeuchi wishes to draw attention to a certain centrality of the body in all acts of knowing, since it is in fact the body—and with it the notions of impressions, feeling and experience attendant upon it—that consciousness must exclude, or rather, as we have said, *disavow*, if it is to secure its own autonomy and integrity. Now this privileging of the body lies in the fact that it is, at one and the same time, that thing which is somehow most familiar

---

9. "Seiji to bungaku no mondai (Nihon bungaku to Chūgoku bungaku I)," p. 104. As is well known, the criticism of visuality in Takeuchi is set forth most thoroughly in "Kindai towa nanika (Nihon to Chūgoku no baai)," where it forms part of the overall strategy of resistance to subjectivity (*shukansei*), modernity and the West. Significantly, this notion of resistance is enabled by its refusal of all "absolute viewing" (*zettaishi*), as Oda Makoto points out in his "Takeuchi Yoshimi no Ajia ron ni tsuite." Collected in *Sengo bungaku to Ajia* (Tokyo: Mainichi Shinbunsha, 1978), p. 228.

and most foreign to us. All people of course have a body (each person is, as one says in English, "some-body"), and yet this body is constructed in such a way as to steadfastly resist any discursive knowledge of itself. Because of this resistance it is impossible to speak of the body as in any sense *mine*, as if it somehow belonged to me and me alone. In fact, it is what we might call here the betrayal of the body vis-à-vis the possibility of ownership, belonging—all propriety—that so fascinates Takeuchi. Hence, as in "Wasurerarenai kotoba," the body reacts in ways that prove to be beyond my control: rather than me dictating to it how it should comport itself, as for example is notoriously the case with Mishima Yukio,[10] I seem to find myself becoming passive and subservient to it. This reversal in hierarchy between body and mind is what plays itself out in "Seiji to bungaku no mondai (Nihon bungaku to Chūgoku bungaku I)" as well. There the body is represented as something that is intrinsically alien to me, to my will, and indeed to all that has its home in that space of interiority that is the subject. It shows itself to be primarily a kind of dull, unreflecting surface, one whose materiality is no different from that of things in the world. In its status as surface the body is given only to "feel" the world, not as its own, something that it could name or identify—and so thereby posit itself determinately in opposition to it—but instead as an openness to the world's "intensity," which continuously "presses in upon" it, producing impressions. If then we are to understand Takeuchi's writing as "sensual," it is because of this lingering concern with the body, and above all with the sense of "anxiety" that at all times haunts what can never be simply *my* relation to it. This anxiety arises directly as a result of the fracture, or the cleavage, that exists within consciousness, within that interiority that is the otherwise unified and self-enclosed system of conscious thought. Insofar as consciousness must necessarily maintain its relation with the body so as to communicate with the world—the materiality of which it attempts ceaselessly to internalize (to simultaneously negate/preserve (*hitei suru/hozon suru*) in dialectical fashion)—it implicitly recognizes the fact of the body's exteriority, that its strangeness and alterity are for it radically irreducible. In this sense, we can see that the self can in truth never but be Other to itself. Making use of the scripturality that lies at the heart of the notion of "impressions," we could say that the body qua impressed or imprinted surface tends precisely to *draw* the self out of itself. This it does by its status as matter, which con-

---

10. See especially *Sun and Steel*, trans. John Bester (New York: Grove Press, 1970). This essentially theoretical relation with the body would be the very obverse of what Karatani Kōjin finds to be so noteworthy in the I-novelist Shiga Naoya, whose work, as he writes, "displays a bodily sensibility which precedes the distinction between the self and the other." *Origins of Modern Japanese Literature*, trans. Brett de Bary et al. (Durham: Duke University Press, 1993), p. 92.

sciousness is always drawn toward in its desire to (derivatively, secondarily) re-present the world to itself. And yet the body resists ever giving itself to consciousness as such: in its retreat, or withdrawal, from consciousness, it incisively marks itself as absent. This absence is indeed a marked one in the sense that impressions appear in (the) place of the body (meaning: at once *upon* the body and *instead* of it). While consciousness desires to internalize these impressions, to literally make sense out of them, the force with which they are drawn in is in fact overwhelmed by that greater force which binds them to the body, to the world, and which thus works to effectively draw consciousness outside of itself.

It should now be clear just how large the stakes are in Takeuchi's so-called "sensuality." Above all, what Takeuchi attempts to think in terms of the body can in principle never be reduced to a determinate ontological *topos*, as for example Yoshimoto seems to believe when he explicitly links this notion with Takeuchi's reading of "China." Without unfolding the very general logic embedded in this "sensuality" as it manifests itself not only in his writings on China but indeed, it must be said, in all of Takeuchi's writings, such a reduction remains dangerously misleading. If, as Lawrence Olson has aptly pointed out in his study of Takeuchi, "what Yoshimoto feared was . . . the kind of emotionalism that he found in Takeuchi's concept of Asia [and China], with its dangerously parochial overtones,"[11] then we would have to respond to this fear through a kind of double reading which would attempt to take into account, and to do justice to, both the legitimacy of this charge and the "emotionalism," or the "sensuality," that apparently provokes it. Now on the one hand, it must be recognized that Yoshimoto's fear is undeniably well-founded: in his attempts to *oppose* the West and that logic of identity which so thoroughly permeates it, Takeuchi all too often falls into precisely this same trap. This is of course the trap of the reversal, that "clamorous declaration of the antithesis," as Derrida puts it,[12] in which the very desire to overturn the opposition leads all the more surely to its reproduction, such that victory is achieved only through the effacement of that difference which otherwise resists all positing or positioning, and which can never simply op-pose anything. Hence the recourse in Takeuchi's text to such extremely problematic notions as that of ethnic nationalism (*minzokushugi*) and Asian identity—both of which, let us repeat

---

11. In *Ambivalent Moderns: Portraits of Japanese Cultural Identity* (Savage, Maryland: Rowman & Littlefield, 1992), p. 61.

12. *Spurs: Nietzsche's Styles*, trans. Barbara Harlow (Chicago: University of Chicago Press, 1979), p. 95. "For the reversal, if it is not accompanied by a discrete parody, a strategy of writing, or difference or deviation in quills, if there is no style, no grand style, this is finally but the same thing, nothing more than a clamorous declaration of the antithesis." To which is added, significantly: "Hence the heterogeneity of the text."

(and this point can never be emphasized enough), are put forth primarily as *strategies of resistance to the West*, to the ongoing homogenization of the world that Takeuchi saw in the twin projects of westernization and modernization. On the other hand, however, Takeuchi's notion of the body in its very "sensuality" opens up a space within which all oppositionality necessarily gives way onto something Other, something that, beyond all calculation, effectively resists the logic of symmetrical opposition and contradiction. This notion of resistance (*teikō*), which, as is well known, provides the guiding force behind Takeuchi's entire path of thinking,[13] resists even his own attempts to articulate a determinate "politics of resistance" in the name of some fictitious national or regional identity. Here, resistance resists all figurality, it is always Other to that which presents itself, whether in the discourse of politics or philosophy, history or literature. (And Takeuchi's writing crosses all of these). As such it can never simply be appropriated, organized into a project or program, since all such attempts to positivize resistance invariably find themselves betrayed in that very act of translation. For Takeuchi, it is the resistance of the body's materiality that allows it to function as a unique site of disturbance, one which paradoxically ungrounds the activities of consciousness and knowing in the very movement by which it grounds them. The traces of this resistance can be read nearly everywhere in Takeuchi's text, and appear in their most radical form in his interrelated notions of negativity, "ways" (*michi*), feeling and the body. Their effect is to abruptly call into question the possibility of any "parochialism" ("dangerously parochial overtones")—that is to say: the possibility of any *particularism*—precisely by exposing this concept, as well as the various projects that it spawns, to a movement of generality which it (and which they) can no longer control. Generality, here, must be understood as essentially bound up with that difference which works to divide all unity or identity from itself, and which the subject in its universality cannot but presuppose in its very *relation to* the ob-jects it poses opposite itself. As a matter of fact, it is this complicity between the universal and the particular that literally prepares the ground (in the sense of *hypokeimenon*) for the subject.

---

13. See in this regard Takeuchi Shigeaki's chapter on Takeuchi, entitled "Takeuchi Yoshimi: teikō no shisō," in his *Sengo shisō e no shikaku: shutai to gengo* (Tokyo: Chikuma Shobō, 1972), pp. 145-161. Takeuchi Shigeaki provides a reading here of what he refers to as Takeuchi's explicitly "bodily (*nikutaiteki*) thinking of resistance" through an extended comparison with Yoshimoto Takaaki's work.

Significantly, it must be noted, Takeuchi conceives of the excess of "resistance" to opposition in terms of "feeling," for this resistance itself resists all theoretical knowledge and determination: "In saying this, however, I do not know what resistance is; I am unable to fully penetrate into its meaning. . . . It is simply that I feel (*kanjiteiru*) something within resistance, something that I cannot extract and logically construct." "Kindai towa nanika (Nihon to Chūgoku no baai)," p. 144.

This it does by allowing (particular) difference to be incorporated as merely difference of the Same, that which in the course of experience gradually becomes absorbed both by and within that unified ground/sub-strate that is the (universal) sub-ject. In this way, as in Hegel, the movement of experience—and indeed of history, understood here as "world-history" (*sekai-shi*)—assumes as its *telos* precisely its own point of origin, a point whose absolute purity of identity can only be recaptured by the subject's constant advance (*zenshin*) in the world, such that all particular difference comes to be revealed as always already universal. So it is that the notion of "experience" is radically deprived of its strangeness, its quality of perpetual surprise, and becomes nothing more than the process by which the subject actively colonizes the world. Now it is entirely against this colonization (both by the subject and by the West, the two of these recognized as historically inseparable) that Takeuchi struggles. His thinking directs itself toward ungrounding the principles of unity and identity in such a way as to incessantly expose the subject (whether defined as the individual or as "China" and "Asia") to an alterity that resists its advances. Hence the subject would be forced to receive the world's otherness primarily passively, in the form of what has been called "impressions" and "feelings." Properly understood, this ungrounding of the subject situates itself in Takeuchi's text in the elusive difference between opposition and resistance—and it is perhaps significant in this regard that the word *teikō*, which Takeuchi of course uses for "resistance," can also mean "to oppose" (*temukai suru*: literally, "to raise one's hand against"). The point here is not simply to *choose* one or the other meaning, that it is a question entirely of our "freedom of choice," as one says. As goes without saying, such a framing of the problem would return one very quickly to precisely that notion of subjectivity which Takeuchi is trying to unsettle, to somehow open up to the disavowed generality of its outside. Rather, much more radically, and so even prior to the moment of decision, it is this *difference between* opposition and resistance that gives itself to be thought. Insofar as thought would here be drawn to an open space, a kind of interval whose shifting economy works to disturb the stasis (or standing) of the terms grounded upon it, it would find itself at the very site that Takeuchi designates as *teikō*. But since it could never be certain that it was in fact occupying that site, it would be unable to escape that sense of "anxiety" which for Takeuchi refers inexorably back to the feeling of pressure one receives from the outside.

At this point we can see that it is not simply a question of reading Takeuchi *against* Yoshimoto, for there are certain important inconsistencies within Takeuchi's own text that would necessitate a reading of this latter against, or rather in dialogue with, himself. The same of course can be said of Yoshimoto's text as well. Inasmuch as our reading is concerned far less with this debate itself than with the matter of "sensuality" that it explicitly, and, as we have seen, very justifiably, raises, the task would be to more rigorously set forth what we have called the generality of the sensual (impressions, feeling, bodily experience, etc.). While this generality will constitute the central problematic of this essay, let us for the moment return to the passage we originally quoted from Yoshimoto so as to better understand the nature of this strange "sensuality" that he finds in Takeuchi's writing. A reexamination of this passage will finally round off our reading of this debate and so allow us to investigate other instances where Takeuchi attempts to come to grips with some of these same questions. The passage is given as follows: "As concerns my reading of [Takeuchi's] work, no matter how theoretically dense [that work may be], I can always feel that he interprets China on the basis of something like sensuality." Now this final clause can in fact be rendered more literally; directly translated, Yoshimoto writes that "I can always *receive the feeling (kanji wo itsumo uketoru koto ga dekiru)* that he interprets China on the basis of something like sensuality." At issue here is the manner in which, as we stated earlier, this remark seems to uniquely perform that "sensuality" which Yoshimoto attributes to Takeuchi's reading of China, but which we found on the contrary to be much more general, because intrinsically bound up with what is for Takeuchi the essential limits of all knowledge and production of meaning. Specifically, the remark's performativity centers on the notion of "feeling": while appearing to thematize "sensuality" as something that distorts and so detracts from Takeuchi's understanding of China—an understanding that is otherwise "theoretically dense," as he writes—Yoshimoto is nevertheless forced to describe his own reading of Takeuchi in terms that directly reproduce the general logic within which "feeling" becomes linked to the sensual. That is to say, as we saw in Takeuchi's formulation of these concepts, the innate "sensuality" of "feeling" lies precisely in the body's openness to the world, its ability to "always receive (the) feeling" that is the constant inscription of experience. In essence, the notion of "sensuality" that Yoshimoto attempts here to isolate or thematize creates effects at that level of language within which the intended thematization takes place, such that in speaking of the sensual Yoshimoto is forced to say too much, as if "sensuality" were not something that could be simply determined, or delimited, by a speaking subject, but rather in fact *generated in and of itself* all utterances, including of course those that attempt to capture its meaning. The difficulty that Yoshimoto is confronting springs from his desire to reverse the order of meaning: insofar as the subject's intentional acts are necessarily grounded upon the body's prior receptivity to the world—a receptivity which, as we have argued, takes the inscriptional form of "feelings" and "impressions"—any attempt to objectify the sensual is by definition doomed from the start, for it could not but presuppose that which it sets out to show. This reversal would not however fail completely. Rather it would produce a kind of split at the level of the utterance between that "sensuality" which was successfully objectified and that which somehow overflowed, or exceeded, objectification.[14] Hence the unsettling remainder of "sensuality" in Yoshimoto's remark that appears in his own use of "feeling," a term which otherwise functions to set off and create the necessary distance between the speaker's position and that of his object (i.e., Takeuchi). That space which properly separates Takeuchi's "sensuality" from Yoshimoto's own "feeling" about it—on the basis of which alone subject and object may come into being in their mutual difference—is nevertheless compromised by that more profound linkage which holds these notions together. The primordiality of "sensuality" is such that the subject can never fully raise itself above it, speak of it thematically (or objectively) beyond the reach of its "feeling." Nor can the subject ever gain access to a language in which all traces of the sensual have been eliminated, thus allowing it to function as nothing more than a *medium* which would itself remain distinct from the "sensuality" it thematizes. Even at the level of language feeling makes itself felt, it produces effects within the utterance which, while captured in part within the delimited scope of the thematization, yet constantly exceed it, open it up to the generality of its outside. Clearly Yoshimoto desires to restrict the bounds of the sensual: they circumscribe neither his own position nor Takeuchi's theoretical rigor—and yet he finds that he can do so only through recourse to a notion of "feeling" that belongs to it through and through. What we have called the performativity of this remark lies in precisely this, that it somehow *says* more than it *means to say*. For Takeuchi, "sensuality" is to be understood as the ability to receive feelings (*kanji wo uketoru koto ga dekiru*). In this sense, Yoshimoto's ascription of this quality strictly to Takeuchi's reading of China is belied or betrayed by the very words with which he attempts to take up a theoretical stance vis-à-vis that sensuality. In truth, "feeling" and the sensual is what language always says, what it necessarily must say, and this regardless of the content of the said. In so saying, language declares that its foundations are in the world. This being the case, we can see that all utterances cannot but testify to their grounding in man's exposure, or receptivity, to the world's otherness, an otherness that in fact writes itself upon the surface of man's body. Yoshimoto's remark presents itself as an example of this generality, one which in its attempt to explicitly

---

14. Cf. Naoki Sakai's discussion of Itō Jinsai's disagreement with Song rationalism on this point: "Whereas [for the Song rationalists] feeling must be objectified to be deprived of its spontaneity and thereby rendered tameable, Itō now defines feeling as exactly outside of what can be objectified, that is to say, outside of the thinkable. . . . Hence, feeling is that which cannot be present or made present to the mind: it always flees the arresting reach of the mind." *Voices of the Past: The Status of Language in Eighteenth-Century Japanese Discourse* (Ithaca: Cornell University Press, 1991), p. 65.

thematize the sensual allows us to glimpse the essential limits of all thematization, the manner by which sensuality traces itself outside the scope (or the "frame" (*waku*)) of the theme even as it seems to be captured by it. And yet this remark is by no means extraordinary; the movement that we have found within it by right takes place in all utterances. Because language is irreducibly sensual, that is, because it is a language *of* feeling—and through this, necessarily, of the body, the world—it can never be made equivalent to the realm of signification that is the home of the subject.

"ALL CONSCIOUSNESS EMERGES FROM THE INSTANT"

Takeuchi's attempt to think outside the subject leads him to ask, very literally: what is the subject's outside? Needless to say, this outside cannot be understood in terms of the object (*taishō*), which is nothing more than what the subject throws or projects opposite (*ob-, tai-*) itself so as to thereby constitute itself in reflective relation to it. Objectification creates the illusion of symmetry between man and the world: the universal determination in modernity of man qua subject and world qua object makes it appear as if these two somehow exist apart from one another, as if man's existence were not fundamentally in the world—where, because of his corporeality, he is given first to feel and to suffer— but rather distanced from it, in some significant way *above* it. This "above" points to a shift in emphasis from man understood as agent of action (or *shutai*) to man as cognitive or knowing subject (*shukan*), and with this obviously a privileging of consciousness and mind (i.e., the above, that which is closest to God) over the body, the entire region of affectivity (the below). It is this effacement of man's practical relation to the world that Takeuchi wishes to uncover, and this because he regards man as a radically "sensual" being, immediately bound up with the world in his exposure to it. Because of this exposure the world's alterity cannot ever be domesticated, set off in objectified form as distinct from the self: man, as Kan Takayuki writes in his work on Takeuchi, must in his very "sensuality" be recognized as "an internalized otherness (*tashasei*), a self that is externalized as Other."[15] Takeuchi's attempt to call attention to the immediacy of the relation between man and world finds particular expression in his writings on Lu Xun. In contrast to the subject who sets out to reduce the world (or being) to representation, what Takeuchi will refer to critically as the "modern self" or the "European self," Lu Xun is read as in some sense exemplary of man's general receptivity to the world's otherness: "His fiction is poetic and his criticism endowed with sensibility (or

---

15. *Takeuchi Yoshimi ron: Ajia e no hanka* (Tokyo: Sanichi Shobō, 1976), p. 65.

"susceptibility": *kanseiteki*). His thinking as well as his temperament are far from grounded in the conceptual (*gainen*). He thinks by analogy, he does not reason by deduction. He intuits, he does not constitute (*kōsei wa shinai*). He does not confront (*tachimukau*: literally, "to stand against") the world with goals and methods, that is, he lacks a position (*tachiba*)."[16]

Now immediately apparent in this passage is the binary logic with which Takeuchi wishes to situate Lu Xun in relation to the notion of subjectivity that he finds to be so characteristic of the modern West. The subject owes its being entirely to the intellectual, the cognitive: the traits which make up and consequently sustain the subject are those of conceptuality, deduction, constitutivity, goals (or "aims"), methods, and positionality. Outside of this lies the sensible, the very different traits of which include the poetic, analogy, and intuition. What we critically noted earlier about Takeuchi's thought appears now again, in very clear form: this being the notion of *reversal* which articulates resistance strictly on the basis of oppositionality. By way of general comment, and without the slightest bit of exaggeration, let us say here that the entire difficulty of Takeuchi's thinking comes down to precisely this, the desire for reversal. This is not of course to deny the importance of such a move, an importance which we believe, following Takeuchi, to be above all historical, or contextual. But if the reversal is to be anything more than dialectical, that is, if it is to *do more* than simply affirm in inverse manner the value of the previously subordinate and excluded term (whether this be the "Orient" (*Tōyō*) or the notions of intuition and sensibility), then a kind of displacement becomes necessary, one which no longer merely situates itself within this binary logic but rather works to change it, to deform it, such that the very meaning of these terms themselves is put into question. Specifically, despite their difference both of the binary terms alike can be seen to ground themselves upon a notion of presence, which indeed allows them to maintain themselves as such in the reciprocity of their negative difference. This presence, in other words, reveals that identity is always at the bottom of what otherwise seems to be difference. Because of this, we can perceive that the terms in fact constantly feed off each other, and that their complicity and mutual dependence function to create a larger, more comprehensive unity within which each are essential parts. Thus in the context of Takeuchi's attempt to overturn the value of subjectivity and knowledge, he appeals somewhat predictably to the "lower" elements of knowledge, that which while required for the translation of being into meaning is yet demoted to the status of mere departure point from which the operation of knowledge truly begins. Sensibility (or

---

16. From *Ro Jin*, in *TYz*, vol. 1, pp. 158-159. This text was originally published in 1944. The essay from which these lines are taken, however, entitled "Shisōka toshite no Ro Jin," was added as an appendix to the book's third edition, published in 1952.

"sensuality"), at this point, becomes privileged, it is very strategically high-lighted against conceptuality and the intellectual so as to in some way bring into focus that which knowledge has hitherto unfairly neglected. Now the problem with such a move is this: insofar as we understand knowledge to be the *union* of the sensible and the intellectual, Takeuchi's efforts at reversing the implicit hierarchy of these terms, his *desire for us to recognize* the right-ful but misunderstood (because silent) value of sensibility, can be read paradoxically as strengthening this overall synthesis that is knowledge. In which case, Takeuchi's "resistance" against knowledge could be understood as ultimately working in the service of knowledge. Indeed, doesn't Kant teach us that knowledge comprehends within itself *both* the intellectual *and* the sensible, that it in fact needs the one just as much as it needs the other? So for example in the *Critique of Pure Reason* we can read the following lines: "Our knowledge springs from two fundamental sources of the mind; the first is the capacity of receiving representations (receptivity for impres-sions), the second is the power of knowing an object through these repre-sentations (spontaneity [in the production] of concepts). Through the first an object is *given* to us, through the second the object is *thought* in relation to that [given] representation (which is a mere determination of the mind). Intuitions and concepts constitute, therefore, the elements of all our knowl-edge, so that neither concepts without an intuition in some way correspond-ing to them, nor intuition without concepts, can yield knowledge."[17] And from this Kant concludes, "It is, therefore, just as necessary to make our concepts sensible, that is, to add the object to them in intuition, as to make our intuitions intelligible, that is, to bring them under concepts. . . . *Only through their union can knowledge arise.*"[18]

Now the concern here is that Takeuchi can easily be read as assimila-tionist, that the overturning of the value of the conceptual in favor of that of the intuitive (and with this, of course, the inversion of the "West" in favor of the "Orient") works merely to reinforce the solidity of knowledge's over-all union. In this respect, the desire to bring intuition and sensibility to the fore, to allow us to—quite literally—*regard them* as in truth superior to the conceptual, contains within it something of that "slave nature" (*dorei konjō*) of which Takeuchi is otherwise so critical.[19] Very generally, this "slave na-ture" can be said to reveal itself in the sense of *ressentiment* with which the slave considers the master. His envy of and hatred for the master point to an inferiority that is indeed far more profound than simply his official under-

---

17. *Critique of Pure Reason*, trans. Norman Kemp Smith (New York: St. Martin's Press, 1965), p. 92.
18. Ibid., p. 93. Emphasis ours.
19. See here especially the section entitled "Hyūmanizumu to zetsubō" in "Kindai towa nanika (Nihon to Chūgoku no baai)," pp. 154-159.

privileged status: this inferiority lies in the fact that he desires nothing more than to replace the master, to in other words *become* him. But in this craving for recognition, the slave shows himself to be essentially no different from the master, and the change that he effects in the reversal of hierarchy between himself and the master in fact changes nothing in the overall structure that is the master-slave relation. In terms of the criticism of knowledge that Takeuchi here articulates, we can say that unless the relation between conceptuality and sensibility is configured otherwise, unless the notion of presence that entirely supports or grounds this relation is itself ungrounded, then this criticism remains ultimately a very traditional one, and as such easily recuperable. In order to call into question the very possibility of synthesizing these terms within the universal "union" that is knowledge, it seems that sensibility must be thought in a way that radically displaces the traditional understanding of this term.

The question thus arises as to whether Takeuchi's attempt to think outside the subject can be understood *simply* as a reversal of the dominant traits that otherwise make possible the unity and self-identity of knowledge. If, as we have alluded to, there is in the operation of reversal something like an excess (a "more"), which in fact comes into being in the very *act* (*kōi, kōdō*) of inverting these binary terms, and which moreover produces as effect a radical distortion of their symmetry, then it is incumbent upon us to try to locate this excess within Takeuchi's text. Here it is not at all a matter of arbitrarily projecting something onto the text which it itself originally lacks, a something that would represent merely the subject's active (or spontaneous) addition to the thing;[20] what is at issue rather is the unfolding, or uncovering, of those moments within the text that seem to themselves effectuate a displacement of the notion of sensibility. This displacement would necessarily take the form of a generalization, what we tried to bring forth in our reading of the "debate" between Takeuchi and Yoshimoto Takaaki under the heading of the generality of the sensual. As general, this "sensuality" or sensibility would resist being conceived on the basis of presence. Unlike the notion of sensibility which has traditionally been understood as appropriable by knowledge—since conceptuality has the capacity to interiorize, to literally raise impressions up to the level of the mind—a properly general sensibility would disturb the possibility of cognitive synthesis by

---

20. Again, this manner of reading would directly return us to a thinking of subjectivity that Takeuchi explicitly argues against. In this respect, the Marxist literary critic Honda Shūgo's contention that Takeuchi's criticism of Japanese literature is guided by his finding in this latter an unfortunate "absence of spontaneity (*jihatsusei*)" must be described as only half true. While remarks to this effect can indeed be found in Takeuchi's texts, it should nevertheless not be forgotten that action is conceived by him as profoundly passive, something that always exceeds the subject's control. *Monogatari sengo bungaku shi* (Tokyo: Shinchōsha, 1975), p. 509.

marking itself otherwise, in ways that the subject is fundamentally un-equipped to take into account. That is to say, sensibility would no longer represent the first stage of subjective interiorization but rather the point at which the body originally opens itself to the world, where it begins to re-ceive the imprint of the world's alterity in the form of "impressions." This openness works to irrevocably *draw* the subject out of itself: it reveals that even the conceptual remarking of impressions is but one instance of that more general remarking that is man's experience of the world. For this rea-son it becomes impossible to simply oppose conceptuality to sensibility, for the generality of the latter shows that this relation is in fact one of inscrip-tion—that conceptual interiority is, in other words, necessarily inscribed within that infinitely greater exteriority (or alterity) to which sensibility points. This notion of sensibility would represent a decisive break with any philosophy of empiricism, as for example the pragmatism that Takeuchi astutely criticizes as grounded upon a thinking of presence,[21] and which we shall more fully turn to later on in the essay.

The excess which resists the apparent governance of the text by binary logic, and which Takeuchi brings out through his generalization of the sen-sual, can be recognized in the criticism of the notion of positionality found in the passage quoted above. There it was a question of thinking the imme-diacy of man's experience of the world as somehow Other to the opposi-tionality that regulates the subject's reflective relation to the object. Already here we can see that Takeuchi's appeal to "sensuality" springs most directly from his dissatisfaction with the binarity inherent within the traditional sub-ject-object relation, a binarity that in fact fosters an expressly theological notion of the subject as "that which looks from the [world's] outside," with-out actively engaging within it.[22] Specifically, by refusing the subject the possibility of positioning itself Takeuchi wishes to conceive of man's exis-tence as radically irreducible to a mode in which he simply "confronts" the world, stands opposite to it armed with "goals" and "methods." (This would be rather the relation between man and world as set forth by pragmatism). Precisely because man originally exists without a position, according to Takeuchi, he is ridden with "anxiety": this anxiety signifies the lack of an identifiable boundary between man and the world, such that it becomes im-possible for him to in any way safeguard or guarantee the internal purity that is nevertheless required by consciousness. It is this boundary between man and world that articulates the intimate relation between positionality and op-positionality, a relation that can be seen in Takeuchi's own text in his implicit linking together of the notions of "position" (*tachi-ba*: literally,

---

21. See "Ko Teki to Dūi," in *TYz*, vol. 5, pp. 42-57. Originally published in 1952.
22. "Kindai towa nanika (Nihon to Chūgoku no baai)," p. 159.

"the site where one stands") and "standing-against" (*tachi-mukau*). Here we can begin to understand that all positioning is necessarily a positioning against, it is what allows the subject to gather itself qua itself through its dialectical negation of the other. Only in this way, moreover, can the subject effectively offset the sense of anxiety that otherwise haunts it, and which threatens constantly to take its feet out from under it, make it come to lose its standing (*tatenakunaru*) in the world. What we must not fail to grasp in this ungrounding of positionality is, literally, the *ecstasy* of experience, in which man's openness to the world forces him to radically stand outside of himself, such that, whether he wishes to or not, he is always already historically situated. This is why, as Takeuchi writes, the self does not originally "constitute" the things of this world. Constitution, in this context, refers to the activity by which the subject is believed to freely or spontaneously make the world over, and in so doing properly make it its own. As the universal making of the world by an active subject, constitution contains within itself the notion of positionality as the specific form through which the subject produces *itself* in relation to the world that it objectifies.[23] In the act of positioning itself, the subject in fact constitutes a determinate exteriority in relation to which alone it is able to settle itself within the well-defined borders of its interiority. In which case, the constitution of the other is revealed to be always coterminous with the constitution of the self (and vice-versa), as for example Naoki Sakai demonstrates on the basis of what he has called *tai-keishōka no zushiki* (or "the schema of co-figuration").[24] At the same time, however, it must be understood that this dual positioning is never able to fully eliminate the presence of alterity within the self, since it is only upon this alterity that positioning operates, or maintains itself. The paradox here is that while positionality is necessarily grounded upon the world's— and so, by extension, the self's—otherness, it nonetheless comes into being as the very negation of these latter. And yet, hypothetically speaking, if it were in fact to ever succeed in that negation and so absorb the entirety of this otherness within itself, it would then no longer have any ground upon which to stand. All standing, or positionality, therefore, can be seen to found itself upon a ground that is yet radically heterogeneous to it: while it allows for the possibility of the subject-object relation, this ground at the

---

23. Cf. Rodolphe Gasché's discussion of this point in *The Tain of the Mirror: Derrida and the Philosophy of Reflection* (Cambridge: Harvard University Press, 1986), p. 158.
24. "Nihon shakaikagaku hōhō josetsu: Nihon shisō toiu mondai," in *Iwanami kōza: shakai kagaku no hōhō*, vol. 2, ed. Yamanouchi Yasushi et al. (Tokyo: Iwanami Shoten, 1993), esp. pp. 23-27. This essay has since appeared in English translation in revised form. See *Translation and Subjectivity: On "Japan" and Cultural Nationalism* (Minneapolis: University of Minnesota Press, 1997), pp. 40-71.

same time marks that relation's impossibility, its essential limits, since experience (as ecstatic) always exceeds the boundaries of this division.

In this regard, what Takeuchi is trying to think under the notion of experience needs to be examined more closely. So for example in "Kindai towa nanika (Nihon to Chūgoku no baai)," in the context of inquiring into the possible relativity of all truth, Takeuchi writes the following: "However, if I were asked whether truth (shinri) is relative, it seems that now, that is, within my environment of today, I would have to say that it is relative. I know this experientially (keikenteki ni)."[25] Now the strangeness of this remark makes itself felt only several lines later, when Takeuchi will, let us not quite say reverse himself, but at least decisively throw these words into relief: "In any case, what I am thinking of now, in this place, is that my judgment on the relativity of truth might itself be European."[26] What follows at this point is a radical questioning of the possibility of knowledge in the face of experience, a questioning which, although admittedly veiled because couched in a language more allusive than analytical, is nevertheless no less powerful for all that. Here, however, let us call attention to what we believe to be taking place in these words, for in fact their force lies above all in the movement which they uniquely reveal while remaining at the same time entirely caught up within it. Now Takeuchi's concern is to set forth a notion of experience which at once grounds knowledge and destabilizes it. To this end he articulates two statements, both of which very explicitly signal what we might refer to as the fact of their situatedness in the world. This situatedness takes the form of a pair of spatial and temporal markers—what in linguistics has been called "indicators" or "shifters"—and are repeated over from the first passage to the second: these are of course the "here" (the "environment (or: milieu) of today" (kyō no kankyō), "this place" (kono yō na basho)) and the "now" (genzai, ima). Such marked attention to the speaker's situatedness at the instant of the statement's enunciation (énonciation) might appear to be odd, if not indeed completely superfluous, since what is after all at issue in these lines is the notion of experience, and with this the possible relativity of all truth claims. And yet it can be seen that this situatedness is precisely what Takeuchi wishes to express by this notion, that the immediacy of experience, in other words, is best demonstrated (not signified) through recourse to these indicators. Experience, of course, is radically singular—something like a "one-time matter," as he says in another context[27]—and as such resists all repetition in the form of representation. Nevertheless, thought does not simply respond to that singularity by observing a respectful and wondrous silence, thereby all the more

---

25. "Kindai towa nanika (Nihon to Chūgoku no baai)," p. 138.
26. Ibid., p. 139.
27. Ibid., p. 134. The phrase used here is ikkai kagiri no mono.

effectively (if unwittingly) raising experience to its representation as, precisely, "mystical experience," or rather experiential mysticism. In a sense, the singularity of experience cannot help but be raised to the level of representation, or signification: just as there exists a law of experience which dictates that all experience be absolutely singular and unrepeatable, so too can we see in effect another law, one which, without in any way contradicting the first, sets forth the necessary possibility that singularity leave or divide itself, that it literally *give itself up* to the operation of repetition. So it is that we must somehow try to think the singularity of experience *both* as a "one-time matter" *and* as something that necessarily always leaves open the possibility of its betrayal. In this respect, it is no doubt significant that Takeuchi refuses to content himself with what is, in point of fact, the security of the relativist position. As is well known, this security derives from its covert grounding upon the notion of truth, since relativism cannot ultimately avoid determining its *own* position as a true one. Takeuchi's sensitivity to this trap can be seen in the hesitancy with which he asks himself: could it be that my own (experiential) judgment that truth is relative is actually European, and hence not relativist but rather "absolutist"? As the broader context of this essay reveals, what is highlighted here is the underlying complicity between empiricism (*keikenshugi*)—which Takeuchi signals by his use of the term "experience"—and rationalism (*gōrishugi*)—which is introduced through the word "knowing."[28] Hence in the statement "I know this experientially" we can see, as we indeed noted earlier in Kant, that experience and knowledge (or empiricism and rationalism) come together to form the seamlessness of a "union" within which each plays an essential part. This is why Takeuchi is forced to question not simply the particular content of this experiential knowledge but rather, much more radically, the very possibility of experiential knowledge as such. In the act of casting doubt on the confidence with which the belief in the foundedness of experiential knowledge is initially expressed, by saying that this knowledge might also be "European"—and therefore in fact less experiential than abstract, or conceptual—Takeuchi implies that man is fundamentally incapable of grounding knowledge in experience, that these two are for him in principle irreconcilable, unbridgeable. If we say then that man experiences

---

28. As the section of "Kindai towa nanika (Nihon to Chūgoku no baai)" entitled "Tōyō no kindai" (pp. 129-136) makes clear, empiricism with its attendant notion of experience as specifically *present* experience is in no way to be understood as outside of, or resistant to, the West. There is here then no simple reversal of the conceptual chain "West-knowledge-rationalism" in favor of that of "Orient-experience-empiricism." On the contrary, conceived in these terms the former by definition always comprehends the latter, takes it up into a "union" with itself. As we have emphasized throughout the essay, Takeuchi is concerned ultimately less with either of these poles as such than with trying to think that generality within which each of them is necessarily inscribed.

the world, as we of course must, we are yet unable to say that he ever knows the meaning of those experiences, or *what* they are, without thereby distorting them in that very "act of knowing" (*shiru toiu kōi*).[29] The temporal deferral from experience to knowledge (or, as we said earlier, from (passive) sensibility to (active) conceptuality) ensures that experience can be known only *jigoteki ni*—or retroactively, after the "blow" (*coup*) that is the instant of the imprint of experience—and yet this deferral creates a radical difference between what we might call the "now" of knowing and the "then" of experience.

What can be said to survive this questioning into the (im)possibility of experiential knowledge is Takeuchi's peculiar attention to the situatedness of his own discourse, that is, to the *taking place* that is the instant of the enunciation. Let us insist that this notion of "situatedness" is not to be conceived syllogistically as a third term, it is not something that unites within itself both knowledge and experience as their higher synthesis: there can be here no speculative resolution of this antinomy. Instead, we must try to understand "situatedness" as that which simultaneously grounds and ungrounds this division. Perhaps this is not the best way to phrase this problem, for what we are calling "situatedness" (or *jōkyōsei* in Japanese) is not a universal essence (*sei*) which exists in some way prior to and independent of those real particular situations which manifest it, i.e., which translate it perfectly into being. As we have maintained throughout the essay, what is at issue here goes beyond the universal-particular relation. That relation is precisely the structure within which subjectivity is made possible, whereas Takeuchi's concern is to think outside the subject, and thus to think its ultimate *impossibility*. Before all else, "situatedness" refers to the "here" and "now," what he will set forth under the heading of the "instant" (*shunkan*): "The instant is a limit, it is a point within history that lacks extension, or rather it represents the place (*basho*) (which is not an expanse) from which history emerges. Hence it is in fact wrong to describe the instant in terms of that [dialectical] movement in which advance equals retreat. Because all consciousness emerges from the instant, however, even this image of equivalence between advance and retreat naturally comes from it—if derivatively."[30] The traits that we see Takeuchi trying to bring together at this point are those of experience, "situatedness" (the "here" and "now") and the instant. Inherent in all of these is a generalized notion of passivity (or receptivity), one which does not in symmetrical fashion simply oppose itself to that of activity but rather comprehends it, inscribes it. (As Takeuchi very succinctly writes of Lu Xun: "He was passive (*ukemi*: literally, "a body that

---

29. Ibid., p. 139.
30. Ibid., p. 138.

receives") at all times").[31] Thus in the *act* of enunciating a statement, Takeuchi refuses to conceive of his action as something that primarily emanates from a free and spontaneous subject. In this way, the intentionality that is thought to lie behind the statement would in the enunciative act survive what is putatively its "fall" into the material world, such as to yet retain its purity in the form of expressions (*hyōgen*) charged or animated by subjective spirit. On the contrary, for Takeuchi the "place of action" (*kōdō no ba*)[32]—what he refers to above, in apparent reference to the philosopher Nishida Kitarō, as the "place" (*basho*) that is not an "expanse"[33]—is necessarily marked less by activity than by passivity, or rather the action that it names springs most originally from the world as opposed to the subject. However else man may react to this action, then, he is first of all *impressed* by it, such that the one "action" which necessarily attends all his other actions is, literally, that of being impressed with the world. It is this action that can be said to reveal itself in the physicality of the body's reaction to the world, a reaction which, significantly, outstrips the control of consciousness and intentionality, as for example we witnessed earlier in Takeuchi's reading of Lu Xun ("the entire body tenses up, the heart pounds and one breaks out in a cold sweat"). Given the primacy of the world's action, all of man's actions must be understood strictly as re-actions, which unavoidably continue and form part of the totality of the world's activity even as they pose themselves against the world. (And here we can see quite clearly the point at which Takeuchi's project sets itself off from any "dualist ontology," in which activity is believed to be generated not by the world but solely by man). This reactivity on the part of man is another name for his responsibil-

---

31. "Bunka inyū no hōhō (Nihon bungaku to Chūgoku bungaku II)," p. 118.
32. See, among numerous other instances, ibid., p. 117. It should be noted that this "place" is equivalent to what Takeuchi refers to elsewhere as *kōi no ba*, as for example in his 1953 *Ro Jin nyūmon*. In *TYz*, vol. 2, p. 39.
33. For Nishida, "place" can only be understood as an instantaneous taking-place, that is, one in which the self both dies and is born at every instant: "I say, therefore, that the religious self is self-determining by transcending the here and now, by expressing the world of the absolute present, the world of the eternal past and the eternal future, within itself. It lives by being at each instant birth and death, and yet no-birth and no-death. . . . The world of the absolute present thus has the form: 'Because there is No Place wherein it abides, this Mind arises'. . . . Within this framework I endorse the saying: 'The present is the eternal present.' This does not mean that our life transcends time in a merely abstract way. Each instant of time, which does not even stop for an instant, is the simultaneous presence and absence of the eternal present." *Last Writings: Nothingness and the Religious Worldview*, trans. David A. Dilworth (Honolulu: University of Hawaii Press, 1987), pp. 88-89. Originally published in 1949.
    As Tsurumi Shunsuke points out in his *Takeuchi Yoshimi: aru hōhō no denki* (Tokyo: Riburo Pōto, 1995), p. 58, Takeuchi began reading Nishida (specifically his *Zen no kenkyū*) as early as high school, but the effects of this reading did not appear until he began work on Lu Xun. Takeuchi himself makes reference to his rather free reworking of Nishida's conceptual terminology in a note subsequently (1952) appended to *Ro Jin*, p. 157, n. 12.

ity, meaning that whatever the content of his actions, they cannot but respond or answer to the world's action upon him, action that he receives primarily passively. What is more, insofar as man's "place of action" is the singular site of the "here" and "now," each action—which thus bears the material imprint of the world—can come into being only differentially. By emphasizing that all representational knowledge occurs as a taking place, and that this "place" is created through the "act of knowing," Takeuchi calls attention to the fact that the ideal doubling required for knowledge to be representational (i.e., that it repeat the world as it gives itself originally in experience) grounds itself upon the difference inherent in the "instant." In which case, the ideal repetition (or sublation) of experience that is knowledge must be said to give way onto something like "iterability," in which the very possibility of repetition is shown to be inscribed within that otherness named in the Sanskrit *itara*.[34] While knowledge implicitly recognizes that it founds itself upon the alterity of the "instant," such that all knowing (*shiru*) bespeaks its status as, most originally, an "*act* of knowing" (*shiru toiu* kōi), nevertheless it must disavow that fact so as to preserve the confidence in its possibility. This disavowal of both the "instant" and the "act" takes place on the basis of an absolute equivalence posited between the death of singularity and the birth, or emergence, of universals, whose atemporality forms the element within which knowledge appears to operate. As such, Takeuchi's attempt to think the generality of experience may properly be understood as a calling into question of the translatability of action/experience into knowledge, and with this, significantly, that of singularity into universality.

Earlier we pointed out that this attention to the singularity of the instant of discourse was marked by Takeuchi's use of what in linguistics has been referred to as "indicators." Let us now more rigorously explicate this concept as it appears in the work of the linguist Emile Benveniste. In his well-known study "The Nature of Pronouns," Benveniste writes of indicators as follows: "This constant and necessary reference to the instance of discourse constitutes the feature that unites to *I/you* a series of 'indicators' which, from their form and their systematic capacity, belong to different classes, some being pronouns, others adverbs, and still others, adverbial locutions. . . . The demonstratives, *this*, etc., are such indicators inasmuch as their organization correlates with that of the indicators of person. . . . By simultaneous ostension, *this* will be the object designated in the present instance of discourse . . . which associates it with *I* and *you*. Outside this class, but on the same plane and associated in the same frame of reference, we find the

---

34. Jacques Derrida, *Limited Inc*, trans. Samuel Weber et al. (Evanston: Northwestern University Press, 1993).

adverbs *here* and *now*. Their relationship with *I* will be shown by defining them: *here* and *now* delimit the spatial and temporal instance coextensive and contemporary with the present instance of discourse containing *I*." So it is that the concept of the indicator only makes sense by reference to the "instant" that is what Benveniste emphasizes as the "*present* instance of discourse": "The essential thing, then, is the relation between the indicator (of person, time, place, object shown, etc.) and the *present* instance of discourse."[35] Here we can understand that the strangeness of the indicator lies in its resistance to the presenting necessary for re-presentation: whereas representation operates on the level of the universal, that is, on the level of ideality which is equivalent to the possibility of infinite repetition (since what is ideal is that which can be infinitely repeated without the intervention of difference), indicators reveal nothing more than the singularity that is discourse taking place—or rather, following Takeuchi's reading of Nishida, that is discourse taking *a* place (*basho*), each time differently. In this respect, the indicators "here" and "now" that we saw Takeuchi draw attention to above function to situate the present as an elusive site of difference. The failure of representation to grasp this present can be seen in its inability to refer to that site or place as strictly the *same* place on the basis of these indicators, since "here" and "now" ceaselessly disappear into the past in the very act of identifying them. Hence it is the instantaneity—or in other words, the temporality—of the act which ensures that the present "here" and "now" is always already dissolved into the "there" and "then." Takeuchi illustrates this disappearance of the present through adroitly juxtaposing one statement, or utterance (*énoncé*), with another: although both of these statements explicitly mark themselves as the "here" and "now," nonetheless a radical difference at the level of content takes place between them. This difference produces as effect a kind of suspension of the experiential knowledge embedded in judgment. As goes without saying, this suspension is in no way reducible to a mere change of opinion on the part of psychological consciousness, as if the hesitation and attitude of self-doubt redolent in these lines were what is really at stake here. On the contrary, Takeuchi's central concern is to underline what we might call the "objective" structure of presence/the present upon which psychological consciousness is grounded. At this level, it is undoubtedly the impossibility of maintaining the present—that is to say, it is the singularity that divides the present from itself, that effectively differentiates the "here" and "now" in its very punctuality—that works to drive a gap between experience (qua singular) and knowledge (qua universal). What Benveniste refers to then as the "*present*

---

35. *Problems in General Linguistics*, trans. Mary Elizabeth Meek (Coral Gables: University of Miami Press, 1971), pp. 218-219.

instance of discourse" helps us situate man as concretely grounded upon a present whose very immediacy and nearness unsettle the possibility of any reflective knowledge of it. Because man can only mark his situatedness in the world through reference to such indicators as "here" and "now," which simultaneously place and displace him within being, he "lives by being at each instant birth and death," as Nishida writes. For just as the "here" and "now" are incapable of identically repeating themselves, so too does man suffer the intervention of difference at each instant of experience. This intervention, or "interruption" (*danzetsu*) as Takeuchi will often refer to it,[36] is what prohibits the sublation of the singularity of the present into a universal "here" and "now." Clearly such a sublation would represent the very height of meaninglessness, since indicators are by definition resistant to all universalization, pointing only to the "*present* instance of discourse."[37]

In this sense, we can understand desire as the wish to eliminate the intervention of difference from the course of man's being in the world, such that that being is to be understood solely as a process of formation, or *Bildung*. Man's desire is to repeat himself as selfsame, to act upon the world while remaining essentially unaffected by it. As such, the "here" and "now" that otherwise radically displace him at each instant, forcing him thereby to lose himself and become Other, must be reconceptualized in such a way as to preserve difference as above all difference of the Same. Difference, then, is that which strikes an essential ground or substrate that is itself beyond difference. This ground is nothing other than the sub-ject, which does not so much as suffer, or feel, difference (in the manner, for example, of that "receptive body" (*ukemi*) Takeuchi finds in Lu Xun) as it does actively utilize it in the course of its repetition in the world. Here, as we noted earlier, the singularity of experience to which the indicators point is effaced so as to allow for the propriety of the universal-particular relation, in which the alterity of the world is reduced to parts predicated upon the universal ground that is the subject. Difference thus functions strictly to instantiate or manifest the subject: the negation of the subject that it effects must be understood as nothing more than a dialectical negation, which leads only to its strengthening, or "development" (*hatten*), as opposed to its demise. While this difference is required by the subject so as to determinately realize itself,

---

36. See for example "Ko Teki to Dūi," p. 52.
37. As for example Hegel understood perfectly: "When I say 'this Here', 'this Now', or a 'single item', I am saying all Thises, Heres, Nows, all single items. Similarly, when I say 'I', this singular 'I', I say in general all 'Is'; everyone is what I say, everyone is 'I', this singular 'I'. When Science is faced with the demand—as if it were an acid test it could not pass—that it should deduce, construct, find *a priori*, or however it is put, something called 'this thing' or 'this one man', it is reasonable that the demand should *say* which 'this thing', or which 'this particular man' is *meant*; but it is impossible to say this." *Phenomenology of Spirit*, trans. A.V. Miller (Oxford: Oxford University Press, 1977), p. 62.

it remains incapable of ever disrupting this latter's essential identity, since all such differential realization merely brings to light what the subject inherently is. As we saw Takeuchi write above in his formulation of the "instant," the subject maintains itself on the basis of a "movement in which advance equals retreat." This is to say that the difference of the world comes to be domesticated by the subject as simply a *posited* difference, and this loss (or "retreat," retrogress (*kōtai*)) is necessarily equivalent to the subject's gain, its "advance." The subject not only survives the instant of difference; it actively thrives upon it, for the operation of subjectivization that is the translation of world into object has need of an initial materiality that is only subsequently negated, and thus raised to the level of "spirit" (*seishin*). What we in fact see here is the betrayal of the singularity of the instant in the form of consciousness, which consists expressly of universal representations. Just as the instant is singular, and so essentially inimical to consciousness—as for example we witnessed in consciousness' inability to make sense of the indicators "here" and "now," which for it always appears belatedly, or *jigoteki ni*, as the "there" and "then"—so too does there exist the necessary possibility of its repetition, what can be understood as the instant's universalization (or idealization). It is for this reason that Takeuchi will speak of consciousness as in principle derivative of the instant: "Because all consciousness emerges from the instant, however, even this image of equivalence between advance and retreat naturally comes from it—if derivatively." That which "comes from" the primacy of the instant, in other words, is both this image of equivalence and consciousness. Indeed, for Takeuchi the symmetry involved in the (dialectical) movement of the subject's advance and the world's retreat is precisely what enables consciousness to maintain itself as such. Consciousness operates through its ideal repetition of the singular, hence elevating it to the status of the universal. In this doubling the world disappears, leaving behind it solely those representations of itself which belong less to the world than to consciousness. Now if Takeuchi's insistence is upon the *impossibility* of this operation, such that the world steadfastly resists its subjectivization, or, in singular fashion, betrays its betrayal, it is because he finds the instant to be irreducible to consciousness. Here, the relation between the instant and consciousness can in no way be understood as one of "equivalence." Rather the instant in its singularity properly exceeds consciousness, it remains outside of it even as it allows consciousness and its intrinsic operation of universalization to ground itself upon it. Although it is true that consciousness successfully feeds off of what we might call the materiality of the instant, then, nevertheless the instant somehow eludes this appropriation, and in so doing disturbs it, thereby opening consciousness up to the world.

This exposure, or expositioning, of consciousness in the face of the singularity of the instant is what Takeuchi will perhaps paradoxically refer to as "present consciousness" (*genzaiteki ishiki*).[38] Here it is no doubt significant that Takeuchi does not simply dismiss out of hand the value or the possibility of consciousness, but rather makes strategic appeal to it in the very act of ungrounding it, that is, in revealing the strange nature of its situatedness in the world. Consciousness, as we have argued, must be understood as at once possible and impossible. And this precisely because of its grounding upon the present instant—or, what is the same thing, the instantaneous present—such that all consciousness is necessarily "present consciousness." (Which is also to say: consciousness is not to be conceived as a "looking from the outside," as we quoted Takeuchi earlier, in which this "outside" is above all construed as a kind of transcendent beyond to the world and to time). In its locus of the present, consciousness is fundamentally incapable of positing a self which exists opposite the world. In which case, "present consciousness" must not be interpreted as designating a higher, more sophisticated form of consciousness, one in which the self could despite everything still be identified, or isolated. On the contrary, the self is defined now as nothing more than that which suffers the constant surprise of its being in the world. For Takeuchi, this quality of surprise is articulated as an unavoidable "sensation of pain," and is linked, once again, with the figure of Lu Xun: "Incredulous about everything, [Lu Xun] was unable to believe in even the self's despair. He saw darkness, only darkness; and yet the self which thus viewed darkness was undifferentiated from it as its object. It was simply that he became conscious of the self only in the sensation (or "actual feeling," *jikkan*) of pain being inflicted upon it."[39] Just as "all consciousness emerges from the instant," as Takeuchi writes, so too does consciousness of the self appear derivatively upon the flow of sensations—or "feelings," "impressions," as we witnessed earlier—which is here defined as the "sensation of pain." Let us emphasize that "pain" does not simply refer to a particular emotion in this context, one which for example could be opposed to other like emotions. Far from being a specific type of reaction, "pain" rather designates reactivity, or what has been called affectivity, in general. That is to say, "pain," according to Takeuchi, is what invariably takes place at the instant of the body's experience of the world, it is what testifies to the fact of the world's givenness. This "fact" is of course not a static one; instead it dynamically expresses itself by marking up, in incessant and yet "interrupted" fashion, the exposed surface of the body. The pain that is "afflicted" upon, or literally "*given*" (*kutsū wo ataeru*) to the yet selfless body, then, is none other than the fundamental giving of the world to man. Before all else, the world reveals itself to man in the sensa-

---

38. *Ro Jin*, p. 161.
39. Ibid.

tion of the body's pain. In asserting that it is only upon this sensation of pain that the self first comes into being, Takeuchi wishes to draw attention to the original selflessness of experience. This is why it is insufficient to dwell upon what he calls "the self's despair," for at this level "the self which thus viewed darkness was undifferentiated from it as its object." The self comes to the fore strictly in its viewing of the world, since sight is the privileged means by which it mediates its relationship to things, against or in opposition to which alone it is then able to posit itself. And yet even prior to this spectatorial (or theoretical) positioning there exists the immediacy of experience, in which man is given simply to feel the world. Experience in this way shows itself to be not only painful, but as well sightless, or blind. Indeed, it is for this reason that Takeuchi is forced here to speak of experience in terms of "darkness," which must properly be understood to mean the absence of consciousness and its enabling operation of seeing. The body's experience of the world is one of unrelieved darkness; it is unable to see because it is as yet "undifferentiated" (*mibunka*) from that darkness, such that self and world are profoundly ambiguous, interwoven.[40]

Significantly, Takeuchi refers to this blind receptivity to the world that is experience as "despair," a despair which is however not yet attributable to the self. Despair is thus associated with the exposure the body suffers in the absence of a proper site—i.e., the self—from or through which otherness is mediated. Experience can never be reduced to *my* experience for the simple reason that this self is continually ungrounded in the course of its being. Consequently, the emergence of the self signals the overcoming of both "darkness" and "despair," a kind of attenuated lightening of the world in which seeing appears to maintain itself not by any "sensation of pain," but on the contrary by the painlessness (because unsituatedness) inherent in the active *re-presentation* of sensation. This re-presentation ideally repeats sensation, and in so doing seeks to deprive it of its intrinsic pain, to in other words efface the original cut or mark of experience in the very remarking of it. And yet the knowledge that is produced through this remarking always refers back to the present instant of experience, what Takeuchi specifies elsewhere as "the experience that forms 'despair.' "[41] In its grounding of all representational knowledge, the experience of despair nevertheless reveals a

---

40. As Nishida seems to suggest in his "Preface" to *Zen no kenkyū*, experience in its immediacy can never belong to the individual self, which on the contrary is necessarily subject to it: "Over time I came to realize that it is not that experience exists because there is an individual (*kojin*), but that an individual exists because there is experience. I thus arrived at the idea that experience is more fundamental than individual differences (*kojinteki kubetsu*), and in this way I was able to avoid solipsism." *Zen no kenkyū* (Tokyo: Iwanami Shoten, 1999), p. 4; *An Inquiry into the Good*, trans. Masao Abe and Christopher Ives (New Haven: Yale University Press, 1990), p. xxx. Originally published in 1911.

41. "Bunka inyū no hōhō (Nihon bungaku to Chūgoku bungaku II)," p. 124.

more originary groundlessness, one which results from the alterity inherent in the present instant. As Takeuchi writes, this alterity at work within despair may justly be compared to that negativity, or "nothingness" (*mu*), which effectively "disturbs" and resists "being" (*yū*) (in the sense here of determinate, or phenomenal, being) even as it allows for it: " 'Despair' is a conviction. But it is a conviction that cannot be asserted. While 'despair' is a state of consciousness (*ishiki no jōtai*), this state is one of disturbance. A settled despair is not a true despair. Despair is something like a point without extension. It is like the nothing that is able to express itself only by way of being. In other words, despair lacks a self."[42] At this level, "despair" can perhaps be said to mark off a certain between-ness. This is the region (a kind of no-man's land, if you will) that lies between the singular instant of experience and its universal, or ideal, re-presentation on the part of unified consciousness. Hence despair does in a sense participate in the unity of consciousness, but only to more effectively "disturb" that unity, open it up to the generality of its outside. That "being" which consciousness posits in objective form is at each instant undermined by the "nothing" that resists phenomenologization, and yet without which being itself would not appear. In which case, despair must be thought in terms of the strange (un)ground that both being and the self presuppose; it is the instantaneous "place" because of which all situatedness necessarily differs from itself. Takeuchi continues: "In effect, despair is something that is revealed at the place of action (*kōi no ba*), it is not revealed at the place of contemplation (*kansō no ba*). That [Lu Xun] is someone in despair is to say that he is an actor (or "actant": *kōisha*). It is to say that he is someone who lives. 'Where shall I go?' 'There is no place (*basho*) to go.' Such anxiety shows that he has walked, and is walking, along a way." Immediately following these lines Takeuchi quotes from an essay written by Lu Xun in 1926 entitled "Xie zai 'fen' houmian" [Postscript to "The Grave"], and which we in turn repeat here as uniquely illustrative of what we have throughout this essay tried to think under the heading of the "instant of experience": "I do not know what I am doing," he writes, "yet I am doing something."[43]

THE INSTANT OF EXPERIENCE AS CONTINUED IN HU SHI

What we have called the "lightening" of the world in the emergence of the seeing or cognitive subject (*shukan*) which poses itself opposite what are thus ob-jectivized things is perhaps more cogently described, from the his-

---

42. *Ro Jin nyūmon*, p. 38.
43. Ibid., p. 39.

torical viewpoint of Takeuchi, as a process of "whitening." For this lightening, if it has in a sense necessarily always occurred, takes on a particular virulence and force only in the era of modernity (*kindai*), in which the West (which has of course historically represented itself as the "white") has sought to form itself as subject in the course of its invasion, and so, paradoxically, constitution, of the East (the "non-white"). Through revealing the East as a selfsame entity, one entirely contained within itself, the West has attempted to produce its own identity and wholeness "in mirror-like fashion"—to employ here a phrase from Takeuchi[44]—which is to say, in the specularity of reflective opposition. Hence the West does not exist naturally or immediately, in a word, positively. Or rather: the positivity of the West derives strictly from the fact that it is *posited* as distinctly other to that which it is not, i.e., the East. In this way, we see that the West's putative positivity in truth conceals an underlying negativity: the West can equal itself only in its negative status as the non-East. (And it is no doubt significant in this regard that the term "non-West" appears even today as a fixture in both academic and journalistic discourse, since it is strictly through this term, or concept, that the privileging of the West perpetuates itself, continues to be taken for granted. Whereas the term "non-East," precisely because it hints at the negative and so artificial status of the West—thereby implicitly threatening the security of the westerner's own intimate sense of cultural identity, which remains for the most part otherwise unquestioned—is seldom if ever used. What this disproportionality very clearly points to is the notion of the West as tacit norm, and hence the *telos* toward which both the non-West and the West itself *should* aspire. In this sense, the widespread currency of the term "westernization" as well as the concomitant absence and even absurdity of that of "easternization" is especially telling). So it is that the revealing of self and other vis-à-vis one another has effectively served to whiten both, it has allowed for difference to be organized along the lines of identity in what appears to the West as an overcoming of "darkness." Now the problem which thus arises in this universal emergence of whiteness is that the West remains yet insufficiently distinguished from its outside. Whereas earlier no difference was possible between East and West given the darkness that enshrouded both, now it is the fact of their mutually revealed identity that paradoxically obfuscates distinction. Although the East is seen as other to the West, the very fact that it can be seen, or represented theoretically, testifies to its incipient whiteness. As a matter of fact, we may understand this process of lightening/whitening in terms of the movement away from the otherness of the Other (which in principle resists specularization, and instead conveys itself primarily through the reg-

---

44. "Kindai towa nanika (Nihon to Chūgoku no baai)," p. 160.

ister of "feeling," or "sensation") toward the emergent *figure* (or gestalt) of the other, whose presence thus allows for the possibility of all self-figuration—as for example Jacques Lacan demonstrates in his formulation of the theory of the mirror stage.[45] In this manner, the hitherto pervasive sense of "anxiety" which attends the immediacy of feeling is now (quite literally) *focused* into a sense of rivalry or aggressivity, which takes place at the specifically theoretical level.

What is at stake here, of course, is the profound degree of transference that governs East-West binarity as such. Inasmuch as the West maintains itself as the negation of the East, it remains at all times dependent upon this latter. In narcissistic fashion, the West desires nothing more than to see itself, but this is necessarily also to say: it desires nothing more than to see itself as the other sees it. Just as in the Greek myth Narcissus gazes at himself mediately or indirectly by looking at the reflecting pool looking back at him, so too does the West imagine itself (meaning: produce images of itself) strictly in terms of the East. Nevertheless, it would be a mistake to assume that transference simply functions in this regard as the means by which to consolidate the subject's own *particular* identity, thereby leaving intact or undisturbed the integrity of the other. At the same time as the subject actively constitutes this other's identity, it somehow comes to sense the threat that that identity poses to itself, for despite everything this other represents in its exteriority the subject's own finitude. (Which is to say, in slightly different terms, that even the reflecting figure of the other remains a site of otherness, since the Other can never be completely negated (or sublated) in its figuration. Again, this returns us to the question of "resistance" as set forth by Takeuchi). Aggressivity manifests itself in the transferential relation in the subject's desire to eliminate this threat, and so achieve a yet more perfect silence at the heart of interiority. This violence to the other, which has of course already suffered the initial violence of objectification and figuration, is perpetrated by the subject in its explicit translation of that other into itself. In other words, in the eyes of the subject objectification alone is insufficient, and must be complemented by a more fundamental translation of this other not merely qua other, or object, but rather now qua the objecti-

---

45. "The fact is that the total form of the body by which the subject anticipates in a mirage the maturation of his power is given to him only as *Gestalt*, that is to say, in an exteriority in which this form is certainly more constituent than constituted, but in which it appears to him above all in a contrasting size (*un relief de stature*) that fixes it and in a symmetry that inverts it, in contrast with the turbulent movements that the subject feels are animating him. Thus, this *Gestalt* . . . by these two aspects of its appearance, symbolizes the mental permanence of the *I*, at the same time as it prefigures its alienating destination; it is still pregnant with the correspondences that unite the *I* with the statue in which man projects himself." "The Mirror Stage as Formative of the Function of the I as Revealed in Psychoanalytic Experience," in *Écrits: A Selection*, trans. Alan Sheridan (New York: W.W. Norton and Company, 1977), p. 2.

fying subject. Here we can begin to grasp the essential complicity between the processes of transference and translation, as for example the fact of their cognation doubtless already suggests. Specifically, the particular identities created and sustained transferentially, in the reciprocal negativity of their relation, are always under the strain of that universalizing movement which seeks through translation to reduce the other entirely into the one. Translation, in this respect, must rigorously be understood to mark the *end* of transference, in the sense of both aim and cessation. For the absolute subjectivization of the object-other is the ideal toward which all transference strives, since it is only at that point that one's dependence upon the other is finally overcome, and the self-sufficiency proper to the subject attained. And yet, insofar as subjective identity derives its intelligibility solely in negative fashion, as in other words the negation of the object posited opposite itself, such an actualization of the ideal of transference would render senseless the very notion of the subject. In having exhaustively translated the object into itself, such that all trace or remainder is now consumed, the subject's internal inconsistencies—what has traditionally been referred to as its "contradictions"—would definitively come to light. The desire for universalization that inheres within the subject's transferential relation with its object-other, and which is only superficially concealed in this latter's more restricted movement of particularization, can in this way be regarded as an impossible desire, always undermined by its own logic.[46]

In the context of East-West relations, according to Takeuchi, this translation project can be seen most egregiously in the process of westernization so essential to modernity. Although it is obviously the case that the West has posited the East as existing outside of itself, as its symmetrical non-West, there can nevertheless be said to exist latently within this "outside" an inchoate western-ness. In its act of producing the East as a positivity, then, we can at the same time make out something like a desire on the part of the West to destroy this other, or rather erase it dialectically. So it is that these "moments" (*keiki*) of production and destruction in fact reveal themselves to be profoundly indivisible. Now in his analysis of the West's translation of the East (the "Orient") as ultimately part of itself, that is to say, as a particular part that exists within the universal whole that the West constitutes

---

46. This would be the impossibility of the "logic of the absolute," as Jean-Luc Nancy has written of it: "The absolute must be the absolute of its own absoluteness, or not be at all. In other words: to be absolutely alone, it is not enough that I be so; I must also be alone being alone—and this of course is contradictory. The logic of the absolute violates the absolute. It implicates it in a relation that it refuses and precludes by its essence. This relation tears and forces open, from within and from without at the same time, and from an outside that is nothing other than the rejection of an impossible interiority, the 'without relation' from which the absolute would constitute itself." *The Inoperative Community*, trans. Peter Connor et al. (Minneapolis: University of Minnesota Press, 1991), p. 4.

as subject, Takeuchi could not but be struck by the massive *work* undertaken by many Asian intellectuals in support of this project. In a sense, one could perhaps say that these intellectuals figured that moment of westernness that Takeuchi understood to exist dormantly, or virtually, within the non-West. Among those singled out for criticism, for their inability to either think or act the resistance which he believed effectively displaced East-West binarity, Takeuchi returns frequently in his writings on China to the well-known social reformer and pragmatist philosopher Hu Shi. This no doubt in large part because of Hu Shi's multifaceted project of westernization (modernization), which he articulated as necessary for China if it were to successfully maintain itself as an independent nation-state. In this regard, Takeuchi found Hu's thinking unique in its emphasis on pragmatist philosophy as the privileged means by which to effectuate the translation of China as West. Here Hu showed his understanding of pragmatism to be not simply theoretical, or abstract—which indeed would run counter to the very principles of this philosophy, which above all grounds itself upon the notions of concrete action and experience—but instead guided throughout by a concern with practical application. As Takeuchi writes in his 1952 essay "Goshi bunka kakumei" [The May Fourth Cultural Revolution]: "As a thinker, Hu Shi was a thorough pragmatist; he was the greatest westernizer of his time. He regarded all things from the West as valuable, and attempted to transplant European modernity to China as such. In this respect, he stood poles apart from someone like Lu Xun. It is true that he studied pragmatist philosophy, but this is not to say that he expounded it from a rostrum. He learned it as a method and applied it toward practical reform. Thus he in fact opposed the superficial reception of those aspects of European culture which were popular at the time."[47] Similar remarks can be found in "Ko Teki to Dūi," published in the same year, where for example we are told that Hu "did not understand pragmatism as a given theory but rather learned it as a method. He did not study 'philosophy,' he studied 'doing philosophy' (*tetsugaku suru koto*). What this means is that 'doing philosophy' is the essential nature of pragmatism, a spirit that Hu had fully grasped." And again, several lines later: "While Hu indeed called himself a pragmatist, the only essay in which he explained this philosophy was 'Shiyanzhuyi' [Experimentalism], which was written for the purpose of introducing Dewey when Dewey came to China. Hu Shi did not preach pragmatism but rather practiced (*jikkō shita*) reform of the status quo, and this attitude informed all of his work."[48] As Takeuchi's language makes clear, Hu saw in pragmatism far less a formal or abstract system of thought (i.e., "philosophy") than what

---

47. "Goshi bunka kakumei," in *TYz*, vol. 3, p. 34.
48. "Ko Teki to Dūi," pp. 46-47.

he refers to here as a "method"—literally a "way," or "path" (*hodos*)—the sole concern of which is practical doing ("doing philosophy").

Thus it is specifically on the basis of pragmatism that Hu's translation project of westernization is to be actualized, put into practice. In this respect, we might say, China's westernization is understood to be necessarily coterminous with its pragmatization. Now immediately apparent here is Hu's determination of China—and, more generally, Asia as a whole—as in some sense outside of the region of praxis. For it can be seen that the insufficiency Hu associates with China does not simply stem from the absence of pragmatist philosophy as such, but rather from what he believes to be the widespread neglect of the practical. Indeed, for him the effects of this neglect can very clearly be identified in the massive technological imbalance between East and West. Because, that is to say, the West has historically been more attentive to the present here and now, it has succeeded in developing increasingly greater technology with which to satisfy man's concrete needs. In contrast to this stands China, which regardless of the putative wealth of its "spiritual" accomplishments has remained relatively (meaning: in relation to the West) impoverished or undeveloped materially. Let us point out in this context that Hu's determination of the West in terms of praxis and the concrete is radically at odds with what Takeuchi understood to be the West's essentially theoretical, or spectatorial, being, that it has throughout its history sought to pose itself as nothing more than "that which looks from the outside." Accordingly, the notion of resistance comes to be formulated by Takeuchi as an attempt to think the essential limits of the West, and in this way to unsettle the privileging of *theoria* and subjectivity. Because of this the Orient is considered ultimately less as a force of opposition—the paradoxical effect of which, as we have argued, is merely the strengthening of East-West binarity and transference—than it is a site of surplus, as something that incessantly escapes the objectification (or thematization (*shudaika*)) of the West. Indeed, if the Orient gives itself to be thought at all, it does so perhaps only in terms of the "nothing" that Takeuchi at one point ascribes to Japan;[49] in other words, given that the West positively sets itself up strictly through its activity of positing, or positioning, the Orient must now be thought as a negativity that yet resists and is irreducible to dialectical negativity. In a manner that distinguishes itself sharply from Hu Shi's thinking, then, the notions of acting and experience function in Takeuchi precisely to unground the West, to expose it to what we might call the singularity of practical being.

In point of fact, this difference in conceptualizing the relation between action and the West strongly bears upon the notion of translation as it in-

---

49. "Kindai towa nanika (Nihon to Chūgoku no baai)," p. 145.

heres within the project of westernization. Let us recall in this regard that the constant appeal in Takeuchi's text to the primacy of acting and the performative situation in general—what we saw him refer to above as *kōi no ba* or *kōdō no ba*—serves to call attention to the impossibility of fully translating the East into or as the West. And this, above all, because the West itself is judged to be ultimately impossible, that the self-identity which it appears to sustain in the course of its ideal repetition is necessarily opened up, at each "instant," to the "place" of alterity and difference. As we have already discussed, this "place" must be understood in terms of the singularity that is the present "here" and "now." In its desire to repeat itself as self-same, the West is forced to submit itself to the iterability that lies at the heart of all repetition. In this sense, the *itara* of iterability names precisely that unrecoverable loss found in the familiar phrase "loss in translation," and without which in fact all translation would be impossible. What this means is that the act of translation in which one entity is transformed into another takes place most originally in the entity itself, that this entity must constantly translate itself into itself in order to be then translated into a determinate other. Only because the entity is essentially other to itself can one possibly speak of translation in its most conventional sense, as a rendering of a one, in all its identity, into an other that is distinct from or exterior to it. In Takeuchi's language, it is the "place of action" that names this strange impropriety of the self, and thus as well the limits of all conventional translation. For Hu Shi, however, the action (*pragma*) intrinsic to pragmatism is what guarantees the success of such translation projects as that of westernization. It should be pointed out in this connection that both Takeuchi and Hu refuse to see action as in any way separable from experience: since action is necessarily an acting upon things that have already acted upon man given the fact of his worldly being, human activity can never release one from the constraints of the world, it is not an expression of sovereignty and freedom. In the final analysis, there can be no distinction here between activity and passivity, since action is as much experience as experience is action. This is why Hu will determine experience (*jingyan*), quoting Dewey (under whom he studied, and who was without question the greatest single influence on his thought), as "ways of doing and suffering"—or, literally, the "ways in which I deal with things and things deal with me" (*wo duifu wu, wu duifu wo*), as it is translated by Hu.[50] Yet given that man's desire for mastery over the world through "doing," or "dealing with things," is thus frustrated by the various and unforeseen ways in which "things deal with

---

50. "Shiyanzhuyi," in *Hu Shi wencun* (Taipei: Yuanliu Chubanshe, 1988), vol. 12, p. 90. The original passage appears in Dewey's "The Need for a Recovery of Philosophy," in *Creative Intelligence: Essays in the Pragmatic Attitude* (New York: Henry Holt and Company, 1917), p. 37.

me," it seems difficult to understand why Hu does not problematize the project of China's westernization. Problematize it, of course, not simply as regards its specific content or possible consequences for China, but rather in the very terms of the translation itself. For, as we are suggesting, this translation project necessarily presupposes the respective identity and intelligibility of the terms being translated, terms which themselves only came into being as a result of translation. In order for westernization to take place, there must first be a West which exists outside of that non-West into which it is then translated. In this way, translation takes place strictly between these two spaces, spaces which are believed to exist in and of themselves prior to the commencement of translation. Yet this theoretical representation of translation remains derivative upon a prior movement of translation in which identity has not yet emerged: this movement, which exceeds all possible knowledge of it, can be conceived of on the basis of that action and experience which Takeuchi and Hu both try to think. In order to better understand these notions as they are articulated by Hu, and so more comprehensively grasp the essential limits of his own project of westernization, let us now turn to his exposition of pragmatist philosophy as set forth in the 1919 essay "Shiyanzhuyi" [Experimentalism]. Through an attentive reading of this essay, we hope to show that while Hu's thinking of man's practical being at times closely approaches that of Takeuchi's, it nevertheless manifestly withdraws from the more threatening implications of this thought. This withdrawal, it is argued, corresponds to a privileging of the notion of experience strictly in terms of its continuity with knowledge.

To begin with, it should be recognized that the major critical force of pragmatism as a practical philosophy (a "*doing* philosophy," as we saw Takeuchi emphasize, as opposed to philosophy proper) is directed against the modern conception of man as cognitive subject. Because man is primarily an actant as opposed to a knower, all knowledge must be understood as necessarily grounded in experience. Hu attacks in the strongest of terms the philosophical subordination of experience to what he calls "subjectivity" (*zhuguanxing*), in the sense here of a detached or transcendent spectatorship of the world on the part of man: "Yet there were men even more foolish than this who regarded knowledge (*zhishi*) as comparable to watching a play. The knowing mind is there likened to a spectator who, facing the stage, watches the ongoing entrancing and exiting of performers without however being in any way related to them: he is an utter bystander. This is a false understanding" ("Shiyanzhuyi," p. 90). The point is that man's existence is inescapably material; however formidable the achievements of knowledge, he is at all times situated within the world, as opposed to located above or outside of it. As Hu goes on to explain, this notion of subjectivity goes hand in hand with the rationalist view of knowledge as linked most fundamentally to reason as opposed to experience. In this way, knowledge comes to be mistakenly regarded as something fixed and eternal; it is believed that certain truths about the world can be acquired in and of themselves, independently of experience. In rejecting this claim, Hu articulates a notion of the self whose effects must be described as immensely far-reaching, even if he himself fails to appreciate the profound reconceptualization of experience such a notion would entail on his part: "Only through the knowledge that no such eternal or absolute truths exist on earth can there arise a sense of intellectual duty. The knowledge that we human beings require is by no means that of the absolute [principles of] *dao* or *li*; *rather it is that which* [relates to] *this time, these circumstances, and this truth of this I*. Absolute truth is empty and abstract" ("Shiyanzhuyi," pp. 65-66; our emphasis).

Let us proceed slowly here, given the considerable difficulties involved in conceiving of this division between what may provisionally be called the practical subject and the cognitive subject. For Hu—as with Takeuchi also, as we have witnessed—this division is understood for the most part in terms of the relation between experience and knowledge. The cognitive subject (the "knowing mind," as Hu calls it above) is seen as a disembodied figure who views the world from the position of a spectator, without in any way seeming to participate in it; whereas, in contrast to this, the practical subject or agent remains at each instant exposed to the difference of the world in the historicity of its being, such that in fact no border can be said to exist between the stage and itself. (And henceforth the notions of acting and performance will have to be generalized, since even the spectator only *acts* as a spectator). To speak of this latter subject or agent is thus to speak of that which resists all presentation of itself in language: the most one can do, perhaps, is demonstrate (*not* signify) its being by means of what we previously referred to as indicators or shifters. And this is of course precisely what Hu does here. The practical subject, he suggests, is nothing more than "*this* I" (*zhege wo*), which can in turn never be abstracted from its immediate link to "*this* time" and "*these* circumstances." In the singularity of its being, the "this I" evades all capture within the universality of ideal signification, that is to say, within the field of meaning (*yiyi*). Universality would in this case be characteristic of the enunciated, or what can also be called the statement, the said. How would it be possible to reproduce the "this I," "this time" and "these circumstances" within the fixed borders of an enunciated such that they always be read as self-identical? In reading these terms, one is forced to recognize that their intelligibility necessarily depends upon what we saw Benveniste refer to as the "*present* instance of discourse." As if in spite of itself, the said seems to constantly refer back away from the stability of its meaning to that saying which is the singular instant of its taking place. In order that the said emerge in its proper universality, it must first survive the instant of its birth, in which it comes forth into the world at a "this time" that is strictly non-identical to any other "this time." So for example in Hu's notion of the practical subject or agent as a "this I," we must at all costs resist the desire to conceive of this entity in terms of a unity that would putatively underlie its experience of the world—a unity that belongs only to the spectatorial-cognitive subject, whose existence Hu in any event denies—so as to instead think experience as radically un-grounding of all unity and identity, forcing the I at each instant (each "this") to differ from itself. As indicator, the "this" names this incessant movement of difference, the taking place of experience. But so too of course does the "I," which likewise makes sense only with respect to the singular instance of discourse. Indeed, the "this I" of Hu's locution reveals itself to be a re-dundancy, since no "I" can emerge as entirely severed from the "this" which marks its taking place in the present "here" and "now." What is des-ignated by the "this I" is solely the instance in which it is uttered; it reveals the agent of the utterance, or what has more commonly been called the "subject of enunciation."

Now it must above all be borne in mind here that Hu Shi attempts to think the "this I" as the practical subject or agent, in other words as that which somehow disturbs theoretical knowledge even as it makes such knowledge possible in its ongoing experience of the world. In its status as indicators or shifters, the "this" and the "I" call attention to a strange junc-ture in which this subject enunciates itself in a meaningful enunciated—thus identifying itself, or rather (since nothing determinable truly precedes this instant) first giving itself an identity—at the same time as it escapes from this enunciated, given the unrepeatability of the instant of enunciation. The subject gives or presents itself by means of the enunciated that it produces. And in so doing, paradoxically enough, it necessarily sacrifices its singular-ity, since the enunciated once produced represents in its ideality an abstrac-tion of or distantiation from the original site of production, the inimitable "this time" and "these circumstances," as Hu writes. Through the enunci-ated, the subject attains to intelligibility in the very movement by which it loses itself, becomes absolutely anonymous—since in principle anyone can claim the "I" for themselves once it appears in the enunciated: by belonging to everyone, in other words, it belongs to no one. In for example the simple statement (or enunciated, *énoncé*) "I am cold," we can see quite clearly that the attempt at self-expression on the part of the "this I" who feels cold at "this time" and under "these circumstances" of, say, a winter's evening, is in fact fruitless, absurd. This because the "I," once crystallized in the state-ment in the form of a grammatical subject, is purely formal: "I" can refer now to anyone at all, it has no necessary relation to the practical subject that originally produced it. What is more, this statement can be read as an at-tempt by the subject to appropriate experience to itself, and in so doing, precisely, constitute itself as subject in the traditional sense of a unitary ground or substratum that underlies (sub-) difference. For, most originally, the sensation (or feeling) of cold is not experienced by a self-identical I, which then simply reflects this experience in language. Prior to any assumption of subjective identity, experience strikes the practical agent—which thus reveals itself to be, strictly speaking, *not* a subject—corporeally, in the materiality of its body. Or as Hu writes, in the context of his reading of Dewey, one must "reject the notion that experience is subjective, and recognize it instead as man's response to the environment" ("Shiyanzhuyi," p. 89). This "response to the environment" takes place in its immediacy prior to all cognitive reflection, and is not organized on the basis of a sovereign I that exists in opposition to things. In this sense, we should note in the statement "I am cold" a kind of reversal at work according to which the singularity, or thisness, of practical being (i.e., the instant at which cold touches the body) is effaced in the emergence of a subject in relation to which the world is reduced to the mere status of predicate. Clearly, however, the grammatical subject of this statement (the "I" of "I am cold") can in no way be identified with what we have heretofore called the practical subject, which indeed now seems to be far less a subject than a kind of nameless, because singular, agent, someone (or something) that is inextricably interwoven with its "environment."

What then is the proper relation between the enunciated and this nameless someone or something that enunciates it? Which is to ask, in other words, how may we identify the "this I" of Hu's practical agent through what appears to be its own language? The enunciated raises the I to universality, thereby rendering it anonymous, severing it from its immediate context. And yet, undeniably, an instance of discourse must have taken place in which the enunciated first came into being. The problem is that it is impossible to return to this singular instant of the enunciation on the basis of the enunciated; it is impossible to bind together as one the practical agent and the grammatical subject, for the latter cannot be other than the discarded shell of the former, so to speak. Just as the practical agent makes knowledge both possible and impossible in its experience of the world, so too does it constantly produce in its enunciations a grammatical subject which both can and cannot be traced back to itself. Here one is forced to speak of something like an *excess* of this practical agent in relation to all representation. Strangely enough, representation seems to depend upon this excess even as it is invariably threatened by it. In this respect, let us insist that Hu neglects to take into account the disturbing effects of this excess in his understanding of the practical agent, and that, as others have indeed remarked, this failure can be said to derive from an insufficient theorization of experience on his part.[51] What Hu attempts to do, precisely, is mend the rupture that otherwise divides the practical agent from both the grammatical subject and the cognitive subject. In his desire to think experience strictly on the basis of its continuity with knowledge, he succeeds ultimately in "subjectivizing experience," despite the fact that he has explicitly warned us against this danger. So it is that, following the terms of the notion of enunciation that we have introduced here in order to more rigorously think experience, Hu posits as perfectly equivalent to one another the agent (*not* subject) of the enunciation—which articulates its singular experience of the world by saying or thinking "I"—and the grammatical subject of the enunciated or statement. For Hu, the "I" as contained in statements is nothing more than the simple expression of the practical agent, who enunciates itself as this "I." Language is in this way reduced to being the pure medium of man; through the mediation of language, practical agents can successfully identify themselves both to themselves and to others. Language is a "tool" (*gongju*), to use a term favored by Hu and by pragmatism generally, one that can be used in exactly the same manner as ideas (*guannian*) to make sense of experience ("Shiyanzhuyi," pp. 78-79). But what happens is that this sense is then projected in reverse fashion back onto experience, as if experience were in and of itself something intelligible, meaningful, or as if the translation from experience to meaning were entirely unproblematic, merely a question of continuity. As a result, the practical agent becomes determined positivistically as an existing substance, such that a simple relation of correspondence is held to exist between the "I" and that entity which says "I." (And this, let us note, despite Hu's criticisms of such a correspondence theory of truth, which he rightly dismisses as "static and inert" ("Shiyanzhuyi," p. 78)). In thus identifying the practical agent as a kind of pre-linguistic grammatical subject—an I before (and below) the "I," as it were—Hu utterly fails to realize that that which is called the subject is constituted solely in and by language, and that experience is on the contrary something that is most originally devoid of subjects. We can perhaps see proof of this failure in the threat Hu perceives in Humean skepticism. "Hume went to the extreme," as he maintains, "not only recognizing all external things as distinct masses of sensations, but as well claiming that even the 'self' which experiences sen-

---

51. Takeuchi strongly alludes to this insufficiency in "Ko Teki to Dūi," referring to a certain rationalism prevalent in Hu's thought. And he would be joined in this reading by Jerome B. Grieder, Hu's English-language biographer. As Grieder writes, "In his exposition of experimentalism Hu referred with evident approval to Dewey's assertion that reason exists only as a derivation of experience. . . . Yet his own thought reveals a greater debt to a kind of old-fashioned rationalism than he would have cared to acknowledge, and it is precisely such an invocation of reason that lies concealed in his vision of civilization triumphant over the forces of a hostile environment." *Hu Shih and the Chinese Renaissance: Liberalism in the Chinese Revolution, 1917-1937* (Cambridge: Harvard University Press, 1999), p. 117.

sations was nothing more than a large bundle of impressions and ideas" ("Shiyanzhuyi," p. 72). And yet if it is true, as we are arguing here, that the subject only comes into being via language, then it seems necessary to think the relationship between experience and language and subjectivity in terms of a border. In a sense, Hu does this—or at the very least he gestures toward such an approach in his conception of the practical agent in what is doubtless the barest and most fleeting of terms possible, as a singular "this I." Prior to the emergence of language, no subject exists as the proper site of experience. Experience rather exposes the practical agent to alterity in such a way that it remains always open to the new, which, as we have said, is the mark of its historicity (or, if you will, its impropriety, an impropriety that is essentially foreign to the subject). Certainly this is why Takeuchi in his reading of Hu will explicitly link this agent to revolution: given its exposure to the new, which forces it to repeat itself as necessarily other to itself, the practical agent can only be understood as what Takeuchi calls (in a phrase symptomatic of his period) *kakumei shutai*, or the "practical agent of revolution."[52]

Now the border that exists between this practical agent and its own metamorphosis as subject, that is to say, the border between experience and language, is at one and the same time a place of division and relation. If borders by definition enclose, or limit, it is also just as true that they represent lines of passage, a space of opening and communication between things. What is in any event imperative here is that we try to think the border in its very duplicity, as neither exclusively opening nor closing but rather, in an unusual sense, both opening and closing at the same time. The difficulty with Hu is that he will tend to conceive of experience only in terms of its continuity with that which lies beyond its border. In its immediacy, experience is recognized at a certain moment as necessarily preceding knowledge, language and subjectivity. In this respect, Hu's rejection of any conflation of experience with knowledge may be seen as a refusal to reduce experience to language and subjectivity as well. Dewey is quoted in support of this claim for the primacy of experience, in contradistinction to the more traditional conceptions of this notion: "In the orthodox view, experience is regarded primarily as a knowledge-affair. But to eyes not looking through ancient spectacles, it assuredly appears as an affair of the intercourse of a living being with its physical and social environment" ("Shiyanzhuyi," p. 88). But if, in keeping with Hu's empiricism and overall emphasis upon the concrete as opposed to the abstract, a border is firmly erected between ex-

---

52. "Ko Teki to Dūi," p. 45. In "Kindai towa nanika (Nihòn to Chūgoku no baai)," this differential experience will significantly be described as the ever-present "juncture at which the old becomes new. . . . This juncture appears in the individual as conversion (*kaishin*), while it appears in history as revolution" (p. 162).

perience and knowledge, experience will on the other hand never be seen to jeopardize knowledge essentially. Experience is the ground of knowledge in the sense that it makes knowledge possible; that it by that very same token makes knowledge *impossible* is a thought that Hu, following here Dewey and, to a lesser extent, William James,[53] never seriously takes into consideration. Rather in its status as the ground from which all knowledge derives, experience does little more than teach man what can be called, quite literally, the error of his ways. Experience allows itself to be raised up to the level of knowledge so fully and completely that any resistance on the part of experience must be seen as provisional, leading to mere errors (*cuowu*) in man's knowledge of the world, errors which can in any event always be corrected by further experience. This subordination of experience to knowledge allows Hu to dismiss errors quite casually—"errors must not be regarded as shortcomings but instead as stages which are necessary to pass through" ("Shiyanzhuyi," p. 74) he blithely declares, and there the matter is laid to rest—as opposed to undertaking the much more important and fundamental task of inquiring into what might be called here the general possibility of error, or in other words the essential fallibility of knowledge. Because knowledge for Hu Shi is necessarily the knowledge *of* experience (there being no knowledge unrelated to experience), errors are acknowledged as an unavoidable fact, something that is an integral part of man's practical being. As Hu points out, rationalist philosophy finds itself incapable of satisfactorily explaining this fact of error. But precisely because error is treated simply at the level of *fact* instead of at the more fundamental level of *possibility*, the discontinuity of experience vis-à-vis knowledge will be passed over in relative silence. If, as Hu believes, experience gives itself to knowledge, then Takeuchi will reply to this (with of course reference to Lu Xun) that it profoundly resists such knowledge as well. The ground of experience reveals itself to be in truth a double ground: the possibility of its presentation in and through knowledge is inscribed ultimately in its impossibility, its essential withdrawal from all capture by knowledge. Paradoxically speaking, man can know the world through experience only because the space of this possibility is opened up by its impossibility, i.e., that in the final analysis man *cannot* know the world through experience. This inscription of possibility within impossibility in the context of knowledge and practical being (or in other words, theory and praxis) is what Takeuchi will assert so forcefully in his works: "It is through the act of knowing that I do not know," as he writes, and again, translating Lu Xun (as quoted earlier),

53. Hu's differences with James, which are openly set forth in "Shiyanzhuyi" (pp. 81-83), are noted by Wang Wei in "Hu Shi ji qi shiyongzhuyi zhexue," as collected in *Hu Shi yu xiandai zhongguo wenhua zhuanxing*, ed. Liu Qingfeng (Hong Kong: The Chinese University Press, 1994), p. 310.

"I do not know what I am doing, yet I am doing something." The primacy of practical being is what ensures that the "errors in knowledge and thought" of which Hu speaks cannot simply refer back to experience as if for a quick fix, but that, directly to the contrary, these errors necessarily inhabit and haunt knowledge in its possibility insofar as knowledge depends upon this strange double structure in which experience gives itself in the very movement by which it withdraws, or conceals, itself. Because Hu focuses so excessively on the translation of experience into knowledge, he is led to underestimate the severely limiting effects that the border produces in this relationship. As a result, practical being becomes more and more to resemble the theoretical realm of subjectivity, again despite his arguments against such a conflation. Nowhere can this more clearly be seen than in his determination of man as a "combatant" (*canzhanzhe*), whose existence in the world is marked by an oppositionality with things, an oppositionality that belongs by right not to the register of experience but rather to that of knowledge. At this point the separation between experience and knowledge has been all but erased: "[M]an is a combatant within the world's activities. Knowledge is obviously an activity of combat, the value of which depends entirely upon the effects it is capable of producing" ("Shiyanzhuyi," p. 107).

With this reconciliation between experience and knowledge, the "this I" that Hu initially presents as radically distinct from the "knowing mind"—which, to recall, "watches the ongoing entrancing and exiting of performers without however being in any way related to them," precisely in the manner of "a spectator facing the stage"—is effectively robbed of its negative force. What comes into being in its stead is a unified subject of experience and knowledge. This subject is seen, typically enough, as an existing substance. For how else can the relation between man and world be interpreted in the terms most proper to the subject-object relation, in which, for all its physicality, this "combat" is still one in which opponents "face" or "face off" (*duizhe*) vis-à-vis one another? What Hu Shi is describing in his determination of man as "combatant" is literally the theater of battle, in which the enemy must at all times be kept in the line of sight. In this way, the generality of practical relationality is reduced to the restricted terms of oppositional logic, and the excess of agency (i.e., the singularity of "this I") in relation to subjectivity cleanly erased. Let us note that this substantialization of the subject represents, following Kant, an unqualified confusion between the levels of being and logic. For if the subject as I must be understood as the logical condition for all experience, this subject is nevertheless in no way an existing being. Hu's error lies in attempting to fuse together two aspects of the "subject" which are in fact fundamentally incompatible with one another. The subject I is after all nothing more than a formal or logical unity, it possesses no actual existence. (And we should point out in this regard that

Hu, much like the pragmatist philosophers before him, spares no effort in attacking Kant ("Shiyanzhuyi," pp. 72-74), without ever really attempting to come to grips with the enormous consequences of the Kantian insight into the split subject). Because of this the experience of what we have been calling the practical agent (which Kant refers to alternatively as the empirical or psychological I, as distinct from the transcendental or logical I) must be understood as profoundly decentering, for nothing real underlies this difference of experience as a self-identical ground. Hu's attempt to think the practical agent as a unity of experience thus deprives experience of its inherently unsettling effects. Experience is most properly allergic to such a notion of unity, just as the transcendental or logical I qua the (merely) formal condition of experience cannot in any way be thought on the basis of the category of substance. To confuse these two levels, Kant maintains, is to fall prey to what he calls the "dialectical illusion in rational psychology": "The dialectical illusion in rational psychology arises from the confusion of an idea of reason—the idea of a pure intelligence—with the completely undetermined concept of a thinking being in general. I think myself on behalf of a possible experience, at the same time abstracting from all actual experience; and I conclude therefrom that I can be conscious of my existence even apart from experience and its empirical conditions. In so doing I am confusing the possible *abstraction* from my empirically determined existence with the supposed consciousness of a possible *separate* existence of my thinking self, and I thus come to believe that I have *knowledge* that what is substantial in me is the transcendental subject. But all that I really have in thought is simply the unity of consciousness, on which, as the mere form of knowledge, all determination is based."[54] The refusal on Hu Shi's part to rigorously separate experience out from knowledge leads him to illegitimately smuggle in notions from this latter so as to think the former. By positing a unified subject of experience and knowledge, he is able to set forth an empiricism in which, as he quotes James, "the bewildering accidents of so much finite experience" ("Shiyanzhuyi," p. 86) may be effectively mastered, put in their place. Determination of the practical agent (the self of experience) takes place by abstracting from the sum total of experiences as undergone by this being, and, in what is a flagrant leap of logic, "I conclude therefrom that I can be conscious of my existence even apart from experience and its empirical conditions." It is this "separate existence" that lies concealed within Hu's unified subject, drawing him back to the detached

---

54. *Critique of Pure Reason*, p. 380; emphasis in the original. For a discussion of many of these same questions regarding the relation between experience, knowledge and subjectivity, see Giorgio Agamben, *Infancy and History: Essays on the Destruction of Experience*, trans. Liz Heron (London: Verso, 1993), pp. 11-63.

"knowing mind" of his criticisms precisely at the moment that he believes himself free from it.

Surely the impoverishment of experience that results from thinking the practical agent on the basis of the subject of knowledge can be seen in the inordinate value that Hu accords to consciousness. The threat that experience in its immediacy might seem to pose to consciousness is dismissed, and instead there emerges the view that consciousness is, if not a necessary component of all experience, at least the *telos* toward which experience *should* strive. Experience in its generality infinitely transcends conscious experience, and yet, ideally, experience is something in which man is keenly aware of the world that affects him. For Hu, this is what distinguishes human existence from animal existence, the latter understood as primarily "unconscious" (*wuyishi*). But man himself possesses an unconscious side as well, one which needs to be overcome so as to, for example, "enable experience to distance itself from behavior [motivated by] unconscious sexual desires" ("Shiyanzhuyi," p. 90). What Hu calls after Dewey "the need for training thought" is described as follows: "Thus it is that the initial efforts involved in the training of thought lie in providing people with living knowledge. And the greatest source of this living knowledge can be found in the conscious activities of life. Experience derived from these activities is knowledge that is real and dependable" ("Shiyanzhuyi," p. 100). It will perhaps not come as a surprise that this *telos* that is conscious experience represents not only a development from animal to man, but as well what is seen as a corresponding development from "savage man" to "civilized man."[55] Authentic experience is what defines civilized man in his difference from both the animals and the savages, it is what makes him properly human. Clearly this view represents a marked departure from the more romantic accounts of experience, which no less problematically attempt to locate experience in its most perfect form in the animalistic and savage. Civilization would thus be another name for the process in which man comes to increasingly experience the dilution or attenuation of experience itself. Hu Shi would rightly discern in such an account a strong sense of nostalgia, emphasizing instead that experience is linked most fundamentally not to the past but to the future: "to use past and present [experience] as a ground (*genju*) upon which to respond to the future" ("Shiyanzhuyi," p. 107). Or as he once again quotes from Dewey, experience "is characterized by projection, by reaching forward into the unknown; connexion with a future is its salient trait" ("Shiyanzhuyi," p. 88). Just as the future for Hu

---

55. These are the terms which Dewey employs in the section entitled "The Need for Training Thought" in *How We Think* (Buffalo, NY: Prometheus Books, 1991; originally published in 1910), p. 15. It must be borne in mind that Hu's introduction of this notion of "training thought" explicitly presents itself as a reading of this section from Dewey.

marks the advancement from the unconscious to consciousness at the level of the individual, so too does it signify the historical process in which man gradually raises himself up from savagery to civilization. In each case, one arrives at a form of experience that can be said to be truly human. Now if we agree here that experience is something that can never simply be restored or returned to, if it is always in a sense caught up with the knowledge (language, consciousness, etc.) that forms in part its future, this is most certainly not to say—as pragmatism does—that the relation between experience and the future is best understood in terms of preparation or prediction, a conscious foreseeing of the world that remains "grounded" upon the past. On the contrary, prior to any specific determination as to *what* the future will be, there takes place a sort of bare and unsettling awareness *that* there will be a future, or *that* the future will come. This "awareness" (if indeed that is the right word for it) is neither conscious nor unconscious, but rather can be said to take place only at the border between these two levels. It is an awareness *of* the future in the sense that it belongs wholly to it, and in this way the future is perceived before all else as a threat, as something that is infinitely beyond all consciousness. But given that Hu, in quite classical fashion, determines the essence of man on the basis of consciousness, such awareness of the future is at the same time an awareness that man is in the final analysis not man, that there can in fact be no such thing as the truly human. In incessantly exposing man to the alterity of the future, experience may thus be understood as that which most dehumanizes man.

3. Nothing Resists Modernity: On "Kindai towa nanika (Nihon to Chūgoku no baai)"

In this third chapter, I examine the relation between history and subjectivity as it is worked out in the essay "Kindai towa nanika (Nihon to Chūgoku no baai)." Specifically, focus is directed to Takeuchi's attempt to think the meaning of "Japan," and with this of course the status of the notions "West" and "East" which form in large part the context of this meaning, in light of Japan's defeat in 1945. For Takeuchi, the necessity to rethink the subject (and above all the national subject) *on the basis of* history was clear: unless one understood the logical priority of this relationship, that is, that the subject is not a given entity which merely has a history, but rather initially becomes possible only in or through history, then the desire for subjective identity which so massively informed the Fifteen-Year War would remain unquestioned, unshaken. For to realize that the subject's formation is inscribed in its possibility within history is also to grasp that history threatens this formation essentially, that it contains within it the conditions of impossibility of subjectivity as well. Here one must confront the unsettling implications of this insight for our understanding of history. The elusive movement or force of history cannot be domesticated by a historiography which insists upon taking as its object of research the subject, which poses itself in all its unity and integrity. Viewing history as a history of subjects (e.g., *Japanese* history, *Chinese* history, etc.) reveals that the empiricity that is the putative domain of historiography is in fact contained within, or subsumed under, the ideal unit that is the individual subject. As Takeuchi suggests, this understanding of history is inescapably a theoretical one in the sense that it is based upon the primacy of vision (*theoria*), regardless of course of whether historiography consciously recognizes this character or not.

What disturbs this traditional relationship in historiography between the subject and history may here be understood as historicity, according to which the subject's thoroughly historical being reveals in the end less the activity of its formation than its fundamental passivity in the world. This passivity, let us emphasize, is originary. Before the subject assumes its proper unity qua subject, then, it is necessarily already exposed to alterity— or difference—which ceaselessly haunts its projects of self-appropriation. It is due to the subject's historicity, Takeuchi suggests, that resistance (*teikō*) against subjectivity first becomes possible. In this regard, Takeuchi calls attention to the manner in which subjective identity has been created in modernity through institutional identification with the signifiers "West" and "East." By virtue of the oppositionality that holds between these terms, the subject comes into being by positing its self in negative relation to its other, such that, for example, "Westerners" are defined as that which "Easterners," or Asians, are not. The importance of this insight must in no way be underestimated, as the Fifteen-Year War was widely seen as a historical conflict between East and West. Through exposing the historical constructedness of such signifiers, the fact that history steadfastly resists (and so exceeds) any reduction of itself to oppositional logic, Takeuchi points to that which he calls the "nothingness" of subjective identity. Because of this "nothingness," what can no longer be understood as the "subject" must now be rethought in its openness, or exposure, to history.

THE EUROPEAN SIGNIFICATION OF THE ORIENT

In his 1948 essay "Kindai towa nanika (Nihon to Chūgoku no baai)" [What is Modernity? The Case of Japan and China], Takeuchi Yoshimi paradoxically begins speaking about the West and the East—what he refers to respectively as "Europe" and the "Orient" (*Tōyō*)—by denying their real existence. The Orient does not exist in and of itself but rather depends somehow on Europe: "What makes the Orient possible is situated in Europe. Not only does Europe become possible in Europe, the Orient also becomes possible there."[1] Appearances to the contrary, Europe necessarily participates in this dependency as well. While it is true that "Europe become[s] possible in Europe," it must also be said that this becoming Europe of Europe cannot take place without the Orient: "Resistance in the Orient is the historical moment (*keiki*) at which Europe becomes Europe. Without Oriental resistance Europe would be unable to realize its self" ("Kindai," p. 143).

---

1. "Kindai towa nanika (Nihon to Chūgoku no baai)," in *TYz*, vol. 4, p. 137. Hereafter referred to as "Kindai."

The paradox here is however only an apparent one, and may be explained by the distinction Takeuchi seems to be making between being and signification. Following this distinction, we find that the possibility of any existing thing in the world which in and of itself is identifiable as either "European" or "Oriental" is ruled out from the start. Rather, the relation between the thing and its signifier is understood to be wholly conventional (that is to say: historical), there being in principle no natural or necessary bond between them. What Takeuchi calls in the above passages "Europe" and the "Orient" refer above all to these signifiers themselves. This is attested to by his insistence on their strange interdependence. In order for the Orient to be itself, he claims, there must be a Europe—just as Europe must have recourse to an Orient so that it may itself come to be realized. Clearly this relationship is a logical and not an empirical one. As goes without saying, an empirically existing Orient (assuming such were possible) would be, qua existent, utterly indifferent to the existence or non-existence of an empirical Europe (and vice-versa). The relation between the two could be fruitfully compared to that between two disparate things, say, a pencil and a wineglass: the existence of the one obviously in no way presupposes the existence of the other. If however there does exist a relation of necessary interdependence between Europe and the Orient (between, in other words, West and East), it is due to their status as signifiers. Historically, the signifier "Europe"/"West" has remained meaningful not in relation to the fixity of its putative referent—nothing could in fact be further from the truth[2]—but rather merely through its opposition to the signifier "Orient"/"East." This signifying pair is, in Takeuchi's words, an "oppositional notion" (*tairitsu gainen*): "Europe and the Orient are oppositional notions, just as are the notions of the modern and the feudal. Indeed, there are differences in the categories of time and space between these two pairs" ("Kindai," p. 136). In fact, it is precisely this quality of formal oppositionality that accounts for the relation of interdependence that holds this pair together. Unlike a hypothetical empirically existing Orient whose existence would be independent of that of Europe, the signifier "Orient," insofar as its intelligibility derives from its historical status as the negative of the signifier "Europe," requires

---

2. As Stuart Hall reminds us, it is impossible to understand the distinction between Europe/West and the Orient/East through recourse to geography. Indeed, this distinction between the two sets of terms is threatened once the couple Europe and West is shown to be itself divisive: "But 'the West' is no longer only in Europe, and not all of Europe is in 'the West'. . . . Eastern Europe doesn't (doesn't yet? never did?) belong properly to 'the West'; whereas the United States, which is not in Europe, definitely does. These days, technologically speaking, Japan is 'western,' though on our mental map it is about as far 'East' as you can get. By comparison, much of Latin America, which is in the western hemisphere, belongs economically to the Third World, which is struggling—not very successfully—to catch up with 'the West.' " "The West and the Rest: Discourse and Power," in *Modernity: An Introduction to Modern Societies*, ed. Stuart Hall et al. (Cambridge: Blackwell Publishers, 1996), p. 185.

or depends upon this signifier as its self-enabling opposition. In other words, it is through their very opposition that the two signifiers are inseparable. Each requires the existence of the other since self-identity is gained only by reference to—that is, the negation of—the opposing term.

In this sense, what we may provisionally call here the structure of interdependence through opposition[3] is shown to operate not at the level of being but rather at the level of signification. For Takeuchi a distinction between these two levels is necessary in order to show that subjective identity is not something naturally given but is, first of all, *produced*. The production of subjective identity, Takeuchi suggests, occurs through the medium of signification. Operating at the level of the signifier ("Orient"-"Europe"), what this structure of interdependence through opposition nevertheless calls attention to are the expressly material effects generated therein. That is to say, the formal oppositionality that is characteristic exclusively of signification comes, in a kind of reversal, to make its presence felt materially at the level of being. Traditionally, of course, the order of signification is understood to be strictly derivative of being. Insofar as meaning is necessarily the meaning of something, or some thing, this thing is believed to precede the signifier which, in reflecting it, raises it to the level of meaning. As posterior, signifiers would then function to merely re-present the thing: being nothing themselves but the transparent double of the thing in language, signifiers are consequently powerless to subvert this relationship and trace their effects upon the world of things. Now it is precisely against this representationalist conception of language that Takeuchi directs his remarks. In witnessing firsthand the force of such oppositional signifiers as "Europe" and the "Orient" to shape material practices—I am referring here specifically to the Fifteen-Year War, which was globally represented as a struggle between East and West—Takeuchi could not but perceive a certain penetrability between the levels of being and signification. Although apparently distinct from being, signifiers were yet capable of producing material effects within being. The tensions which developed in trying to maintain a pure opposition between those spaces known as "Europe"/"West" and the "Orient"/"East" led to the realization that these signifiers could not possibly represent, or reflect, any naturally existing opposition. On the contrary, there was a need to actively create that opposition at the level of being since this latter was inherently devoid of it. Appeal was therefore made to the purely formal opposition existing between these two signifiers. Desire for

---

3. This structure owes much to what Naoki Sakai has called *tai-keishōka no zushiki*, or the "schema of co-figuration," in his essay "Nihon shakai kagaku hōhō josetsu: Nihon shisō toiu mondai," in *Iwanami kōza: shakai kagaku no hōhō*, vol. 2, ed. Yamanouchi Yasushi et al. (Tokyo: Iwanami Shoten, 1993), esp. pp. 23-27. This essay has since appeared in English translation in revised form. See *Translation and Subjectivity: On "Japan" and Cultural Nationalism* (Minnesota: University of Minnesota Press, 1997), pp. 40-71.

subjective identity, which requires that the self be posited against an other which it negates, was accordingly directed towards identification with one of these signifiers. The formal purity of that signifier served not only to highlight the gap between the levels of being and signification (or between the actual and the ideal); in so doing, it incited a desire to actively shape material practices so as to teleologically reduce that gap, hence raising being as far as possible to full conformity with signification.

Here it becomes necessary to reread the passages quoted above so as to better understand the material effects of signification at the level of being. As we will try to show, these lines reveal that Takeuchi is unwilling to rest content with his insight into the formal symmetry between the signifiers "Europe" and the "Orient" (signifiers whose very ideality, let us repeat, creates the paradoxical desire for their actualization in the world). On the contrary, this insight functions as a kind of departure point from which to then call attention to a radical dissymmetry within history. We may state this more precisely: while it is essential to bring to light the structure of interdependence through opposition which massively organizes all "East-West cultural discourse" ("Kindai," p. 137), Takeuchi does not overlook that dissymmetry which has historically marked the relations between those spaces commonly known as Europe and the Orient. Here we need to examine what is doubtless the intended ambiguity of the word "Europe": "What makes the Orient possible is situated in Europe. Not only does Europe become possible in Europe, the Orient also becomes possible there." As the structure of these lines indicates, Europe is strangely double: it is the site at which not only the possibility of the Orient emerges but as well the possibility of Europe itself. We already understand why the possibility of the Orient requires the implicit presence of Europe as its opposite, just as in turn the possibility of Europe requires the presence of the Orient. Yet Takeuchi remarks here that, in a certain sense at least, the possibility of Europe is inscribed within Europe. It seems clear that this break in the otherwise perfect symmetry between Europe and the Orient is intended to draw focus toward those spaces which have historically been identified with these signifiers. At this level, Europe has without question distinguished itself as the site at which these signifiers first came into being. As Takeuchi's continued emphasis on the fact of Europe's invasion of the Orient suggests,[4] it was in

---

4. "I do not know if the European invasion of the Orient was based upon the will of capital, a speculative (*tōkiteki na*) spirit of adventure, the Puritan spirit of pioneership, or perhaps again still another instinct for self-expansion. In any event, it is certain that there existed in Europe something fundamental that supported this instinct, making the invasion of the Orient inevitable. Perhaps this something has been deeply intertwined with the essence of what is called 'modernity' " ("Kindai," p. 130).

   Similar remarks can be found scattered throughout this essay, as well as indeed throughout Takeuchi's entire corpus.

Europe that the encounter with cultural difference first generated the desire to identify with that signifier which in this context articulated the distinction between self and other. Only through identification with the signifier "Europe" could an actual Europe ever come into being as self-identical, or internally homogeneous. While it is of course true of Europe that "its self was confirmed inversely by encountering the heterogeneous (*ishitsu na mono*)" ("Kindai," p. 131), it must be remembered that that heterogeneity was first of all experienced within the self, as it were, hence belying any notion of natural or original self-identity. It was therefore in order to exorcise that difference that the very distinction between self and other became necessary in the first place. That is to say, difference qua the difference between selfsame entities was posited so as to produce (not simply maintain, as no self preceded this positing) homogeneity. *In thus positing difference for the purpose of eliminating difference*, Europe effectively illustrated what in contemporary philosophy has often been called "difference in the service of the same." As is required in all exorcisms, this exorcism of difference made skillful use of what William James, in another context, referred to as a "formula of incantation."[5] This magical formula was of course nothing other than the signifier "Europe." Through a kind of ritualistic repetition, Europe worked towards the goal of its own "self-realization" (*jiko jitsugen*) ("Kindai," p. 132) by identifying itself with that signifying image at the same time that it negated its projected Oriental other. What can thus be seen in this work is a double trajectory, one whose lines may be metaphorically described as simultaneously vertical and horizontal. Vertically, Europe attempts to produce itself as subject on the basis of that ideal signifier "Europe," and this it does through its task of expressing, or actualizing, its putatively latent European nature in the world. In so doing, however, it utterly forgets that "Europe" is nothing more than an *idea*, in the sense that no object of experience can possibly be adequate to it. "Europe," that is to say, is inaccessible, out of play: there can be no *actual* Europe which ever sufficiently *actualizes* "Europe." For essential reasons, each such instance is condemned to fall short of the ideal object that is its goal. Nevertheless, it is paradoxically this very inaccessibility that incites the desire for a distinct and concrete expression of Europe in the world. In this desire we may recognize the force that drives European movement horizontally.

---

5. "Metaphysics has usually followed a very primitive kind of quest. You know how men have always hankered after unlawful magic, and you know what a great part in magic *words* have always played. If you have his name, or the formula of incantation that binds him, you can control the spirit, genie, afrite, or whatever the power may be. Solomon knew the names of all the spirits, and having their names, he held them subject to his will. So the universe has always appeared to the natural mind as a kind of enigma, of which the key must be sought in the shape of some illuminating or power-bringing word or name." *Pragmatism* (New York: Longmans, Green and Co., 1910), pp. 52-53.

In order to understand this horizontal trajectory, one must not assume that the impulse behind it derives from what we have found to be the inaccessibility characteristic of the vertical movement towards the ideal signifier "Europe." Let us emphasize here that such a horizontal course is, despite appearances, neither a response to nor compensation for the impossibility of European manifestation. For that would misleadingly suggest a moment in which Europe's desire for subjective identity existed prior to its positing of an oppositional other. Rather, as we have already noted, the two trajectories are by right simultaneous. It is impossible to conceive of the one without thereby conceiving of the other, and this because the emergence of the signifier for self is meaningless in and of itself. The positing of the self necessarily implies an other *in relation to which* the self equals itself. For this reason, Takeuchi will go so far as to describe Europe's encounter with its Oriental other in terms of "destiny": "In order for Europe to be Europe, it was forced to invade the Orient. This was Europe's inevitable destiny, one that accompanied its self-liberation" ("Kindai," p. 131). In seeking itself, Europe was destined to invade not a naturally existing Orient the objective knowledge of which somehow preceded its invasion. (Such an invasion would be merely contingent, not a matter of destiny). On the contrary, invasion appeared most originally in the very act of this positing of the "Orient" as that which opposed "Europe's" own self. In other words, *the identification of a determinate other produced an interiority within that other where none had previously existed, an interiority which in its emergence was thus already violated from the outside.* This is to suggest that the very concept of invasion is unintelligible outside a logic of interiority-exteriority, and that this logic belongs by right to the level of signification as opposed to that of being. In the gesture by which Europe signified its Other as such (that is, as its posited or represented other), a delineation between the otherwise nonexistent spaces of Europe and the Orient came into being. Although it cannot rigorously be said to have preceded this moment, Europe's act of signification nevertheless revealed it to be somehow already inside this Other—for "Europe itself was originally a kind of mixture (or "confusion": *konkō*)" ("Kindai," p. 131), as Takeuchi will write. Without this prior relation, in which self and Other are originally exposed to one another, always in a sense inside each other, signification would be impossible. Indeed, signification begins as the attempt to deny this relationality, such that the self's exposed encounter with the Other is transformed into a calculable negotiation (or exchange) between distinct and theoretically identifiable entities. We may for this reason say of signification that it presupposes as its ground an unmediated experience of the Other before it has been determined qua other. Paradoxically, then, Europe's identification of the "Orient" hints at this experience at the same time that it conceals it. In order to deny that exposure to the Other and claim for oneself an already secured self-identity, it was necessary to posit an "Orient" whose difference from "Europe" at the level of signification functioned to dissimulate the fact of Europe's presence in the Orient (or, rather, pre-presence, since at this point these two spaces were not yet marked as such).[6] Three points should be mentioned in this regard:

1. The historical emergence of the "Orient" as a product of Europe determined the originally indivisible experience of self and Other as one in which Europe alone occupied the position of self, that is, the position of dominance. In this way, the pre-significative encounter with the Other qua self and with the self qua Other was displaced onto an epistemological framework in which self and Other were rendered as distinct entities: this difference was of course coded as the difference between Europe and the Orient. Here it must be emphasized that the *cut* by which being opened up or gave way to signification was by no means innocently traced. The incisional act of naming the Orient on the part of Europe—which, as we have said, came into being as Europe only in that very naming—revealed a relationship of dominance to subtend the order of signification. Such dominance was grounded, precisely, upon the ordering of positions available within signification. Through a positioning of oneself as subject of signification, it was discovered that the Other could be effectively isolated and made meaningful as object (*taishō*). That is to say, the Other was through the means of signification forcibly reduced to that signifier with which it was now identified. It is in this context that Hegel calls attention to the structure of dominance implicit in what he believes to be the necessary dependence of being upon signification.[7] In this sense, then, we may better

---

6. This impossibility of speaking of Europe (or the West) when one is referring to a time prior to signification has been addressed by Jean-Luc Nancy, for whom signification is to be understood as an "invention" of the West. The West desires to conceive of itself prior to signification, and yet this attempt is necessarily condemned from the start insofar as such an outside can only be constructed on the basis of signification. "But the experience of the West, since it invents signification, and since it creates, within its modern form, the will to signification, does not proceed, in reality, from lost signification to rediscovered or restored signification. It is rather the experience of an entry within the order of signification from out of a different order. This different order perhaps never *was*: for the historian, in any case, the half-millennium before the birth of the West is 'the night,' to quote Braudel, meaning that one must not try to give to this moment . . . a signification, even a 'nocturnal' signification. There was then *another* day, to which we are unable to confer the meaning of any of our days and nights. The question of an order outside of signification poses itself neither within the conditions nor in the terms of signification. . . . Even if there has been an order outside of signification, and even if it is still present somewhere among us, or in us, we would be unable to name it or describe it in our discourse, we would be unable to give it meaning in the logic of signification." *L'oubli de la philosophie* (Paris: Éditions Galilée, 1986), pp. 37-38.

Following this reasoning, one may say that just as signification is an "invention" of the West, so too must the West be an invention of signification.

7. "The first act, by which Adam established his lordship over the animals, is this, that he gave them a name, i.e., he nullified them as beings on their own account, and made them into ideal

understand how Europe's subjection of the Orient was directly related to its historical determination of that other as "Orient."

2. In Europe, the merely "formal difference" (*keishiki no chigai*) ("Kindai," p. 136) between the signifiers "Europe" and the "Orient" created the belief that there exists an actual difference at the level of content to which these signifiers refer. Needless to say, such a belief grounded itself upon a silent representationalism, in which language was understood to be capable of representing things whose putatively innate self-identity preceded and was independent of representation itself. In this regard, any serious questioning of signification (or representation) in its relation to being was considered superfluous, for it appeared self-evident that the signifier "Orient" simply—or innocently—reflected that which was naturally opposed to the immediately familiar space signified by "Europe." What this assumption in truth concealed was a certain anxiety (*fuan*) on the part of Europe resulting from the unavoidable fact of its own internal heterogeneity: the presence of differences existing within Europe which threatened the otherwise presumed validity of the distinction Europe-Orient ironically functioned to reinforce the very desire for such signification. What we have described above as the material effects of signification were here taken to their extreme, producing as a result a kind of self-generating circularity. Undeniably, the difference at the level of signification between "Europe" and the "Orient" functioned all too effectively to eliminate difference and create a more homogeneous Europe. From this standpoint, one sees clearly how European self-identity derives not from any naturally existing Europe but rather from an institutional identification with the idea of Europe. (That is to say: it is the historical process of identification which both grounds and ungrounds what is understood to be natural identity, not the reverse). And yet this process by which Europe sought to realize itself as subject inevitably encountered resistance in the form of the non-European within Europe. At such moments recourse to violence became necessary so as to ensure conformity to the idea/ideal "Europe"—whose full actualization, as we have said, is impossible—which was itself intelligible only in relation to, or as the negation of, the "Orient." In this way, appeal to such signifiers gradually became an institutional part of those material practices which were themselves, strangely enough, shaped by this very signification to begin with. In circular fashion, each moment reinforced the next to effectively *naturalize* Europe and the sense of European identity.

3. The emergence of a determined Orient through European invasion necessarily presupposes a moment of encounter between that which is not yet, and can only retroactively be understood as, the Orient and Europe. As

---

[entities]." *System of Ethical Life and First Philosophy of Spirit*, ed. and trans. H.S. Harris and T.M. Knox (Albany: SUNY Press, 1979), pp. 221-222.

we have emphasized, this moment occurs prior to the formation of these oppositional signifiers (or "oppositional notions," following Takeuchi's language).[8] For this reason, it must not be conceived of according to a principle of identity but rather one of relationality—what we referred to earlier as "exposure," in which the self pre-conceptually *experiences* the Other as that which somehow disrupts or unsettles its otherwise proper domain. The self is here not yet constituted; it does not exist thing-like outside of this exposure, and is in fact nothing more than the loss incurred therein. (In other words, the self is not to be understood as something which through exposure incurs loss so much as that very loss itself). It is in this sense that Takeuchi's repeated insistence upon the non-existence of the self is perhaps best understood. "[T]he self (*jiko*) itself does not exist," he writes ("Kindai," p. 145). This because it always encounters a "juncture" (*jiki*) which disturbs its identity and forces it to be Other: "The self changes by one's holding fast to it. (That which does not change is not a self). I am 'I' and yet not 'I.' If I were simply 'I,' that would not even be 'I.' In order that I be 'I,' there must necessarily be a juncture at which I am outside of 'I' " ("Kindai," p. 162).[9] Only through identification with an ideal signifying image does the self begin to actually come into being as a fixed and coherent entity. This integrity of the self, then, is but an effect of signification; it can in no way be understood as originally present. Nevertheless, insofar as the self is incapable of fully appropriating that idea or ideal with which it identifies, complete self-integrity remains strictly impossible, always out of reach. Hence although self-identity first reveals itself as a possibility at the level of signification, it is never in fact realized at that level. Consequently the self is haunted by the sense of its own incompletion, which, in turn, generates an even greater desire to overcome this lack. Takeuchi notes this unremitting desire for self in the case of Europe: "Through incessant tension, Europeans attempt to be their own selves. This constant activity to be their own selves makes it impossible for them to simply stop at themselves. They must risk the danger of losing the self in order for the self to be itself" ("Kindai," p. 131). The difference between this frenzied search for self and the activity of

---

8. In his "Takeuchi Yoshimi no Ajia ron ni tsuite," Oda Makoto aptly calls attention to that historical period preceding modernity in which relations between those spaces now designated as the "Orient" and "Europe" were not yet marked by oppositionality. Nevertheless, we would have to take exception to any description of this period as one in which, as he writes, "the world everywhere existed like brethren (*harakara*)." The historical emergence of such oppositional signifiers as "Orient" (East) and "Europe" (West) was not preceded by any as yet undivided natural community, as the term *harakara* (or *dōhō*) seems to suggest. Rather, differences and antagonisms proliferated within the social, just as they do in modernity; they were merely represented in other ways. *Sengo bungaku to Ajia* (Tokyo: Mainichi Shinbunsha, 1978), p. 233.
9. As Nakagawa Ikurō explains, this notion of "self-negation" (*jiko hitei*) is central to Takeuchi's political project of "permanent revolution." See his *Takeuchi Yoshimi no bungaku to shisō* (Tokyo: Orijin, 1985), pp. 131-137.

"self-negation" lies in this, that the latter is centered upon avoiding the temptation—or, more fundamentally, acknowledging the impossibility—of identifying with that signifier which has been culturally and historically produced so as to signify (or represent) one's self. Knowing that the self cannot be actualized in the world, it resists positing an oppositional other against which to realize itself. In marked contrast to this, the self which Takeuchi associates with Europe falls easy prey to this type of positing, what we earlier referred to as the structure of interdependence through opposition. "Self-negation" in this instance yields to a negation of the other, an other which is posited only so as to be then negated. As the whole of modern history amply demonstrates (and particularly, in the immediate context of the writing of this essay (1947-1948), the history of the West's imperial violence in Asia, which then merely replicated itself in the form of Japanese aggression in Asia), the "movement of European self-preservation (*jiko hozon*)" ("Kindai," p. 131) has proceeded through a coinciding between this negation of otherness and Europe's own "self-expansion (*jiko kakuchō*)" ("Kindai," p. 137): "Europe's capital seeks to expand markets while its missionaries are committed to their mission of expanding the kingdom of God" ("Kindai," p. 131).[10]

Whether in the spheres of economy or religion, the expansion of the self through the negation of the other is motivated by the self's underpinning desire to *return* to that state of integrity or wholeness which it imagines to have existed in the past. This desire for return arises as a reaction against the presence of the other, which in its intractable resistance forces the self to constantly adopt positions in relation to it, hence depriving the self of its putative independence. As we have discussed, this state of dependence of the self upon its oppositional other takes place at the level of signification. Signification is here that level at which identity is paradoxically promised to the self on the condition that it be relative; so it is that the very intelligibility of such self-identity derives from the presence of a nonself in relation to which alone the self may equal itself. In this sense, self-identity is revealed to be divided from within: the lack of original integrity on the part of the self necessitates a detour through an outside which affirms the self qua self only in its return. Insofar as the self can be itself only in reference to its outside, then, it can equally be said that the self can never truly be itself, that its dependence upon its outside reveals, quite literally, the cracks or breaches (in other words: the writing) in its interiority. As in the case of Europe, self-expansion offers itself as a reactive measure against this self-division. Return to what is fantasized to be the self's as yet undi-

10. Kan Takayuki summarizes this point as follows: "Self-expansiveness is the essence of Europe. Europe's self-maintenance was sustained only through its self-expansion." *Takeuchi Yoshimi ron: Ajia e no hanka* (Tokyo: Sanichi Shobō, 1976), pp. 107-108.

vided natural being is believed possible through Europe's continued self-expansion. Through the gradual elimination of all Oriental heterogeneity (e.g., the Chinese, the Indian, the Jew, etc.), Europe would thus finally overcome its alienation at the level of signification and arrive at the point of its original coincidence to self. The ongoing loss of self Europe experienced in its historical encounter with the other would in this way prove to have been merely provisional, since "the *return* thus first of all signifies that nothing had been truly lost."[11] Here, the return to origins effected by Europe proceeds not in a backward but instead a forward motion. Or rather, to express it in all its strangeness, the return backward is accomplished precisely by the movement forward. The teleology inherent in the work of westernization is such as to ideally restore that state of pure interiority which putatively existed in Europe even before the emergence of the signifiers "Europe" and the "Orient." This restoration of interiority can be attained only through the elimination of exteriority, as Takeuchi suggests in his notion of "self-expansion." We can see here that the very division at the level of signification between "Europe" and the "Orient" gives rise to the desire to overcome this division, and so return to the level of being which these signifiers appear to transparently represent. What is however forgotten in this desire is the fact that the self can be nothing before or outside of signification: "the self *itself* does not exist," as Takeuchi writes. Again, Europe can in no way be conceived of prior to signification since it comes into being originally as an effect of signification. This effect, however, has no identifiable cause which could be understood in and of itself without retroactive determination.

"JAPAN IS NOTHING": GROUND, TRANSLATION, BETRAYAL

Analysis of the structure of interdependence through opposition, in which self-identity is gained by a positing of difference in the other, should not however blind us to the ways in which the self acquires identity by positing a sameness in the other. Here, the other functions as a kind of mirror for the self, providing it with the opportunity to see itself reflected in what appears to be its own image. This determination of the other as same is of course possible only through an elimination of that other's alterity, an alterity which the image is incapable of accommodating, or taking into account. In this way it can be said that the image is instrumental in the effacement of the other. At the same time, however, the importance of the other's presence for the self's act of mirroring must also be recognized, for it is that which serves as the very prop or support of this image. The other is in this sense

---

11. *L'oubli de la philosophie*, p. 16. Emphasis in the original.

double: while it freely gives itself to be shaped by the self's imagination, it also ultimately resists that shaping in its unimaginable (or unsublatable) materiality. The mirror-play that takes place between the self and its other allows the self to transform this other into potentially anything. Play is by no means limited since the mirror does not reflect an already identical self but rather, directly to the contrary, actively constitutes that self in the very process of its mirroring. In this play, the alterity of the other remains always out of sight; it belongs to that unreflected—because essentially unreflect-able—"tain of the mirror" which, while making the exchange of such mir-ror-play possible, nevertheless constantly exceeds it, overflows it as its sur-plus.[12]

For Takeuchi, the image is associated above all with the West, and has he believes functioned throughout modern history as the driving force be-hind the advance of westernization: "Thus of course the image (*imēji*), which was produced in the Europe of advancement, is not produced in the retreating Orient (within the equivalence between advance and retreat)" ("Kindai," p. 137). This same phenomenon can be seen in the relations be-tween China and Japan, the latter understood as already thoroughly western-ized. As exemplified in the Japanese reception of the Chinese writer Lu Xun, respect for the otherness of the other is forced to yield to a reflective seeing of that other strictly in terms of oneself: "When Japan [which, ac-cording to Takeuchi, "remains within the fantasy of progress"] sees Lu Xun, he is distorted (like everything else) into a thinker of progress (*shinposhu-gisha*), a superior enlightenment figure. He is *distorted in mirror-like fash-ion* (*kagami nari ni*) into an enlightenment figure that desperately chased after Europe in trying to improve backwardness. He becomes a Chinese Ōgai" ("Kindai," p. 160; emphasis ours).[13]

The mirror image must be understood as a kind of "distortion" (*yugami*). In its distortion, paradoxically enough, it allows the Other to come into focus as visibly present before the eyes. We have already dis-

---

12. I am of course referring here to Rodolphe Gasché's *The Tain of the Mirror: Derrida and the Philosophy of Reflection* (Cambridge: Harvard University Press, 1986).

13. It must be said that, throughout his works, Takeuchi shows himself to be extremely sensi-tive to the role of this reflective mirroring in the constitution of subjective identity. Thus for example in "Son Bun kan no mondaiten" we read the following: "The divisions within the thought of Sun Yat-sen as seen in Japan are [in fact] a reflection (*hanei*) of the divisions within Japan itself." *TYh*, vol. 3, p. 337. Originally published in 1957.

And slightly earlier in "Kindai," concerning the *regard* Japanese literature has for other foreign literatures: "In the eyes of Japanese literature, Chinese literature appears backward. And yet Russian literature, which like this latter did not abandon resistance [against the West], does not appear backward. That is to say, Japan sees only that aspect of Russian literature which incorporates European literature, while it overlooks that aspect which resists it. Dosto-evsky's stubborn Oriental resistance is overlooked, or at least was not directly reflected (*utsuranai*) in the eyes of Japanese literature until it was reflected (*hansha shite kuru*) in Europe" (p. 159).

cussed how this distortion is foremost one of reduction of the Other's alterity, an alterity which qua material can never fully be brought into presence (or represented) as the object of the scopic or knowing subject (*shukan*). Alterity is nonphenomenologizable in the sense that it resists appearing to consciousness as such. Clearly, this is what Takeuchi attempts to show in the Japanese reading, or rather misreading, of Lu Xun.[14] From the viewpoint of Japan, Lu Xun becomes the embodiment of the desire for westernization—which is, not surprisingly, what Japan itself is.

And yet things become very complicated at this point. For, Takeuchi asserts, insofar as Japan cannot be anything before its representation of itself, "Japan *is* nothing" ("Kindai," p. 145; emphasis ours). Meaning this: that Japan "is" only the desire to be (something), and nothing more than that; it is akin to that *manque-à-être* of which Jacques Lacan speaks—or indeed, following Takeuchi's own path of reading, it is what the philosopher Nishida Kitarō tries to think in *Zen no kenkyū* (1911) as the selflessness of the desiring self.[15] Because Japan is inherently nothing, in other words, it must project its being upon an other who can thus be for it. Takeuchi is here not simply attacking the Japanese *bundan*, or literary establishment, for its inability to appreciate Lu Xun on his own terms as opposed to unjustly projecting its own identity upon him. No doubt this reading is valid, but only, we believe, up to a certain, very limited point.[16] Much more profoundly, Japan's lack of identity is revealed in its understanding of Lu Xun as that figure most centrally defined by its desire to be something else, a something which it is not but which serves as its own formative "model" or "type" (*kata*) ("Kindai," p. 167)—i.e., the West. This, at bottom, is the meaning of Japan's projection of its own identity upon Lu Xun. Being

---

14. In his 1947 article "Fujino sensei," Takeuchi singles out Dazai Osamu's 1945 novel *Sekibetsu* as particularly egregious in its misrepresentation of Lu Xun. *TYz*, vol. 1, pp. 192-195.

    Indeed, even a cursory reading of Dazai's text reveals to what extent Lu Xun is "distorted" into a figure who merely confirms the idea many wartime Japanese had of Japan as a nation and of themselves as citizens thereof. Hence the character Shū-san's (Lu Xun's) great esteem in the novel for the Japanese imperial system as well as for the Japanese "spirit" in general—a fabrication that of course says more about Dazai (and his reading public) than about anything else. See *Sekibetsu* (Tokyo: Shinchōsha, 1973).

15. "When a motive is developing, we might be able to predict the next desire, but otherwise we cannot know beforehand what the self will desire in the next instant (*shunkan*). It is not so much that I produce desires, but that actualized motives are none other than me. People usually say that a transcendent self (*chōzen taru jiko*) outside desire freely decides motives, but of course there is no such mystical power." *Zen no kenkyū* (Tokyo: Iwanami Shoten, 1999), pp. 44-45; *An Inquiry Into the Good*, trans. Masao Abe and Christopher Ives (New Haven: Yale University Press, 1990), p. 25.

16. Kitagawa Tōru discusses some of the problems that arise in Takeuchi's "strong resistance against or will to negate the methods of reception of foreign literature (and thought) in Japan, which understands even Lu Xun as a modernist," in his "Takeuchi Yoshimi to sengo nashonarizumu." This essay is collected in the volume entitled *Sengo shisō no genzai* (Tokyo: Dentō to Gendaisha, 1981), pp. 61-71.

"nothing" (*nanimono demo nai*) as such, Japan must pose its being outside of itself. This projection first of all reveals the impossibility of conceiving of Japan as an existing thing, as part of any given reality. Japan cannot be seen, or represented, since it is capable only of actively seeing—and, hence, of identifying itself solely in terms of those things which it sees. Yet it is through such theoretical representation, paradoxically, that Japan succeeds in denying the fact of its nothingness. Here, self-identification proceeds by the internalization (or assumption) of those images of things which it sees in the outside world, and which constitute the sum total of its theoretical knowledge. This knowledge is thus not simply objective in that it concerns objects external to Japan itself. Rather, in a much more complex, detour-like fashion, objective knowledge reveals itself to be precisely the means by which knowledge of the self is attained. In this sense, Japan's narcissistic desire to locate its self is comparable in scale only to that of the modern West, to the desire of those "Europeans" who "through incessant tension attempt to be their own selves" ("Kindai," p. 131).

We now better understand how Japan's nothingness reveals itself in its imaginary projection of "itself" onto others which, in being represented, allow Japan *to be* through them. The motor force which drives such projection is that desire for determinate identity which itself stems from the original lack thereof. While the source of Japan's projection of being is thus its underlying nothingness, that very projection nevertheless functions to occlude this fact, such that Japan appears now to be something as opposed to nothing. Otherwise stated, attention is focused in this exteriorization on the object (or objects) of projection rather than upon the very movement of projection itself. As a result, the determinateness of Japanese identity appears to be self-evident. Yet before any object can be posed before it in the apparent stability or stasis of its being, the subject must first ecstatically go beyond itself in the act of its positing. This ecstatic movement not only by right precedes the existence of each and every posited object; it moreover transcends all such objects, since none are capable of fully coinciding with the subject. For this reason the passage of the subject to its outside does not end upon its seeing of itself in its own mirror image. Instead, each image in its failure to adequately represent the subject inevitably gives way onto another, thus ensuring the proper endlessness of this movement. It is this endlessness which allows one to understand this movement as not simply one of deferral from image to image, but rather as one in which this very deferral points to the ultimate emptiness—or nothingness—of the image in general. Insofar as each of the subject's self-representations is invariably negated in the ongoing movement of its projection, the latter shows itself to be far less a projection of images than a *projection of nothingness*. Let us here emphasize that the genitive in this phrase functions doubly. First, the projection is one of nothingness since nothingness lies at the heart of the subject, which through its projections attempts to compensate for this absence and so become something instead of nothing. This means of course that no subject can be positively identified prior to these projections (what we saw Nishida refer to as the "transcendent self"), that the site of the subject is rather one of utter negativity. As Takeuchi suggests, the underlying ground or *hypokeimenon* from which these projections spring is literally "nothing" as such. That is why the subject's activity of positing mirror images in the world can only very tentatively be described as narcissistic: the image does not after all reflect or represent a subject that is already present as given reality; on the contrary, it actively creates that reality in a kind of retroactive (*jigoteki*) effect.[17] Secondly, just as the projections originate in "nothing," so too do they end in nothing. The movement of projection ensures that the subject remain always one step ahead of itself, so to speak. While it is the act of its positing that literally *draws*—in the double sense here of "to pull" and "to write"—the subject outside of itself and in the direction of the image (through which it alone comes into being), the force of that movement nevertheless carries the subject well past its goal so that it can never simply "be." As we have argued, the subject transcends—without, however, being transcendent—every self-representation since there can be no point at which it ever sees itself perfectly mirrored. The projection is thus one *of* nothingness both because its images reflect what the subject is ultimately not and because, in the movement which ensues from this unreflectability, the multiplicity of images produced and negated functions to indefinitely defer subjective identity, hence keeping the subject in a state of constant abeyance or suspension (what Takeuchi will refer to both here and elsewhere as *danzetsu*, or "discontinuity").[18] If then the subject's relation to the world must be described through the metaphor of the mirror, according to which objects solipsistically reflect the subject who gazes out upon them, this mirror now reveals itself to be fundamentally nothing. For what these external images reflect in their projection of the subject is, precisely, the negativity that inheres "within" the subject, or the negativity that the subject essentially "is" (quotation marks are here necessary insofar as the subject's underlying negativity by right deprives it of any interiority as well as of any essential being). This negativity cannot be understood merely as the symmetrical opposite—or the antithesis—of positivity. On the contrary, as Takeuchi

---

17. Perhaps this helps explain Takeuchi's explicit linking of this structure of retroactivity with Lu Xun. For, to briefly recall the departure point of our argument here, it was the Japanese "distortion" of Lu Xun "in mirror-like fashion" against which Takeuchi protests so strongly. In which case, one could say in a certain sense that Japan's image of Lu Xun precedes Japan since it is in fact formative of Japan. See here the opening section devoted to Lu Xun in "Kindai," titled "Kindai no imi," pp. 128-129.

18. Among many other places, see here "Kindai," p. 163 as well as the 1952 essay "Ko Teki to Dūi," in *TYh*, vol. 3, p. 347.

emphasizes throughout "Kindai towa nanika," such a logic is in fact wholly consistent with the thinking of the West, and is moreover required of the West so that it may conceive of the subject (i.e., itself) as that which represents the unified synthesis of positivity and negativity, as that which is in other words capable of maintaining its self (*jiko wo hoji suru*) ("Kindai," p. 145) in its own appropriable negativity.[19] As should by now be apparent, it is in order to effectively dismantle this notion of subjectivity—and in so doing set forth criticism of the West—that a thinking of negativity makes its urgency felt. Negativity disrupts the mirror play that takes place between the subject and its represented objects by ensuring that *what is* reflected can never be the subject, for which being remains essentially off-limits.

Once the impossibility of reflection has been sufficiently traced out, it becomes easier to see its disruptive effects at work within what nevertheless appears to be the actual play of reflection itself. Let us recall in this regard Japan's attempt to see itself in the figure of Lu Xun. The crucial element or point of attraction in this narcissistic projection of oneself onto an other was astutely recognized by Takeuchi: it is because "Lu Xun" desires to be something other that Japan identifies with him (or rather, with it—since, as should be evident, we are dealing here with the figure "Lu Xun" as opposed to the actual person of that name). While it is true that the *object* of this desire has been determined as the West, what is here of central importance is not the desired object as such—which is, after all, ephemeral, contingent—but rather the very *movement* of projection that is generated by desire and that, by right, transcends each and every object. This we have already tried to demonstrate. Now desire in this sense shows itself to be essentially equivalent to negativity. In Takeuchi's language, the desire of something (*nanimono*) turns out to be in the final analysis a desire of nothing (*nanimono demo nai*), since it is precisely through desiring and identifying oneself with the positivity of an individual thing, or being, that that being is transcended and nothingness (that is, negativity) revealed. This mode of revealing is of course paradoxical insofar as negativity is by definition that which resists all revelation. To say that nothing is revealed, therefore, is not to say that a being somehow understood as negativity discloses itself—for this would be patently absurd, indeed a contradiction in terms, since "noth-

---

19. It is for this reason that we must disagree with Yoshimoto Takaaki, for whom Takeuchi's thought remains essentially Hegelian. While elements of a certain "Hegelianism" unquestionably exist within Takeuchi's writings, and are in some cases quite overt, we would nevertheless insist that Takeuchi's primary concern (as, for example, it is expressed in "Kindai") lay in the thinking of the ultimate impossibility of speculative dialectics and of the *Aufhebung*. For us, this is what Takeuchi's notion of "resistance" (*teikō*) tries so profoundly to accomplish.

Yoshimoto refers to Takeuchi's thinking as "Hegelian" in "Jōkyō e no hatsugen— Takeuchi Yoshimi ni tsuite," *Shikō*, #50, June 30, 1978, p. 5, as cited in Lawrence Olson, *Ambivalent Moderns: Portraits of Japanese Cultural Identity* (Savage, Maryland: Rowman and Littlefield, 1992), p. 163, note 64.

ing" can never appear in the form of something. Here, what we above all wish to call attention to is the essential distinction between negativity and individual beings. Negativity cannot take the form of a being since it is the very condition of possibility (and of impossibility) of beings in general. This is why beings, which are thus ultimately inscribed within negativity, cannot ever appear or present themselves as simply positive. *Contra* positivism—which Takeuchi is, significantly, quick to denounce[20]—statements concerning external reality can never be subject to verification insofar as that reality is in and of itself unknowable, beyond meaning; that is to say, it is impossible to determine a being in its positivity (X is Y) since its inherent negativity allows it always to withdraw or retreat from that determination, giving itself instead as something other (X is other to Y) (which is not at all to say that X is non-Y in the fashion of *tairitsu gainen*, or "oppositional notions").

Now on the one hand, being essentially grounded in negativity, beings cannot but reveal that negativity in their appearing. Because of this it may be said that negativity is preserved in and through beings, there being no separate and independent realm in which negativity alone would exist as such, that is, in its pure distinction from beings. In order to reveal itself, then, negativity remains necessarily dependent upon those beings by way of which it is translated. Although there is here a radical division between the realm in which beings appear and that concealed realm of negativity which is its ground and which is thus always in retreat from it, the translation of this latter by the former ensures the presence of a kind of continuum between the two realms, such that positive beings are at the same time thoroughly imbued with negativity. On the other hand, however, to speak in this instance of translation is for essential reasons also to speak of mistranslation. This because the revelation of negativity in beings functions invariably to betray that negativity, that is, it positivizes it, in the act of translation itself. Indeed, how is it possible that nothing show itself without thereby becoming something in the course of that exposure? As we have said, negativity in no way exists apart from beings; and yet once translated as or into beings it immediately loses "itself," existing then only in alienated form (from the moment it becomes, precisely, an "itself"). It would seem that this contradiction is a fundamental one, irresolvable insofar as it involves the dependence of antithetical terms upon one another. Either: we agree that

---

20. "Kindai," p. 131: "Europe's invasion of the Orient resulted in the phenomenon of Oriental capitalism, and this signified the equivalence between European self-preservation and its self-expansion. For Europe this was accordingly conceptualized as the progress of world history (*sekaishi*) and the triumph of reason (*risei*). . . . From within this movement were born the distinctive characteristics of modernity: a spirit of advancement that aims at the infinite approach toward greater perfection; the positivism, empiricism and idealism that supports this spirit; and quantitative science that regards everything as homogeneous."

beings are capable of revealing negativity, and so are understandable as the medium of negativity itself. In which case, positivity is not to be grasped simply as the symmetrical reverse of negativity. The relationship between the ground and that which it grounds is now rather one of reflection: positivity, although *appearing* to differ from its ground in negativity (i.e., through its very appearing), nevertheless essentially reflects that negativity, is never in other words truly other to it. Or: in contrast to this, we set forth a radical difference between positivity and negativity, one that constitutes this relationship of grounding in such a way as to allow for, precisely, the betrayal of negativity by beings. Although incontestably grounded in negativity, beings would then not at all reflect that ground. Rather they conceal it, and this concealment is effected, paradoxically enough, through their very unconcealing, or appearing. In this regard we may speak, if metaphorically, of a certain kind of vain intentionality at work in the relation between negativity and beings. Negativity, which is nothing in and of itself, operates through ex-pressing itself outside itself so as to produce in its effects an incarnation in which it may be said to be. What lies at the origin of this movement of ex-pression is thus an empty cause whose sole force (or, as it were, "intention") is to replicate or double itself. Insofar as this doubling is strictly a doubling of nothing, however, the effects produced by this cause must inevitably differ from it. As should be apparent, a profound irony distinguishes this grounding in which cause is destined to remain at odds with its effects: not only does the ex-pression of negativity by right end in its betrayal, such that negativity always *is* its other; even more strangely, this non-identity of beings with negativity illustrates at the same time the very betrayal of that betrayal, since it is after all the essential principle of negativity to be non-identical with itself.

It is certainly true that translations of negativity are necessarily mistranslations in being what negativity is not. And yet this is also to say: translations of negativity are mistranslations in *not being* what negativity "is." Phrased in this way, the underlying negativity of beings now better comes to light. In other words, *it is in betraying that negativity from which they derive, being different or other to it as its errant mis-translations, that beings reveal their essential grounding in negativity.* Beings are thus most revelatory of negativity in that they are not negativity, since nothing can be more truly expressive of negativity than the differing from negativity that is accomplished by positive beings. But let us be clear about the status of this betrayal. In the final analysis, it is not simply that beings betray that negativity which is their ground, thereby confirming (or revealing)[21] that ground

---

21. In order to better understand this relation between betrayal and revealing, it must be remembered that, in addition to its more obvious meaning of "leading astray" or "deception," which is of course intended here, "betrayal" also signifies a revealing, in the sense of "to reveal

in the process. Rather, in a manner that is both active and passive, the betrayal must be described as one of negativity itself. Negativity betrays itself—it is both betrayer and betrayed—in its translation as beings the better to remain faithful to its own negative essence. That is why, moreover, it is in a sense impossible to maintain this distinction between ground and grounded, whatever the theoretical importance of such a distinction might be. For negativity is nothing other than its translation as beings, it always appears in a form that represents its betrayal. But if negativity refers only to beings, those beings are in turn never other to negativity itself, they are merely instances of what Hegel calls, in a resonant phrase, the "disporting of Love with itself"[22]—yet on the condition that this "itself" rigorously obey its own principle of betrayal, one which forbids it the possibility of any ultimate gathering or self-appropriation in which it would maintain itself in or as its difference from itself. (In other words: that all grounds, regardless of the manner or the very disparate contexts in which they are defined—e.g., here, negativity, Love (or "God," as Hegel clarifies in the same passage), the West, Japan, the self qua *hypokeimenon*, etc.—fall prey to the overwhelming and uncontainable movement that is their play, their "disporting"). What takes place then, primarily, is neither the ex-pressive movement from ground to grounded nor the return movement from grounded to ground, since both of these movements are conceivable only in terms of the prior distinction between ground and grounded. Here, this distinction comes down to the *difference* between difference (or negativity) and identity (positivity). In order that the grounded that is positive beings be identical to itself, it must be different from the ground of negativity, just as negativity itself must be different from positive beings so as to maintain its own identity as ground. In each case, difference—or negativity—proves to be the underlying condition for identity, and so as well for the operation of grounding as such. If this is true, however, then the relation between negativity and positive beings is now revealed to be non-original, derivative instead of *another negativity* which is not identical with that negativity understood as ground but which rather accounts for the difference between ground and its grounded. Insofar as we understand the concept of ground to imply an essential unity or oneness capable of comprehending within itself all difference, even a negative ground would be unable to account for that difference between itself and that which it grounds without thereby collapsing that difference—in which case it would no longer function as ground, since such a term loses all meaning in the absence of its opposite. In other

unintentionally." Thus one says, for example, "His demeanor betrayed his feelings." The point here may be summed up as follows: negativity betrays (deceives, reveals) itself in betraying (deceiving, revealing) itself.

22. G.W.F. Hegel, *Phenomenology of Spirit*, trans. A.V. Miller (Oxford: Oxford University Press, 1977), p. 10.

words, granting that a ground comprehends everything founded upon it as part of itself, how is it possible that a difference exists at the very heart of this universal identity? It is this difference which functions as the very condition for this ground, and so, while it is in a way internal to the operation of grounding—since all grounds must contain this difference in order to act as ground—it nevertheless at the same time escapes or exceeds the ground's essential unity, being the condition of possibility (and of impossibility) for that ground. So it is that the formal structure of the ground divides that ground internally from itself; it introduces difference within the same as its enabling condition. Having in this instance specifically determined the ground of beings to be one of negativity, we may say that this negativity is from the start always encroached upon by another negativity, or difference, irreducible to itself which interrupts its functioning as ground.

In this interruptive opening up of the ground to its outside, a kind of abyssal movement is set off. And yet we might ask here: why is it necessary to describe this ungrounding strictly in terms of movement? Indeed, the presence of negativity outside negativity seems merely to suggest another ground more fundamental or universal than itself. The incapacity of the ground to support its grounded would accordingly be conceivable in terms of the negativity left unaccounted for in that relation, but which that relation must nonetheless presuppose as its condition of possibility. In this way, the essential dependence of positive beings upon negativity is reproduced in the relation between this negativity and that other negativity which functions as its own ground. But let us remember that this grounding incapacity is a kind of structural feature, as it were; as such, it does not exist simply in this or that ground but rather, inescapably, in all grounds in general. Like the decaying house located at the bottom of the sandpit that threatens constantly to become buried under sand in Abe Kōbō's *Suna no onna* (1962), the ground is inherently defective. That is why this negativity of negativity is unable to escape its own ungrounding, which is of course already at work the moment it begins to function as ground. Just as it is found to lie at the heart of the relation between negativity and positive beings, so now does it suffer the same fate as its grounded in revealing the need for its own ground. If Abe's house is comparable to a ground in its structural defects, the movement by which this ground suffers its ungrounding may perhaps be likened to the sand which, collapsing under its own weight, slides inexorably downward into the pit.[23] What must be emphasized here is that negativity is at once inside and outside of the grounding relation: insofar as it ar-

---

23. Indeed, as Abe's protagonist reflects at one point, "Things with form were empty when placed beside sand. The only certain factor was its movement; sand was the antithesis of all form." *The Woman in the Dunes*, trans. E. Dale Saunders (New York: Vintage Books, 1964), p. 41.

ticulates the difference between ground and grounded, marking each of these terms as self-identical vis-à-vis the other which it *is not*, negativity is less the "invasion" of an element outside this unity than the internal force generative of its own dissolution. Yet at the same time that it appears within or even as the interval of these two terms, negativity nevertheless has its origin outside them; it is that exteriority which has from the very beginning in-formed the grounding relation as such. In thus explaining why negativity must ground all grounds—even those grounds explicitly determined as negativity—we also see how it inevitably falls subject to its own logic. It is precisely in its capacity as ground that negativity reveals the impossibility of all grounding. Because difference exists at the center of identity, the ordering of heterogeneity within an essential unity or oneness that is required of grounds by right yields to a movement that goes beyond each ground, and that is properly abyssal. Negativity ungrounds itself, but in so doing it unwittingly forms other grounds more fundamental and universal than before. Incapable of ever bringing this movement to a halt, these grounds rather constitute the path of negativity's transcendence.

It is against the background of this radical ungroundedness of negativity that Takeuchi's assertion that "Japan is nothing" is best understood. As Takeuchi keenly realized, it is only upon the advent of modernity that Japan first becomes Japan in the sense of a sub-ject, that is, that ground (or substratum) uniquely capable of containing difference within itself. To ask then, "What is modernity?" (*kindai towa nanika*) is necessarily at the same time to ask, "What is Japan?" The response that Japan is in fact nothing should not be read here as an attempt to subjectivize negativity, such that Japan becomes the privileged exemplar of negativity in a way that is distinct from other (presumably Western) national subjects whose mode of being would be strictly—and, by implication, inauthentically—positive. This for instance would be the wartime position of the philosopher Nishitani Keiji, whose participation in the 1942 debate titled "Kindai no chōkoku" [Overcoming Modernity] is discussed by Takeuchi in his article of the same name.[24] In his paper for this symposium, Nishitani sets forth the notion of what he called the "standpoint of subjective nothingness" (*shutaiteki mu no tachiba*), in which all reified and objectivized determinations of the self are rejected so as to uncover its true underlying nothingness. Significantly, Nishitani goes on to claim that Japan's difference from the West may ultimately be explained in terms of its unique embodiment of this subjective nothingness, hence revealing that "standpoint of religion" putatively absent

---

24. In *TYz*, vol. 8, pp. 3-67. The following expressions of Nishitani appear on p. 22. (Originally published in 1959). Nishitani's contribution to the debate, titled "'Kindai no chōkoku' shiron," is included in the collection *Kindai no chōkoku* (Tokyo: Fūzanbō Hyakka Bunko, 1979), pp. 18-37.

in the West. The problem here is obvious: notwithstanding the importance of Nishitani's insight into the essential negativity of subjectivity, how is it possible that a subject appropriate this negativity to itself, that it in other words stand as the *manifestation of negativity* without thereby objectivizing both negativity and itself? As we have argued, insofar as its effects consist in the undoing or interruption of all grounds, negativity can only be conceived of as resistant to the foundational identity that is the subject. Because of its negativity the subject resists identification. Above all, it cannot be posited against a determinate other which it negates without thereby assuming a certain positivity in respect to that other, since it would then be identifiable as that which the other is not. And yet this is precisely what happens in positing Japan as opposite to the West: its alleged negativity negated, Japan can now only *be* the nothing that the West is not. Which is really to say that it can no longer be that negative nothing, for in the end negativity is determinable solely as that which lies beyond, or is radically Other to, all determinations.

In marked contrast to this attempt to subjectivize negativity, Takeuchi's efforts in "Kindai towa nanika" may be described as directed toward the goal of negativizing subjectivity—that is, toward deconstructing the subject qua underlying ground. In finding Japan to be nothing, Takeuchi suggests that the modern subject represented as Japan is not to be understood as an existing being, that it is not something of which one could have experience. Just as Japan is nothing that exists, so too is it impossible to speak of anything like a negative Japanese essence. For essence, understood as that which allows a thing to be what it is, is ultimately irreconcilable with negativity, which works rather to disrupt the thing's integral unity, introducing alterity within it such that it be always Other to itself. It must be emphasized in this regard that Takeuchi's critical analysis of *what* Japan *is*—i.e., that its ungrounding negativity as subject deprives it equally of the possibility of essential whatness and of any substantial existence—cannot be read simply as the expression of a desire, widespread among Japanese intellectuals in the immediate postwar period (on both the left and the right), to more authentically reform Japan, resituating it this time properly within that "European advance" whose movement is equivalent to "Oriental retreat" ("Kindai," p. 136). For this would merely, in his words, "leave the slave structure of Japanese culture intact" ("Kindai," p. 169), precisely that same slave structure "which accommodates Europe" ("Kindai," p. 168). This structure is none other than that of modern subjective identity. Hence: "Ultranationalism (*kokusuishugi*: literally, "the ideology of national essence") and Japanism were once fashionable. These were to have banished Europe, they were not to have banished the *slave* structure that accommodates Europe. Now modernism is fashionable as a reaction against these ideologies, but the structure that accommodates modernity is still not problematized. Japan, in other words, attempts to replace the master, it does not seek independence" ("Kindai," pp. 168-169).

Given the complexity of Takeuchi's argument here, it seems difficult to incorporate such criticism of Japan merely within the framework (*waku*) of "Japanese thought," as if the fact of the author's nationality were sufficient to read "Kindai towa nanika" as a particular instance of national *self*-criticism, in which Japan is denounced by one of its own so as to emerge through this internal differentiation all the more unified or universal. On the contrary, the dismantling of the subject undertaken here must be read as strictly *useless*, in the sense that Georges Bataille gives to this term. In this way, it effectively distances itself from what may on the surface appear to be similar criticisms, as for example that offered by Takeuchi's contemporary, the Burai-ha writer Sakaguchi Ango. In his companion essays of 1946 titled "Daraku ron" [On Decadence] and "Zoku daraku ron" [On Decadence, part II], Ango calls for the decadence, or degeneration, of a Japan which is in his eyes however already decadent.[25] It is all too clear that this negation advocated by Ango is in fact a negation of negation (a decadence of decadence), in other words, it is part of a dialectic whose endpoint would be the higher synthesis represented by a positively unified Japan. Although it is true that Takeuchi addresses issues which are similar to those touched upon by Ango, and that he moreover makes significant use of this same notion of "decadence" within his writing,[26] nevertheless one would be mistaken to regard Takeuchi's project as motivated by the desire to conceive of difference or negativity simply in the service of identity. Indeed, it is on account of his sensitivity to this trap of what we might call differentiated identity that Takeuchi attempts to think the possibility of negativity as sheer resistance (*teikō*).

In so saying, however, we must not neglect to call attention to another, much more troubling strata of Takeuchi's discourse, one that unwittingly replicates the subjectivist logic of the West even as it resists it. Or rather: in

---

25. In *Teihon Sakaguchi Ango zenshū* (Tokyo: Tōjusha, 1975), vol. 7, pp. 197-204 and pp. 239-246.

26. Among other passages, see "Kindai," p. 140: "The proof of this [i.e., the loss in modernity of a pseudo-spirit within the Orient which "was not spirit in the European sense of development"] can be seen by viewing the history of words in Japan, for words here either disappear or fall into decadence (*daraku suru*). . . . It is true that new words are born one after another (while new words become necessary inasmuch as words fall into decadence, they at the same time cause the decay of old words), but this is due to the fact that they are originally rootless"; and also p. 145: "For me, the argument over whether the Orient exists or not is a meaningless one, it is a regressive argument that takes place only in the minds of scholars. The real problem is that of the intellectual makeup of scholars, for whom this argument is conceived of as a matter of objectivist (*kyakkanshugiteki na*) scholarship. This itself seems to symbolize the history of decadence in that Japan which belongs to the concept of the Orient, and hence also the history of decadence within scholarship in general."

his *reaction against* the West—against not only its prewar expansionist policies in Asia, but as well the implicit violence of the American Occupation of Japan in the postwar—Takeuchi allows a certain element of reactivity to shape, or perhaps even "distort," his notion of resistance. Here we are not referring to the essentially modernist desire on his part to create a collective sense of Asian identity which would be capable of disrupting, or disfiguring, the West's "monistic view of civilization" (*bunmei ichigen kan*), according to which, as he writes elsewhere, "history is the locus of a self-movement in which civilization permeates barbarianism."[27] Rather what seems most reactive of Takeuchi's attack of the conceptual chain that binds the West together with the notions of subjectivity and modernity lies in his appeal to a certain notion of immediacy. This we can see in his condemnation of postwar Japan: "Japan, in other words, attempts to replace the master, it does not seek *independence*," as we have quoted above. Now it seems clear that this remark is directed in the first instance against the Occupation, and particularly the political and economic forces in Japan which recognized the enormous benefits to be gained from American patronage. Takeuchi identifies these forces in his 1954 essay "Bungaku ni okeru dokuritsu towa nanika" [What is Independence in Literature?]: "There are actually those within Japan who gain profit by, and thus take pleasure in, this subordination [to the United States under the Occupation]. In terms of class, these people include the capitalists who subcontract for munitions, those finance capitalists with whom they are linked, and their political spokesmen. Yet it would be a mistake to think of these people purely as traitors. . . . Depending upon domestic and foreign conditions, they could also be patriots."[28] On another level, however, the desire for "independence" from the West can be said to function for Takeuchi as a means by which to escape the mediation (*baikai*) ("Kindai," p. 133) that is paradoxically required of all (European) "self-recognition" (*jiko ninshiki*) ("Modernity is the self-recognition of Europe as seen within history" ("Kindai," p. 130)). What is at issue here is the rejection of that transference relation which has historically maintained western identity, what we earlier referred to as the structure of interdependence through opposition. Only by becoming "independent" from the West can Japan (and ultimately Asia in general) disengage itself from the master-slave relation, and thereby interrupt the mediation constitutive of subjectivity. And yet, as has been the fate of innumerable other attacks against modernity, Takeuchi's refusal of the notion of mediation gives way at a certain point to a desire for immediacy—which is to say, of course, a desire for presence. This can be seen (beyond the parameters of "Kindai towa nanika," and particular in the essays subsequent to this piece) in his

---

27. "Nihon to Ajia," in *TYh*, vol. 3, p. 232. Originally published in 1961.
28. "Bungaku ni okeru dokuritsu towa nanika," in *TYz*, vol. 7, p. 67.

articulation of the notion of a "people" (*minshū*), or a "folk" (*minzoku*), whose being is that of a natural community, one which exists both prior to and outside of the advent of modernity, subjectivity, and the West. In this sense, we can say that Takeuchi's modernity is in fact of a piece with his "premodernity." In which case, his remarks on Lu Xun can perhaps be read as in some way applicable or relevant to himself as well: "Although there is much of the premodern contained within Lu Xun, this very presence of the premodern means that he can only be called modern" ("Kindai," p. 128). As goes without saying, the condemnation of (mediated) subjectivity in favor of (immediate) community—i.e., the people, the folk—merely resituates subjectivity at a higher level, for the absolute indivisibility that this community represents marks the very *telos* (and origin) toward which the subject constantly works.

REPLICATION OF THE INSTITUTION "JAPAN"

It would not be too much to say that Takeuchi's sensitivity to the trap of subjectivity (a trap from which, as we have just seen, he does not fully escape) was honed during his experiences of wartime and postwar Japan. Unlike the modernists for whom Japan's ultranationalism during the Fifteen-Year War was seen as proof of its distortion of an otherwise universally rational modernity, Takeuchi understood that, on the contrary, such a spirit of violence represented modernity's very realization.[29] Insofar as this violence accompanies every attempt to manifest subjective "national essence" (*koku-sui*), it was in principle impossible to make any qualitative distinction between wartime ultranationalism and postwar nationalism. Both were committed to the same goal of bringing the essential ground of Japan into being, and this through a process of homogenization of national space (which was itself unstable, Japan being forced in 1945 to surrender those colonies which were regarded at that time as part of Japan) in which various institutions were created or reshaped for the purpose of embodying Japanese-ness. The modernist desire to see postwar nationalism as a decisive break from its immediate predecessor was then symptomatic of a blindness to its own underlying essentialism. Takeuchi's dismantling of the subjectivity of Japanese identity through recourse to a notion of negativity (defined as a movement of ungrounding) can be in large part understood as an attempt to redress this blindness.

---

29. For a recent discussion of these and related issues, see J. Victor Koschmann, *Revolution and Subjectivity in Postwar Japan* (Chicago: University of Chicago Press, 1996), esp. pp. 149-230.

In the final pages of "Kindai towa nanika" Takeuchi speaks of an "honor student culture" existing in the modern nation Japan. This culture represents that ideal of modernity upon which Japan must model itself if it wishes to be recognized as a unified or selfsame national subject, as is putatively the case in the West. As both a symbol and practical component of modernity, and so of subjective identity as well, the honor student culture naturally bridges the gap between wartime ultranationalism and postwar nationalism. What differs is merely the particular kind of culture operative before and after 1945, not the actual presence of this culture itself. Yet this point is misunderstood by the modernists, who in naively condemning the honor student culture of the war—the principle representative of which was of course Tōjō Hideki—unwittingly condemn themselves to repeat the same violence. As Takeuchi writes, "Those who claim that 1945 was a mistake are trying to preserve Japan's honor student culture; it is just that they recognize the honor students of the imperial universities [i.e., the architects of postwar reconstruction] rather than those of the military academies [i.e., the wartime leadership]. Leaving the *slave* structure of Japanese culture intact, they merely substitute that part which rides on top. This then does not become a negation of Tōjō. It is also impossible to negate Tōjō when one stands upon the same ground (*jiban*) from which he grew. It is impossible to negate Tōjō by opposing him; one must go beyond him" ("Kindai," p. 169). The modernists who believe in the possibility of a Japan, undistorted by ultranationalism, taking its proper place alongside other modern nations must first of all deny any complicity in their project with that of the wartime militarists. Thus a stance of opposition is adopted. And it is through this opposition that Japan's postwar identity may come into being, one that is defined in terms which appear to be the reverse of those employed during the war. Yet this very reversal reveals a continued dependence upon those terms, which in their merely opposed "negation" (*hitei*) are simultaneously conserved, or "preserved" (*hozon*), so as to shape Japan as modern subject. The desire for such subjective identity shows the modernists to be, despite themselves, "stand[ing] upon the same ground from which Tōjō grew." This ground is made to bear the weight of all projects that call for the instantiation of a Japanese national identity, regardless of political stripe ("fascist" or "democratic"). For Takeuchi, the need to "go beyond" Tōjō is necessarily also a need to go beyond this ground, to in other words remove oneself from the illusion that there *is* such a ground. Paradoxically, it is perhaps only in this way that the "nothingness" of subjective identity begins to reveal itself.

4. In Excess of the West: On "Kindai towa nanika (Nihon to Chūgoku no baai)" II

Asia is Europe's food.
— Yoshimoto Takaaki, "Jōkyō e no hatsugen—Takeuchi Yoshimi ni tsuite"

In the following pages, I continue my reading of "Kindai towa nanika (Nihon to Chūgoku no baai)" as initiated in the previous chapter. Here the relation between East and West is examined in such a way as to not simply take these entities for granted, as, for example, the empirical departure point from which to then launch an attack against the West for its imperialist "invasion" of the non-West. While such an attack is not unrelated to the aims of this chapter, nevertheless attention is given primarily to the nature of the relation between these entities as opposed to these entities themselves. In this way, it is argued, the deepest strata of Takeuchi's essay are brought out most fully and faithfully. The question is this: how is one to understand the West's appropriation, or "comprehension," of the East that is the avowed project of westernization? What are the essential limits of this comprehension? For Takeuchi, the West is seen as a subject that desires to reduce history entirely to the history of westernization, such that everything existing outside the West is understood, through the process of subjective reflection, to be in truth latently western. Just as the truth of the outside material world is considered to be the subject, so too does the truth of the non-West reveal itself to be the West. Alterity vis-à-vis the West is thus seen as provisional, for it cannot stand the test of reflection. That is to say, western reflection takes as its goal the absolute reduction of difference to the *meaning* of difference; because this difference somehow gives itself to be identified by the West, it shows that it is in the final analysis nothing other than the West itself. This reduction of course coincides with the West's gradual self-expansion within history, which Takeuchi identifies as one of the core features of modernity. Through carefully explicating this process of western self-expansion, however, Takeuchi finds that the outside of the West is not in fact entirely reducible to the West, that there exists rather a kind of excess which steadfastly *resists* internalization. The present chapter draws attention to and elaborates upon the gestures Takeuchi makes in "Kindai towa nanika (Nihon to Chūgoku no baai)" to determine the movement of westernization precisely to the point where this movement reveals itself to be finally impossible.

INCOMPREHENSIBILITY AND THE QUESTION OF WESTERN FINITUDE

For Takeuchi, the West's desire to comprehend the Orient (*Tōyō*) is a desire that must necessarily end in frustration, for as a rule the latter never fully gives itself to comprehension. Indeed, the West (or "Europe," as it will alternately be called) is keenly aware of this failing. As Takeuchi notes in "Kindai towa nanika (Nihon to Chūgoku no baai)" [What is Modernity? The Case of Japan and China]: "Although Europe has comprehended (*hōkatsu shita*) the Orient, it seems to have felt that something remains which cannot be fully comprehend. This is something like the root of European anxiety (*fuan*)"[1] Let us point out here that this resistance to full comprehension does not simply arise from what we might call the finitude of the West. In such a conception, the West is generally understood as a concrete subject whose finitude derives from its situatedness in history: insofar as it is in history that the West comes into being and passes away, it is naturally unable to transcend its own limitations and attain to complete and perfect knowledge of the object it desires to know. The object in this case represents a totality of infinite meanings which can be known only partially, never exhaustively or absolutely. However much the West knows of the Orient, it can always know more, or at the very least know differently by virtue of the varying perspectives it is forced by history to take up and abandon. Knowledge thus presupposes a radically unequal relationship between the knower—or the *subject* of knowledge (*shukan*) ("Kindai," pp. 145 and 155-158)—which is trapped by the historical constraints that attend its finitude, and the known—or the *object* of knowledge (*taishō*) ("Kindai," pp. 155 and 170)—the infinite richness of which precludes the possibility of totalization that is the ultimate goal toward which all knowledge strives.

---

1. In *TYz*, vol. 4, p. 133. Hereafter referred to as "Kindai."

It can be seen here that finitude functions as the prior condition of knowledge: in order to *know* something, the knower must itself *be* something, that is, it must have first come into being as an entity whose concreteness in a sense puts it on equal terms with that other entity which it desires to know. The explicit determination of a thing that takes place in objective knowledge always carries with it an implicit determination of the subject itself, and this is that the subject is in fact a concrete thing which exists not separated or detached from but rather very much in the midst of other things which are similar to itself. Proximity to these things and their proximity to the subject is what then allows for the possibility of knowledge in the first place. Indeed, it is this proximity and the potential reversibility it implies which can be said to equalize the otherwise unequal relationship between knower and known. For if the object of knowledge appears to be privileged over the subject in its semantic richness, of which the latter can comprehend only part, it is nevertheless also true that this object is really both object and subject, just as this subject is both subject and object. In other words, there is in the world no simple oppositionality that can finally be maintained between finite subject and infinitely knowable object. This opposition is shown to be merely formal and abstract—what Takeuchi will call *keishiki no chigai* (or "formal difference") ("Kindai," p. 136)—since all real particular subjects are at the same time necessarily objects as well. Although the West is barred from full comprehension of the Orient, it too resists such comprehension in its capacity as object of the Orient's own (subjective) attempts at knowledge. This reversibility between subject and object by right precedes all determinations of an entity as either subject or object, and hence it precedes also the relationship of knowledge insofar as we understand this relationship as one between a knowing subject and a known object. In similar fashion, the impossibility of totalization which seemed to result from the asymmetry between subjective finitude and the infinity of objective meaning now comes full circle to reveal the ultimate incomprehensibility of the subject itself. Because the subject is always also an object, the absence of full comprehension that confronts (and in turn incites)[2] its attempts at objective knowledge must be generalized to include its attempts at subjective- or self-knowledge as well.

---

2. Takeuchi is quite clear on this point: the Orient's resistance to the West has had the effect of aggravating the desire for its comprehension, and in this way has paradoxically hastened the moment of its own disappearance: "The European invasion of the Orient produced resistance there, a resistance that was of course reflected (*hansha shita*) in Europe itself. . . . [I]t was clear that through resistance the Orient was destined to increasingly Europeanize" ("Kindai," p. 132).

There seems in this way to exist a kind of circularity in the relation between subject and object, since it is the latter's exteriority vis-à-vis the former that initially sets in motion the work of comprehension. This work can continue only on the condition that there exist some-

As an explanation of what Takeuchi refers to here as "the resistance of the Orient" ("Kindai," pp. 132 ff.) to any claim of absolute knowledge of itself, this account of the West's finitude helps guard against a viewpoint which insists upon seeing the West as a kind of pure and disembodied consciousness, one which has existed throughout history without any delimitable beginning and end mark. Such a viewpoint would be thoroughly rejected by Takeuchi, since it fails to recognize that the self-identity of the West cannot be determined prior to and independently of its instantiation in discourse, discourse being itself here something like the index of historical change. That is to say, the unity of this ostensibly transhistorical subject must now be understood as constituted discursively, to come into being only belatedly as an effect of historical discourse, rather than preceding it. To speak of the West as the pre-existing author (or source) of its own discourse—e.g., here, the western discourse on the Orient—would in this sense be equivalent to a confused reversal of cause and effect. Such an understanding of discourse as derivative of or belonging to the West would be, in respect of this point of precedence, analogous to a scholarship which posits the West as a material object, something which exists in and of itself prior to all our representations of it. In each case, the misconception lies in regarding the West as a real referent (whether essential or empirical), one to which all language *of* the West necessarily returns as to itself. This point can be demonstrated by the futility of any investigation into, say, "western history" or "western literature" which does not begin by acknowledging the incontestably ideal status of its object of study but rather, on the contrary, claims in all innocence to be engaged in strict empirical research. (As goes without saying, this applies equally to all inquiry of objects classed within the field known as "Japanese literature"). For such investigations are incapable of providing an account of the origins of their very object: desiring to empirically trace these "western" phenomena back in time so as to reveal their seemingly natural or necessary genesis, they can explain everything except the emergence of the idea "West," the validity of which must be simply taken for granted as an article of faith. This idea functions to organize and make sense of the otherwise meaningless raw material of historical experience, hence providing a universal form on the basis of which alone knowledge becomes possible. What must be underscored here is the fact that the "West" does not and cannot represent any preexisting thing of which we could have direct experience, outside of the mediation of discursive language. In its capacity to shape that content which is immediately given in experience, the "West" does not itself derive from experience but is

---

thing *against which* it can apply itself, something that is therefore other to itself. And yet at the same time, it is this other that is constantly eroded in the process of this work.

instead, *jigoteki ni* (or: after the fact), actively projected upon it.[3] It is, in other words, a construct produced by the imagination.

This insight into what is thus the irreducibly discursive being of the "West," which forces us to refer to it only in quotation marks, yet poses a threat to any conception of the West in terms of finitude. While this notion of finitude is clearly valuable in allowing us to situate the West historically, nevertheless it proves ultimately insufficient in its insistence upon seeing the West as a concrete entity, that is, a "given thing" ("Kindai," p. 142) which is actually present in the world. To speak of the West as finite is in other words to determine its being empirically, on the basis of our putatively direct and unmediated experience of it. As goes without saying, this objective experience is invariably both grounded in and confirmed by the experience we seem to have of ourselves, insofar as we assume these selves to be inherently western. Here we can detect a certain complicity between the discourse on finitude and that abstract, transhistorical conception of subjectivity which it sets itself against: despite the fact that the former's historicization of the subject brings to light the impossibility of its projects of comprehension, both accounts nevertheless show themselves to be in profound agreement in determining the subject on the basis of presence and self-identity. What has been changed merely is the specific mode of subjective presence; the possibility of this presence itself is not put into question. For that view which regards the West as existing continuously throughout history, such that its presence assumes the form of a disembodied and universal consciousness, the notion of western finitude substitutes a concretization (or particularization) of the subject West, hence reformulating presence along the lines of its embodiment in the world. If then we realize that the emergence of the West as a particular being within history is necessarily followed by its disappearance, it nevertheless becomes possible now to speak of the West as a kind of thing, something whose ontological status is on par with the material objects of everyday experience.

Takeuchi carefully avoids this trap of ontologizing the West. And this, no doubt, because of his understanding that criticism of the West's comprehension of the Orient on the basis of a notion of finitude accomplishes precisely what it does not wish in setting the problematic upon a strictly empirical level. For the West (Europe) is not empirically present, he insists, it *is not*: "History is not an empty form of time. It includes an infinite number of instants (*shunkan*) in which one struggles against obstacles so that the self (*jiko*) may be itself, without which both the self and history would be

---

3. In his dismantling of the notion of the mother tongue, Naoki Sakai discusses this *jigoteki* quality as essentially bound up with the imaginary status of the subject of enunciation. See "Nashonaritī to bo(koku)go no seiji," in *Nashonaritī no datsukōchiku*, ed. Sakai Naoki et. al. (Tokyo: Kashiwa Shobō, 1996), pp. 31 ff.

lost. Simply being (*de aru koto*) Europe does not make Europe Europe" ("Kindai," p. 130). Or rather, the West's mode of being is such that it neither simply is nor isn't; hence one can say only that it "barely maintains itself": "The various facts of history teach that Europe barely maintains itself through the tension of its incessant self-renewals" ("Kindai," p. 130). This same suspension of being applies of course to the westerner himself, whose identity is never immediately given—his own protests to the contrary—but can in fact only be acquired: "Through incessant tension, Europeans *attempt to be* their own selves (*jiko de arō to suru*). This constant activity to be their own selves makes it impossible for them to simply stop at themselves. They must risk the danger of losing the self in order for the self to be itself" ("Kindai," p. 131; emphasis ours). Full comprehension of the Orient presupposes the possibility of totalization, whereas it is precisely this *impossibility* that the West can be said to demonstrate. And yet this impossibility is not to be attributed to the West's finitude. In this instance, the belief that the finite subject is incapable of grasping the infinite meaning of its object due to its own historical constraints reveals a certain lingering positivism. Thus it becomes linked, from Takeuchi's standpoint, to the ongoing quantification and homogenization of the world so essential to modernity and westernization ("Kindai," p. 131). The notion of finitude reveals itself here to be a product of the West—"for which everything is homogeneous" ("Kindai," p. 132), he adds—not simply because of its geographical place of origin, but rather in the sense that the empirical assumptions embedded in this notion are grounded upon that possibility of presence upon which homogenization depends. Insofar as the translation of heterogeneity (i.e., the Orient) into identity that is the avowed project of westernization requires that this West be initially selfsame, or present to itself, it undeniably shares with a notion of western finitude the belief in the West's given reality. While it is true then that this notion provides a framework within which to critically examine the West, that it brings the West down to earth in exposing its pretensions to universal, transhistorical presence in its capacity as knowing subject, nevertheless it consistently fails to think the possibility of conceiving the West otherwise than in terms of being.

EAST AND WEST ACCORDING TO REALISM: THE CRITICISM OF "OBJECTIVIST SCHOLARSHIP"

Regardless of how we understand it, Takeuchi suggests, the West does not owe its apparent unity and self-identity to such observable and concrete factors as, for example, (to cite only the most commonly named) geographic location, linguistic traditions, or sociocultural practices, etc. In this instance in particular, it is clear that form—i.e., the idea "West"—is in no way immanent within matter. On the contrary, in analyzing this entity one is forced to speak of a kind of "technical" (in the sense of man-made, something that is produced and not simply given in nature) *application or imposition of form upon matter.* For this reason it is impossible to lay claim to an actual experience of the West, just as it is impossible to claim either for oneself or for others an intrinsic identity as westerner. In fact, such claims can be said to reveal a deep-seated longing for subjective being, as well as the attendant sense of "anxiety" provoked by the possibility that such being is forever unattainable, or even simply chimerical ("Kindai," p. 133). More to the point, there can be detected in these claims a kind of reversal at work between reality and the representation of reality. What for Takeuchi is the purely conventional status of subjective representations of objective being is, in other words, forgotten, giving way to the mistaken notion that these representations in fact reflect or derive from reality itself. At issue here is the reification of discursive representation: a strictly abstract form whose original function is to render intelligible an existing thing comes to covertly usurp the place of this latter. In this regard, it should be pointed out that the danger of this reversal is constantly present within language, since it is after all impossible to rigorously distinguish between a thing and its representation outside of the very medium of representation. Whether we like it or not, the scales are for all such distinctions overwhelmingly tipped in favor of representation. Even were one to adopt a stance of realism and attempt to conceive of the thing independently of its representation, i.e., as how it really is in and of itself, this *conception* would have the unintended effect of contaminating the thing, robbing it of its ostensible purity in the simple exchange of one representation for another. That other, second representation might well be issued with the intent to eliminate all idealization and return to the thing itself. But this project must necessarily fail insofar as representation yet remains the medium through which the return to reality is carried out.[4]

Takeuchi directly addresses this problem as part of his general attempt to dismantle the notions "East" and "West." Commenting on the long historical dispute between idealists and realists, he writes: "But neither the

---

4. Judith Butler outlines this same problem in her discussion of the transition from consciousness to self-consciousness in Hegel's *Phenomenology of Spirit*: "The object of Explanation becomes curiously ambiguous as well; in being explained, the object is revealed as having certain properties that consciousness itself can elucidate. But what the object reveals, and what consciousness contributes, remain indistinguishable, for the only route to the object is through the Explanation itself, so that we cannot appeal to the object what exists outside this explanation in order to see to what extent the Explanation adequately expresses the object itself. Indeed, the object itself is no different from the object-as-explained; it exists in the form of the Explanation which has become its actuality." *Subjects of Desire: Hegelian Reflections in Twentieth-Century France* (New York: Columbia University Press, 1987), p. 29.

idealists nor realists attempt to pull reality back to themselves (*genjitsu wo hikimodosō towa shiteinai*). They do not try to bridge the discord between reality and concept (*kannen*) by pulling reality back to themselves. Nor do they think about whether such a project is even possible in the first place" ("Kindai," p. 149). As we have remarked, realists fall into self-deception when they believe themselves capable of dealing with a reality entirely un-tarnished by ideal significations—significations which are only subse-quently projected upon reality, and which it itself, as pre-significant, lacks. In their desire to guard against abstraction and grasp entities in their proper objectivity, they are careful to dissociate being as it exists in itself and being as it exists for us. (This as opposed to a more naïve realism, which in its notion of being as *immediately* One rejects the possibility of any such dis-tinction). The realm of appearances that is the latter (i.e., being-for-us) must, if one is to avoid the trap of "linguistic immanence,"[5] be conceived as necessarily grounded upon real being, or being-in-itself, which thus serves as the touchstone against which all subjective truth claims may ultimately be judged. In spite of this division into two types of being, therefore, a nec-essary relation is shown to exist between them, hence preserving being's overall unity. This relation may be described as a natural doubling: the in-telligibility that exists merely in latent form within being comes to develop from this latency to emerge finally in the shape of a determinate entity. In this way, being is able to meaningfully appear to man in and of itself, in objective fashion, without the mediation of idealizations which are merely supervenient and arbitrary.

As Takeuchi realizes, however, this epistemological confidence evinced by realism in its professed ability to distinguish between objective and subjective reality (or between reality and appearance) is undermined by those historical attempts, current especially during Japan's Fifteen-Year War, to identify what was universally recognized as the *essential reality* of East and West. Here, these terms were understood to refer to essences which existed objectively, that is, independently of consciousness. These essences in turn grounded the sum total of those particular eastern and western things most familiar to us in everyday experience. Takeuchi ex-presses a deep suspicion of this so-called realism, in which he sees the roots of a merely superficial and unreflecting "objectivist scholarship." Question-ing the widespread assumption of the "Orient's" objective being, he re-marks: "However, I do not believe that such a general Oriental nature exists as an essence (or *ousia: jittaiteki na mono*). For me, the argument over

---

5. Or "semiological reductionism," as M.C. Dillon calls it. This is "the thesis that there can be no meaning (or relatedness, etc.) found within the empirical domain that has not already been projected upon it through the agency of the immanent structures in question [i.e., the structures of language]." *Merleau-Ponty's Ontology* (Evanston: Northwestern University Press, 1997), p. xi.

whether the Orient exists or not is a meaningless one, it is a regressive argument that takes place only in the minds of scholars. The real problem is
that of the intellectual makeup of scholars, for whom this argument is conceived of as a matter of objectivist scholarship (*kyakkanshugiteki na gakumon*). This itself seems to symbolize the history of *decadence* in that Japan
which belongs to the concept of the Orient, and hence also the history of
decadence within scholarship in general. Actually, in terms of practice, such
scholarship was and still remains very forgiving of the militarists' self-
interests in the name of scholarship" ("Kindai," p. 145).[6]

For our purposes here, the insights that Takeuchi reveals in this passage
are two: 1. the non-derivative nature of appearance, or being-for-us; that is,
the impossibility of tracing representation back to an originary objective
source of which it would be but the passive reflection; and 2. the parasitic
ability of such phenomenal representations to pass for reality, such that the
historically *productive activity* which enables them to come into being is
effaced, forgotten, thus forcing us into the absurd position of inquiring after
their referents in objective reality—precisely in the manner of "objectivist
scholarship." Whereas realists maintain the primacy of the objective world
over all subjective interpretations of such, Takeuchi acknowledges that the
boundary which marks this division remains by right unknowable, or unde-
cidable. Indeed, how is it possible that the difference between consciousness and world be articulated in such a way as to eliminate all possibility of
ambiguity between them? Would this difference exist objectively, in and of
itself, or would it be instead a representation of such, one that is to some
degree already contaminated by consciousness?

In speaking of an external Oriental "essence" which underlies those
particular Oriental objects ostensibly given in experience, realism shows
that it underestimates the power of representation to convincingly disguise
itself as reality. What realism remains blind to is the fact that experience
cannot be understood as a purely passive reception of external reality; that
passivity, which as it were lures one into speaking of experience in general
as *reflective* of the world, is ultimately nothing more than an ideal, one that
is thus never attained in any actual experience. Inseparable from all experience is a certain active force that can be linked, Takeuchi implies, to the
imagination. Although inaccessible in and of itself, the imagination never-

---

6. Takeuchi takes up this point again several lines later: "However, it must be said that the
inquiry into the Orient's existence does in fact emerge from a kind of resistance, as there is
here an aspect of defiance against any concept of the Orient as self-evident. This aspect is
correct qua scholarship, and was thus unpopular with the militarists. Yet when it sought to
establish itself as scholarship, in which the thesis of the Orient's existence was opposed to that
of its non-existence, i.e., when it became a method to compare extractions (*toridashita mono*),
this aspect *fell into decadence*. For such scholarship represents the sole scientific method"
("Kindai," pp. 145-146).

theless produces "representations" (*hyōshō*) ("Kindai," p. 140) of objects in an entirely originary fashion, that is, these representations are in no sense duplicative of real objects already perceived. Which is to say, therefore, that these representations can be understood to refer back neither to reality, which it effectively transcends, nor in fact to imagination itself, which is after all nothing present. These representations, or "images" (*imēji*) as Takeuchi will also refer to them ("Kindai," p. 137),[7] yet carry within themselves a potency whose effects are invariably felt at the level of the material world, at times with a truly destructive intensity. The "Orient" is of course such a representation.

We should here keep in mind that, appearances to the contrary, the emergence of this representation in modernity does not signal a desire on the part of a nascent Orient to represent itself to itself. What it points to rather is a West that has not yet come into being, and that thus requires an imaginary unity posited outside of itself *against which* it may represent itself in determinate fashion. Reflecting no pre-existing reality, the "Orient" nevertheless comes to shape in its historical effectivity an Orient whose status is primarily negative, being merely the symmetrical opposite or other of the West. In this way, the Orient's negativity may be seen to have functioned as the requisite mediation through which the West was able to positively determine itself. Ironically enough, the realists in their desire to identify an objectively existing Orient so as to reaffirm, in their struggle against the West, the belief in the foundedness (or naturalness) of their own collective non-western identity—thereby explaining, incidentally, the manner in which "such scholarship [was] very forgiving of the militarists' self-interests"—reveal a strange complicity with the West's own project of self-identity. Insofar as both "easterners" and "westerners" alike assume these identities to be in some way grounded in reality itself, they are similarly unable to, in Takeuchi's phrase, "pull reality back to themselves," to in other words question the historical sedimentation due to which these images or representations have come to appear as natural and self-evident.

---

7. Takeuchi's sensitivity to the place of imagination within experience, and hence to the impossibility of any pure or unadulterated knowledge of the experienced object, may be gleaned from this deceptively simple admission he makes regarding his own scholarship on Lu Xun: "What I wish to write about is the image of the man Lu Xun that exists in my imagination." Quoted in Tsurumi Shunsuke, *Takeuchi Yoshimi: aru hōhō no denki* (Tokyo: Riburo Pōto, 1995), p. 144.

As goes without saying, this statement does not imply that, for Takeuchi, Lu Xun is simply reducible to "the *image* of the man Lu Xun." Nothing could be further from the truth. What it does suggest, however, is an awareness that all claims to objective knowledge contain an ineradicably "subjective" element of which one must be extremely self-conscious. Only through rigorously confronting this problem is there found to be a beyond or a limit to the imagined. It is in fact precisely this unimaginable which makes possible something like respect for the otherness of the other.

WESTERN IDEALISM: THE EXPANSION OF THE WEST AS SUBJECT

Let us recall at this point that Takeuchi directs his attack not only against realism, but equally, and indeed with greater force, against idealism. Nevertheless, it would be a mistake to read "Kindai towa nanika (Nihon to Chūgoku no baai)" as in any way a philosophical discourse. To be sure, it is Takeuchi himself who warns us against such a reading, as much by the extremely allusive and fragmentary manner with which he treats these philosophies as by his admission that the arguments presented are based on nothing more substantial than what he calls his "literary intuition" ("Kindai," p. 138). The criticism of realism and idealism as set forth in the essay is above all else a political criticism, in the sense that Takeuchi sees the geopolitical tensions which resulted in Japan's Fifteen-Year War as in some sense grounded upon notions of the "East" and "West" which were at once realist and idealist. From his perspective, writing in the years 1947-1948 in the aftermath of Japan's defeat, these philosophies each in their own way functioned to perpetuate gross misunderstandings regarding the issues of modernity and westernization. It is, then, strictly in the context of these particular issues that his criticism is formulated: Takeuchi is less concerned with these philosophical positions as such than with the very concrete manner in which they historically informed these issues. Taking as our point of departure his insight that both positions effectively prepared the ground for wartime aggressions, we must now try to, first, provide an account of Takeuchi's general conception of idealism, and, secondly, specify the very distinct ways in which he suggests idealism implicated itself within this historical problematic. In this way, it is hoped, we can come to a better understanding of what in "Kindai towa nanika (Nihon to Chūgoku no baai)" is set forth as the essential relation between idealist philosophy and the West.

In Takeuchi's judgment, the primary fault of idealism lies in its guiding assumption that reality is ultimately reducible to the *thought* of reality. The idealist universe is one in which what appear as things existing outside the self are revealed in truth to be latently part of the self, which thus grounds the world as its own. Insofar as they are constituted by consciousness, objects of knowledge refer not to any external reality from which the self is absent but rather strictly—if indirectly, or mediately—to the subjective realm itself. In other words, what is now brought into play is the self's unique capacity for "reflection," what Takeuchi translates by the term *hansha* ("Kindai," pp. 133 and 159). Here, the subject is seen primarily as a mirror in relation to which the world comes to progressively lose its externality and otherness. No concrete reality is able to resist this reflection, a fact which immediately calls into question the status of reality's very concreteness and impenetrability. In looking outside of itself, the subject takes solace in its knowledge that the world is merely the site of *its own* alienation. The world's difference from the subject is only a superficial difference, an effect of appearance that cannot stand the test of reflection. What this alienating difference indicates then is not the permanent isolation of a self in confrontation with a world perceived to be beyond its understanding and hostile to its interests; all conflict between self and other is rather provisional, that is, dialectically resolvable in a higher synthesis. In a strange manner, the world can be described as awaiting the self's representations of itself in order to be complete: it seems to require the mediation of an external agency so as to realize itself as itself (i.e., as *determinate* reality), just as the self in its act of representing things finds that mediation through which it capably recognizes itself as subject. Without this representational doubling, it is maintained, reality is helpless to raise itself above the level of dumb, inert matter. Trapped at first within the immediacy of material density, from which it cannot extricate itself on the basis of its own efforts alone, this reality is as yet pure spatiality, that is, for idealism, space devoid of time (or history). In Hegelian language—which, let us note, Takeuchi appears to make use of for strategic effect—we may say that this original spatiality is a self-identity that does not yet know itself to be such, that in other words the "self-recognition" (or "knowledge-of-self," *jiko ninshiki*) ("Kindai," p. 130) enabled by reflection must first become explicit in order for this "self" to pass from a stage of latency to one of actualization. Following the logic of the argument set forth here, it can be seen that this actualization is ostensibly accomplished through the intervention of time.

Now time, for Takeuchi, is equivalent to history in the specific sense he gives this term to mean "world history" (*sekaishi*), that is, the history of the West—or the West as the *telos* of history ("Kindai," pp. 130-132 and 137).[8] This point must be borne in mind since, as suggested by this account of idealism, time is understood to refer primarily to man (and specifically to western man). It is through man that time is opened up in such a way that it now becomes possible to speak without contradiction of material things existing temporally, or historically, no longer in the mode of pure spatiality as was the case before their emergence in the human world. As Takeuchi reminds us, this transformation is conceived by idealism as a "movement" (*undō*) ("Kindai," pp. 130 ff.) in which *mono*, or things, lose their initial ontological status as merely positive beings so as to become, more properly, "objects" (*taishō*). Hence the conviction, which Takeuchi finds to be prevalent in, if not indeed fully characteristic of, modernity, that "all things can ultimately be objectified (*taishōka*) and extracted" ("Kindai," p. 132). What

---

8. Takeuchi is of course referring here to the Kyoto School. Greater space is given to this concept of "world history" in the 1959 essay "Kindai no chōkoku," in *TYz*, vol. 8, pp. 3-67.

this conviction in fact points to is a conception of man as essentially negative: just as man is understood to be nothing in and of itself, so too are his relations with the world defined exclusively by negation, or the annihilating of that (spatial) reality that man is not. This activity of negation is not however simply destructive, since another reality necessarily comes into being through this work. This emergent reality is one that is *produced*; it represents a spiritualization of matter that effectively liberates matter from itself, such that it henceforth becomes something other to, or rather higher than, its own original or immediate positive identity. From this moment onward a relationship will exist between things and man, one that uniquely manifests itself in the form of *meaning*. That is to say, things are no longer able to resist man in their material alterity. Gone is their inherent strangeness, replaced by a more profound intelligibility that, always latent within things, nevertheless only now comes to the surface as expressive of what they are in truth. The difference that previously separated man from things is in this way shown to be illusory, transient. That difference is understood to be in no sense indicative of revealed reality; on the contrary, it functions as the immediate departure point from which the "movement" of consciousness to the real and the real to consciousness unfolds, thus giving reality its properly historical character.

The movement from positive being to negated and thus meaningful object is one in which things are progressively *actualized*, manifesting their underlying potential as significant, that is, as a representational form that exists within consciousness. As this word makes clear, the thing's actualization depends upon an intentional "act" (*kōdō*) on the part of consciousness. Serving in this instance as the medium as well as the ultimate content of revelation—since it is after all only through consciousness of objects that self-consciousness is able to reveal itself—consciousness thus effectively assimilates the thing into itself. We can understand this process in both an active and passive sense: through his negative act of extraction, man on the one hand actively transforms the thing into an object; on the other hand, however, this transformation that is actualization may also be described as what passively happens to the object as it manifests its own potential to be. This latter, self-manifestation cannot be grasped in terms of a forced or unnatural incursion of an exteriority upon an interiority that is otherwise allergic to it. Rather the thing somehow opens itself to its own development through the mediation of an "external" agency whose function it is merely to allow the thing to become what it inherently is. In which case, that agency is not to be conceived as ultimately external since it is after all integral to the thing's own internal development, without which it would remain stunted in its refusal of all outside relations.

As is clear from the context of discussion, this notion of actualization is understood by Takeuchi as coextensive with that of "determination"

(gentei). Returning again to this problematic of East/West, he notes that
"Europe's invasion of the Orient extends across time and space, and so the
cutting of this extension at a spatiotemporal point results in these entities
becoming determined, actual things (*gentei sareta genjitsuteki na mono*)"
("Kindai," p. 167). What comes to light here is the dependence of determination upon negation, which as we saw was also constitutive of the process
of actualization. Generally speaking, something can be described as determinate only when it is posited against an other which it is not. In the above
passage, for example, it is clear that neither Europe nor the Orient is determinate in itself, or as such. In order for these entities to become determinate, there must be a kind of "cut" made on their surface, such that they are
irreversibly transformed through that cut. This cut implies an external
agency, someone or something whose historical act of incision allows for
the possibility of Europe and the Orient to first come into being qua
"Europe" and the "Orient." Negation here exists in the form of the relationship between these proto-entities and that mediating agency through whose
work original, indeterminate matter is overcome so as to allow for the
emergence of concrete determinateness. Only by reference to this work,
which is none other than the activity or "movement" of representation, are
we able to understand that Europe and the Orient are first of all *products*,
that is, unnatural and historically created.

In this context, we should also point out a further negation that Takeuchi only tacitly alludes to here, since he has already made this point earlier
in the essay: this is the historical positing of oppositionality between Europe
and the Orient.[9] As is all too clear, these entities have existed in modernity
strictly as binary oppositions, such that through a kind of reciprocal determination the being of the one has necessarily presupposed a negation of the
other. It would in this sense be impossible to speak of, say, Europe without
thereby making implicit reference to the Orient as that which the former is
not. This quality of oppositionality extends to a range of concepts which
have come to be associated with *either* Europe *or* the Orient: "Europe and
the Orient are oppositional notions (*tairitsu gainen*), just as are the notions
of the modern and the feudal. Indeed, there are differences in the categories
of time and space between these two pairs" ("Kindai," p. 136). As Takeuchi
will emphasize, Europe has historically determined itself only by means of
actively negating that Oriental other which it has posited as its own logical
negation. This suggests that insofar as distinct entities are initially posited
as reciprocally negative, self-determination has no choice but to proceed by
continuing that negation already presupposed by this very distinction be-

9. See especially the section entitled "Tōyō no kindai" in "Kindai," pp. 129-136. Cf. also Oda
Makoto's discussion of this issue in his "Takeuchi Yoshimi no Ajia ron ni tsuite," in *Sengo
bungaku to Ajia* (Tokyo: Mainichi Shinbunsha, 1978), pp. 227-228 and 232-233.

tween self and other. As we see, then, once a "cut" has been made on the surface of positive being, identity can no longer refer simply (or naturally, purely) to that being itself but must involve some kind of relationality to an outside, hence explaining the underlying "tension" (*kinchō*) ("Kindai," p. 131) that marks determinateness and identity in general—and, according to Takeuchi, the sense of determinate European identity in particular.

In its necessary link to negation, determination reveals both the presence of exteriority, or difference, and the possibility of the overcoming of that exteriority in the movement of appropriation. We can see here how idealism paradoxically requires alterity just as it consumes it. Or rather: that it is precisely through the existence of alterity that idealist interiority first comes into being, gradually gaining force in its reflexive discovery that reality is indeed reducible to the thought of reality. In this way, of course, the epistemological confidence that "all things can ultimately be objectified and extracted" is confirmed. While this emerging reflexivity appears as the development of self—what Takeuchi refers to by the notion of "self-expansion" (*jiko kakuchō*) ("Kindai," p. 130)—we must also recognize that objective reality undergoes a corresponding development, as was amply revealed in the process of actualization. There a distinction was made between the thing as it exists in itself and the thing as it appears for us, in its phenomenal being. This distinction first comes about when consciousness realizes that the things it intends cannot exist purely outside of itself, that there is rather an essential dependence on the part of things which belies their apparent transcendence and otherwise unsettling indifference. In a manner of speaking, we can say that consciousness reacts to this initial indifference with its own indifference, and that this reaction reflects its "discovery"—which necessarily occurs after the fact, or *jigoteki ni*—that objective consciousness has all along really been *self*-consciousness. What must be understood here is that the self's posture of indifference to the world is bound up with the very function of representation, that is to say, representation is now recognized as instrumental in achieving the idealist goal of subjective autonomy by virtue of its unique capacity to negate empirical reality. In what Takeuchi calls "the adventure or risk of thinking that is abstraction" ("Kindai," p. 137), we can see that representation appears as the presence of the *absent* real thing. Despite its seemingly privileged status as the origin of all representation, the thing in its transcendence strangely allows for the possibility of its own usurpation and treatment of indifference by absolutely refusing to be revealed. For as soon as it is revealed—as soon, that is, as it sacrifices its transcendence—it *shows itself* to be radically other than itself, i.e., no longer the thing in its immediate (and so unpresentable) reality but instead merely a mediated representation of itself.

This paradox can be described as follows: things manifest their force only negatively, on the basis of their powerlessness to manifest themselves in a positively determinate manner. As is clear, manifestation signifies in this case both potency and impotency. What is manifested within being necessarily refers in its positivity to something beyond itself, something whose force resides in its capacity to cause representations of itself to appear while remaining itself behind the scenes, resolutely invisible. The appearance of representation can thus in one sense be said to mark the end of the thing, for the pure potentiality that is the thing is now actualized, it has assumed concrete (or actual) form within being not despite but rather precisely because of "abstraction" (*chūshō*), so becoming something rather than nothing. At the same time, however, representation may also be understood as the very beginning or opening of the thing, since the thing in its transcendence can evidently be nothing outside of representation—indeed, the most that can be said of it at this point is *that* it is, it is not yet answerable to the question of *what*, this being of course entirely dependent upon derivative form. In which case, actualization would be conceivable not as a fixed state brought about by the proper realization of the thing's potential, but instead as a vibrant and necessarily interminable *process* in which things spontaneously give themselves up to the play of representation. This distinction between actualization as state and actualization as process can be read, borrowing the language of Georges Bataille, as the difference between restricted and general economy.[10] The realization of a thing in its truth as the proper and rightful doubling of itself would thus symbolize a kind of restricted economy of representation. This because representation could then claim for itself the exalted status of "reflection" or faithful reproduction of the original thing, hence preserving the integrity of this latter even in its absence. The restrictedness of this economy can be attributed to what we might call the premature exhaustion of the thing's potential or potency: rather than overwhelm the phenomenal world with the infinite products of its activity, the thing instead lodges or *houses* itself (the *oikos* of "economy") in a single reflection or set of reflections that could in principle always return to itself. In this way, the possibility of referentiality is secured, and with it the notion of truth as correspondence between thing and representation. Now in contrast to this, a general economy of representation would begin by challenging the relegation of this "re-" to a position of strict obedience, or derivativeness. Specifically, what would be called into question here is the assumption that the "re-" is capable of a pure passivity, that it is in other words able to efface itself so entirely as to allow the thing to appear as it is in itself, without the least alteration (the well-known "loss in translation") that would make of this double less a re-presentation of something prior and originary than a presentation in its own right. Nevertheless, if we find that this condition of utter passivity is never in fact fulfilled (be-

---

10. See especially *The Accursed Share* (New York: Zone Books, 1995), vol. 1, pp. 19-41.

ing in principle unfulfillable), so disallowing us from using the word "representation" in any rigorous sense, it by no means follows from this that the presentations which now emerge are simply freed from all relation to the thing. For these presentations are unable to attain the status of self-sufficiency; that is, they cannot in their activity ever be *present* unto themselves. Inasmuch as they are for structural reasons forced to respond to their origin—what we might literally call the responsibility of representation in general—these "presentations" would necessarily refer away from themselves to something Other, something (or some thing) that in its transcendence signifies the ultimate dependence of presentation/representation upon negativity. For this reason, the positivity that such (re)presentation acquires in its appearance in the world can never be grasped as full positivity. Rather, it would be more accurate to say that the thing's negativity somehow attends or haunts it from beyond itself, thus determining its status as essentially ambiguous, neither positive nor negative. Understood within the framework of a general economy, the thing may be conceived as a limitless reserve of such (re)presentation: unpresentable in itself, in its immediacy, the thing compensates for this impotency (or this nothingness) by its potential to house itself in—that is, *to be*—anything. That (re)presentation is, in the final analysis, the paradoxical form of this receptivity to the thing's nothingness, is possible only on the condition that it be irreducible to either positivity or negativity.

WORDS

In speaking of the relationship between the thing and its representations, it becomes clear that what is at stake for idealism is a kind of murder, what Derrida has called the "linguistic neutralization of existence."[11] Before representation, the thing in its reality is an unmarked or seamless plenitude, one which, existing entirely in itself, is as yet without meaning. As we have argued, meaning requires an intervention on the part of man; prior to this intervention we can say only *that* the thing is, we cannot in any way identify *what* it is. The relation between a thing and its representation appears as the relation between presence and absence, for the doubling of something is felt to be necessary only when one is in some sense removed from it. In the loss of that immediacy afforded by the thing's presence, representation functions as a restorative device, something that not only temporarily palliates this absence but indeed claims to eliminate it entirely. The strange presence of representation is precisely this: the negation of a nothing. Yet this negation

---

11. *Edmund Husserl's* Origin of Geometry: *An Introduction*, trans. John P. Leavey, Jr. (Lincoln: University of Nebraska Press, 1989), p. 67, note 62.

is not to be grasped as an elimination pure and simple. In dialectical fashion, what is negated is at the same time preserved, lifted up and internalized in what Takeuchi—doubtless alluding here to Hegel, who remains however unnamed throughout the essay—refers to as the "self-movement of spirit": "Spirit (*seishin*) is not the shadow of matter (*busshitsu*), nor is matter the shadow of spirit. . . . The self-movement of spirit certainly seems recognizable enough, as there is here an incessant activity of going beyond oneself, such that no concepts ever stop at the place of concepts. Rather these concepts are advanced like chess pieces" ("Kindai," p. 139). The representation of a thing is thus merely another name for its spiritualization, and just as theology will speak of the soul taking flight after the body's death so too will idealism ground the possibility of representation upon the elimination—or murder—of empirical existence. Only through its destruction, therefore, is matter able to finally give birth to that spirit which was until this point merely latent and slumbering within it.

This operation of dialectical *Aufhebung* can be described more specifically: in the brute fact of its being, the unique and solitary thing seems at first to resist intelligibility, which presupposes by necessity some type of relationality or openness between itself and its outside. While this opening appears on the surface to be effected by the external penetration of spirit, it is revealed that spiritualization actually takes place less as an outside incursion—what in Takeuchi's language is termed an "invasion" ("Kindai," pp. 129 ff.)—than as an entirely *internal* self-development (or a making explicit of itself) on the part of spirit within the thing. The attainment of intelligibility represents a decisive overcoming of the contingency of the thing's empirical existence, hence liberating—again, like the soul in flight from the body—its properly universal essence. In this way, we learn that the thing's universality requires for its emergence the negation of its original immediacy, that the thing must in other words "reflect" (*hansha suru, utsusu*) itself in itself if it is to meaningfully become, or develop into, what it is. Here, the death of immediacy equals the birth of universality, what idealism conceives of as the *truth* of the thing. Truth is thus removed from immediacy and defined squarely in terms of development: "It seems to me that in the Europe of infinite advance, truth (*shinri*) itself is developmental, and I suspect that truth consists only of those things that develop. Hence I suspect that truth does not appear as such in the Orient (as situated within the equivalence between advance and retreat)" ("Kindai," p. 139), Takeuchi observes. What this suggests is that spirit's sublation of matter involves a death that is not a death in the radical sense, that is, death as absolute and irrecoverable loss; rather it signifies the theological dream of life, or immortality, conceived in this context as *presence*. To this end death is not denied but instead incorporated, made to serve a higher and more sublime goal. Grounded upon death through and through, the spiritualization that is representation yet marks its overcoming (the death of death) in the form of the ideal object.

As Takeuchi astutely recognizes, this ideal object is nothing other than the *word*, which means that language is determined as the general site of ideal objectivity: "words are the representations of consciousness" (*kotoba wa ishiki no hyōshō*)," they are that which makes "spirit itself developmental" ("Kindai," p. 140)—hence allowing us to speak of the purely "representational function of words," as Takeuchi writes elsewhere.[12] This insight into the idealist dependency upon language as the sublation of material existence leads to a sustained criticism of words so defined. "I do not believe in *words*," Takeuchi declares in his "Seiji to bungaku no mondai," for words claim to be able to effect the (spiritual) translation from thing into object.[13] In the essay which we are reading here, "Kindai towa nanika (Nihon to Chūgoku no baai)," the relation between words and spirit is made explicit in the context of an analysis of East and West: "No such self-movement of spirit existed in the Orient, that is, spirit itself did not exist. Of course there was something resembling spirit that existed in the Orient prior to modernity, as was present in Confucianism and Buddhism, but this was not spirit in the European sense of development. However, even that disappeared with the advent of modernity. The proof of this can be seen by viewing the history of words in Japan, for words here either disappear or *fall into decay*" (p. 140).

As we have said, words acquire their value for idealism only insofar as they signify life, life that is equivalent to presence. And yet this presence is in fact a re-presence, a secondary and derivative representation of something which seeks to conceal the fact that it is grounded upon the death of this latter. Because, that is, words come into being strictly by way of a prior negation of being, they signify a presence which strangely carries within itself absence and death. In this context, Takeuchi's condemnation of words and language can perhaps best be explained by reference to Mishima Yukio, for whom the relation between words and life and death appears in all its complexity. In Mishima's *Taiyō to tetsu* (1968), for example, we find the

---

12. "Kotoba mondai ni tsuite no kansō," in *TYz*, vol. 7, p. 405. Originally published in 1958.

13. The full title of this 1948 essay is "Seiji to bungaku no mondai (Nihon bungaku to Chūgoku bungaku I) (Chūgoku bungaku to hyūmanizumu)." In *TYz*, vol. 4, p. 102. Emphasis in the original.

This same notion is expressed by Ichimura Hiromasa in a recent text: "In being named, the 'world' became the world for man. Through names, man opens up a rift in the world understood as continuum, thus punctuating the object; he allows things to come into being through mutual separation; by making up each name he understands phenomena . . . Man determines the ideal form of space and things, and therein is revealed the power of names which must take possession of these ideal forms in the experienced world. For naming was 'ownership.' " *Zōho "nazuke" no seishinshi* (Tokyo: Heibonsha, 1996), pp. 134-140. Quoted in Isomae Junichi, *Kiki shinwa no metahisutorī* (Tokyo: Yoshikawa Kōbunkan, 1998), pp. 160-161.

following passage: "Death began from the time when I set about acquiring an existence other than that of words. For however destructive a garb they might assume, words were deeply bound up with my instinct for survival, were a part of my very life. Was it not, essentially, when I first felt the desire to live that I began for the first time to use words effectively? It was words that would make me live on until I died a natural death; they were the slow-moving germs of a 'sickness unto death.' "[14] What these lines bring out so well is the essential ambiguity of the status of words: clearly for Mishima words are associated with life; regardless of the content of their particular significations, which are frequently of course quite "destructive," they seem to signify in their very structure a presence indissolubly sheltered from death. Opposed to the security of this linguistic existence, or being-in-language, would be that "existence other than that of words" which for Mishima marks the beginning of death. This opposition between linguistic existence (life) and real existence (death) is not however absolute, since the former remains necessarily grounded upon the latter. Indeed, the inability of words to ever fully separate themselves from death can be glimpsed in Mishima's own language: while signifying life, "deeply bound up with my instinct for survival," words nevertheless are also described as "the slow-moving germs of a 'sickness unto death.' "

This life founded upon death that are words is what doubtless reverberates in Takeuchi's statement—which we have quoted above—that "words are the representations of consciousness."[15] Here, let us point out that this phrase can be read in two very distinct ways. As we have found, words are the presencing or appearing of a thing as ideal object; in this sense, consciousness meaningfully represents a thing to itself in the form of the word for that thing. "Representations of consciousness" thus refers to words in general in their capacity to serve as mediation of things. They are that unique bridge which allows consciousness to first establish and then continue to maintain a conceptual relationship (i.e., a relationship of identity)

---

14. *Sun and Steel*, trans. John Bester (New York: Grove Press, 1970), p. 67. Let us mention in passing that Takeuchi shares with Mishima the insight into the profound relation between reflection and language. It is tempting to say in this connection that whereas the possibility of a return to immediacy is for Takeuchi ruled out from the start, it can be seen to crucially inform Mishima's work. From there one would be led to articulate this difference as central to the difference in their respective political projects, Takeuchi being of course a member of the left and Mishima of the far right. Yet we suspect that this line of reasoning would be somewhat too easy, and that it would function moreover to obscure those troubling commonalities between the two precisely where the question of politics comes into play. Here, it should be remembered that Takeuchi is quite sympathetic in his reading of the Japanese Romanticists (Nihon Rōman-ha), with whom Mishima is frequently linked.

15. For a more empirically-based account of the relation between language, understood here in the strict sense of Takeuchi's own literary production, and life and death, see Nakagawa Ikurō, *Takeuchi Yoshimi no bungaku to shisō* (Tokyo: Orijin, 1985), pp. 98-111.

with an otherwise constantly changing or differing empirical reality. At the same time, however, this same phrase can be understood in such a way as to emphasize that what is represented by words are not only things, but in fact consciousness itself: "representations of *consciousness*" (ishiki *no hyōshō*). In this case, the relation between words and consciousness is properly one of reflection: words are the means by which consciousness, which is otherwise unable to appear in itself, or as such, succeeds in manifesting itself in the world, becoming that is something instead of nothing. Or as Takeuchi writes elsewhere making use of a slightly different vocabulary, referring to words in this instance as "expression" (*hyōgen*): "Whether understood as *thing* or as means, expression functions as the mediation (*hashiwatashi*) which guides intention [i.e., consciousness] to effect; it constitutes its own realm."[16] In order to be, consciousness has no choice but to present itself as other than what it is. It submits itself to a process of translation in which it becomes other to itself so as to emerge in the world as "effect" (*kōka*). In this way, we see that the necessary condition for the appearance of consciousness is, in fact, alterity. Just as the presence (or life) of words is founded upon the absence (death) of those things which they claim to represent, so too do words present consciousness as absent, as invariably other to those effects that nevertheless appear to be its own proper representations.

To say that "words are the representations of consciousness" is then to grasp the strength and the weakness of consciousness as one, since the unity of consciousness, and consequently the underlying subject presupposed therein, is here tacitly defined in terms of transcendence. On the one hand, consciousness seems to be that unique and all-powerful cause which produces effects, thereby bringing words into being as the representatives of itself. In this sense, words would be before all else the proof of consciousness' generative force, that to which they ultimately refer as their original source. On the other hand, however, consciousness in its transcendence is by definition deprived of the possibility of manifestation, it is in other words condemned to invisibility or insubstantiality. What appears in the name of consciousness is thus, paradoxically, never consciousness itself. Moreover, it is this impossibility of self-manifestation that accounts in fact for the ceaseless proliferation of words (qua effects), since no one word can ever claim to perfectly reflect consciousness. The translation of consciousness—and let us repeat that consciousness can be nothing outside of translation—is a project that is necessarily doomed from the start: insofar as words are required so that it may embody itself, consciousness finds itself com-

---

16. "Hyōgen ni tsuite," in *TYz*, vol. 7, p. 387; emphasis in the original. First published in 1955.

"In order to tie intention to effect," Takeuchi continues, "the independence of this realm . . . must be acknowledged." Nevertheless, this "independence" is not in any way to be understood as absolute, or complete; what is at stake here rather is only "a certain relative independence."

pletely given over to them; and yet in that very giving over, at the precise moment when translation takes place from consciousness (intention) to word (effect), i.e., the moment that is the act of enunciation, a certain stage-fright, as it were, seizes consciousness, causing it to flee backstage, behind the scenes. For it must be recognized here that words in their function as effect mark the *end* of consciousness, that is, its simultaneous realization and death. Although given presence by words, consciousness unavoidably meets its end there as well. It is in this sense that we find, strangely enough, that words present consciousness both with life and death.[17]

In reading Takeuchi's statement that "words are the representations of consciousness" in such a way as to bring out the fact that both things and consciousness lie at the level of the represented, we should now further shed light on the complex interrelationship that obtains between these latter. As we have tried to show, words are the pivot by which the idealist shift from external or objective reality to the expansive interiority of the subject centrally turns. In being represented, things seem to lose their thing-like quality and become intelligible rather than impenetrable. They reveal themselves, finally, as nothing other than the extension of consciousness itself. In this way, words are instrumental in allowing the thing to emerge from its sense-less (or non-relational) particularity and attain that universality which it has always already embodied, albeit only latently or unwittingly. This universal essence which has all along resided within the thing, and which words function to render explicit, is in the final analysis less an Ideal Form, as with Platonic realism, than it is the subject itself. In so saying, however, we must primarily keep in mind that this subject, which qua consciousness is bereft of any substantial existence in the world, does not come into being as the simple replacement of reality, a straightforward and so conceivable exchange of one thing for another. In speaking of this transition as one from real existence to linguistic existence, we should not imagine a movement from one mode of present being to another. While it is in a sense true that language reveals reality, and that reality is unknowable prior to the emer-

---

17. This being the case, Mishima's statement that "Death began from the time when I set about acquiring an existence other than that of words" must now be modified so as to read: "Death began *both* from the time when I set about acquiring an existence other than that of words *and* from the time when I set about acquiring an existence in words." Which is to say, finally, that language not only proves incapable of preventing death; it is structurally the very means by which death takes place.

As the postwar Arechi poet Tamura Ryūichi writes in "Hosoi sen" as if somehow in response to Mishima, "You pull the trigger!/I die in words (*kotoba*)." (Quoted in Naoki Sakai, *Translation and Subjectivity: On "Japan" and Cultural Nationalism* (Minneapolis: University of Minnesota Press, 1997), p. 187). And again, in the final stanza of the poem "Yonsen no hi to yoru": "In order to beget one poem/We must kill the things we love;/That is the one way of bringing the dead back to life." (Quoted in Donald Keene, *Dawn to the West: Japanese Literature in the Modern Era* (New York: Columbia University Press, 1984), vol. 2, p. 369).

gence of language, thus becoming recognizable only *jigoteki ni*, or after the fact, nevertheless this revealing occurs strictly by way of negation. The revealing of things by words, or rather the transition via the mediation of words from things to consciousness, is effected by a negation which introduces negativity at the heart of being. In other words, the negation of positive being radically puts an end to all positivity, not merely certain forms of such. With the emergence of language, being becomes conceivable only as a positivity contaminated through and through by negativity and death.

It is at this point, precisely, that the idealist project, understood here as the becoming-subject of substance and the becoming-substance of the subject, discloses one of its major flaws. As Takeuchi makes clear, the desire on the part of the subject to utilize language so as *to know* substance is expressive of nothing less than the desire *to be*, that is, to be substantial, to assume an actual and concrete existence in the world. Yet this desire is by right impossible, unrealizable, since, as we have argued, the subject is barred from all manifestation. Indeed, this is what Takeuchi reminds us of time and again in "Kindai towa nanika (Nihon to Chūgoku no baai)": regardless of the various ways and different contexts in which it is determined, the subject remains always and irreducibly *nothing*. Hence: "For there is here no resistance, that is to say, there is no wish to preserve the self (the self itself does not exist)" ("Kindai," p. 145). Likewise in the case of Japan: "The absence of resistance means that Japan is not Oriental, but at the same time the absence of the wish for self-preservation (the absence of the self) means that Japan is not European. That is to say, Japan is nothing" ("Kindai," p. 145). Again, in a discussion of the characters/humans (*ningen*) treated by writers in literature: "Even if writers strip a character/human naked, they must leave on the final layer of clothing, for the character/human would disappear if they removed it. That is to say, the character/human is not originally present" ("Kindai," pp. 146-147). And finally, more explicitly: "The person who holds fast to the self cannot change direction, but only walks his own path. However, walking means that the self changes. The self changes by one's holding fast to it. (That which does not change is not a self). I am 'I' and yet not 'I.' If I were simply 'I,' that would not even be 'I.' In order that I be 'I,' there must necessarily be a juncture at which I am outside of 'I' " ("Kindai," p. 162).

We can describe the emergence of this nothing in the world as an act of violence through which culture and signification are founded. In this sense, nothingness must paradoxically be understood not as a simple and utter void but rather as a kind of force whose destructiveness is simultaneously its productivity. It is through violence that the otherwise seamless identity of positive being is breached, thus opening up a field of infinite meanings entirely absent of any stable ontological grounding. Understood most literally, we can say that it is in this breaching that *nothing happens*: the productive force that is negativity begins its activity (its happening) of "representation" only in the wake of the destruction of being. Here it should be noted that this violence is conceivable only as originary, that although it is possible to *think* the event of the breaching of positive being by negativity, it is nevertheless impossible for us to *know* the nature of this breach, this given the fact that all knowledge is necessarily cultural and significant. Such knowledge would be possible only on the basis of a comparison between positivity and negativity as such. Yet this would require on the part of the knower access to a transcendent viewpoint, one which was neither purely positive nor negative, from which both being and meaning could be theoretically grasped. This viewpoint—which for Takeuchi is consistently identified as the vantage of humanism ("Kindai," p. 156)—is here described in terms of the optical imagery employed so effectively throughout the essay: it is at once "a third eye, which belongs neither to Europe nor to the Orient" ("Kindai," p. 135), and "that which looks from the outside," in which the self posits itself as outside history, gazing in upon it in the fashion of a spectator observing a horse-race ("Kindai," p. 159).[18] Adoption of this supra-historical viewpoint is required so as to situate the breach from which history begins in relation to that originally objective purity that is being as such. Insofar as knowledge can only depart from the point of the breach, however, its own negativity ensures that the positivity or plenitude of being be conceivable strictly as originally contaminated.

Now this happening of nothing is such as to render the substantialization of the subject impossible. For if the subject is that which destroys being by language, being itself nothing outside of language, then it is by right deprived of any ontological status. The "I" to which Takeuchi refers in the above passage ("I am 'I' and yet not 'I' ") is inescapably part of that empirical reality which it negates through language. Although this "I" may be understood as the cause or generative source of language, or "words," it nevertheless disappears from the very moment it begins to enunciate itself.

---

18. This passage bears citing in full, if only to provide a sense of the force of Takeuchi's condemnation of that Japanese literature which understands its own being as purely spectatorial, that is, theoretical (from the Greek *theoria*, meaning "a viewing or looking at"): "Chinese literature is reflected (*utsusu*) in the eyes of Japanese literature as a backward nation literature, and this reflection is an accurate one. Accurate—truly 'accurate.' Accurate like a camera, 'accurate' in showing time and space reduced to two dimensions. Japanese literature does not enter history in this way, it looks from outside at racehorses running the course of history. . . . The Chinese horse is lagging behind while the Japanese horse quickly pulls ahead. Such is how things appear, and this view is an accurate one. It is accurate because one is not running." ("Kindai," pp. 159-160).

Relatedly, Takeuchi will speak in an essay published the same year of what he calls "the site of action (*kōdō no ba*)," at which "one feels bodily, putting oneself inside as opposed to merely looking at things from the outside." "Bunka inyū no hōhō (Nihon bungaku to Chūgoku bungaku II)," in *TYz*, vol. 4, p. 117.

If, in this sense, the act of enunciation may be determined as that which destroys the subject, we must also remember that it is the only means the subject has at its disposal to manifest itself. Ideally, the subject's becoming-substance is accomplished by its enunciative acts, in which subjective presence is attained through the negation of its original nothingness. But the *effect* of enunciation invariably turns out to be no more than the emergence of a language in which all traces of an identifiable subject have been eliminated. Far from assuming any substantial existence in the world, the subject may on the basis of enunciation only be imagined, its existence determined strictly retroactively.[19] In this way, the project of the subject's substantialization reveals itself to be a (non-dialectical) contradiction in terms: the subject comes into being necessarily as the very negation of substance, and above all of its own substance. There can be no simultaneous movement of subject becoming substance and substance becoming subject, for subjective negativity decisively puts an end to all ontological projects. This does not however mean that substance, or being, disappears completely, that it is in other words fully internalized or taken up by the subject. Rather its breaching introduces a kind of split between what we might call subjectivized substance—i.e., representation, that which is given to knowledge and functions as the means to its "self-expansion"—and substance as such. It is this latter which, although allowing for the possibility of knowledge that is subjectivized substance, nevertheless resists (*teikō suru*) it, as Takeuchi would say, always ultimately undermines it, in its own unrepresentability.

SEKAISHI: THE *BILDUNGSROMAN* OF THE WEST

We should recall at this point that, for Takeuchi, the idealist project of self-expansion is inextricably linked in modernity to the West's invasion of the East. For this reason, it is impossible to consider the history of modern idealism outside of the East-West relation, just as it is impossible to grasp this

---

19. Following Naoki Sakai, we may refer to this disappearing because "internally" divisive self which conceals itself through the very act of its revealing as *shutai*, a term which he translates alternately as "body of enunciation," "agent of enunciation" and "agent of action." See *Voices of the Past: The Status of Language in Eighteenth-Century Japanese Discourse* (Ithaca: Cornell University Press, 1991).

As Vincent Descombes very clearly explains in his analysis of this problematic of enunciation and subjectivity, it is the act of enunciation itself that produces a split between the subject of the enunciated (*l'énoncé*) and the subject of the enunciation (*l'énonciation*): "the subject who speaks remains distinct, when he speaks of himself, from the subject of his enunciated." Or as Lacan, whom he quotes here, says, "It is not a question of knowing if I speak of myself in a way that conforms to who I am, bur rather if, when I speak of myself, I am the same as the person of whom I speak." In *L'inconscient malgré lui* (Paris: Les Éditions de Minuit, 1977), pp. 138-139.

relation in all of its complexity without sufficient understanding of the presuppositions and aims of idealist philosophy proper. Specifically, Takeuchi finds that the West implicitly conceives of the movement of westernization in terms of the subject's ongoing "extraction" (*toridasu*) ("Kindai," pp. 144 and 146) of objective being. This "extraction" is a *movement*, one which for the West has come to be wholly equated with history itself. History, in other words, is here understood as necessarily western history, the unfolding of the West's universalization through the progressive extraction or consumption of its other. Hence the term *sekaishi*, or "world history," that Takeuchi will refer to in describing this movement. Refusing the possibility of any unsublatable (or unextractable) excess to itself, history is reduced to a kind of *Bildungsroman* of the West qua subject: "Modernity is the self-recognition (*jiko ninshiki*) of Europe as seen within history, that regarding of itself as a self distinct from the feudalistic, which Europe gained in the process of liberating itself from the feudal (a process which involved the emergence of free capital in the realm of production and the formation of personality qua autonomous and equal individuals with respect to human beings). As such, it can be said that *Europe is first possible only in this history, and that history itself is possible only in this Europe.* History is not an empty form of time. It includes an infinite number of instants in which one struggles against obstacles so that the self may be itself, without which both the self and history would be lost. Simply being Europe does not make Europe Europe. The various facts of history teach that Europe barely maintains itself through the tension of its incessant self-renewals" ("Kindai," p. 130; emphasis ours).[20]

According to this conception of history, the West ("Europe") is uniquely endowed with subjective agency: it is the subject around which history in general revolves. Yet this subject is not to be understood as initially given or present, as for example in the manner of things. Objective reality is considered to be in itself ahistorical, static; it can only *become* historical, and this in the process of the subject's own becoming. History emerges through the ongoing interaction of subject and object, such that the difference between these two entities functions as the mediation through which each comes into its own. More precisely, the subject that is the West

---

20. As Kan Takayuki writes in his reading of this essay, "European modernity is unlimited progress. It is the self-movement which incessantly attempts the transcendence of the self. Not only does matter move, but spirit as well. Originally, there was in the Orient no such unfolding of movement. The unresisting Orient can only exist as a one-sided plasticity vis-à-vis Europe as compelling force." *Takeuchi Yoshimi ron: Ajia e no hanka* (Tokyo: Sanichi Shobō, 1976), p. 108.

For a more critical assessment of some of the implications of Takeuchi's attack of this teleological history—referred to here as the "monistic view of civilization" (*bunmei ichigen kan*)—see Kitagawa Tōru's "Takeuchi Yoshimi to sengo nashonarizumu," collected in the volume *Sengo shisō no genzai* (Tokyo: Dentō to Gendaisha, 1981), especially pp. 68-71.

can be seen to develop by way of its objective experience of the East, an experience which in turn reveals this latter as latently historical—and so, according to the terms of this idealist narrative, latently the West as well. As we have emphasized throughout the essay, this encounter between subject (West) and object (East) must be understood as one of reflection. The West, as Takeuchi asserts, "looks" (*nagameru*) at the East, and in this looking realizes that the East stands directly opposite itself as its own mirrored other. That is to say, the West's *prise de conscience* consists in this instance in its awareness that this other is not in fact Other to it, that its alterity is merely provisional, since it cannot be independent of the West's very act of looking. Hence this gaze does not so much disclose the essential dependence of the East upon the West as the strange fact of *the West's own objective alienation*. What the West regards as the East is only an appearance, one which in its immediacy hides the truth for both these entities that the object is always incipiently the subject.

Not only must the East learn this truth; the West, likewise, must come to understand that the object of its experience is actually nothing other than itself, that its appearance of independence and exteriority is an appearance only, testimony to a state prior to reflection—or what phenomenology will call the "natural attitude." This state is characterized by what is revealed retrospectively to be a merely superficial difference between entities, a difference which will gradually be eliminated in the course of that history of reflection that is the West's proper self-development. Or as Takeuchi writes, "History . . . includes an infinite number of instants in which [Europe] struggles against obstacles so that the self may be itself, without which both the self and history would be lost." To speak of the West's experience of the East is to suggest, of course, that this latter transcends the subject as its external object. For if the West is able through this experience to develop, to become that which it was not due to its receptivity or openness to this other, then it must follow that the East is radically irreducible to the West. Experience, in this sense, presupposes an alterity that one can only passively suffer, without ever being able to fully incorporate that outside within the confines of the self. Nevertheless, according to the idealism inherent in the project of westernization, this is precisely what does not happen in the West's encounter with the East. Here, the concept of experience must be reworked so as to signify what is ultimately the self's encounter with itself.[21] The contingency that marks experience and which renders the self Other in its encounter with exteriority is now not so much elimi-

---

21. In "Seiji to bungaku no mondai (Nihon bungaku to Chūgoku bungaku I)," Takeuchi finds this same rejection of difference, that is, the same projection of identity upon the Other, at work in the encounter Japanese literature has of Chinese literature. This encounter, significantly, is for him distinguished by the apparently complete lack of anxiety one feels vis-à-vis one's interlocutor. See here especially pp. 102-103.

nated as it is appropriated within the totalizing movement of westernization. This movement, remarks Takeuchi, has come to be equated with history itself: "In the Europe of infinite advance, that which was previously outside history is consumed within it through European self-expansion, thus becoming historical" ("Kindai," p. 137). We can see here that contingency conceals within itself an underlying necessity, and this is that the object of experience for the West must be itself, that in other words the West can do nothing but make itself explicit as subject in its experience of itself as alienated object. Indeed, what the West comes to realize in its project of westernization is the fact of its unique historical immanence. History is grasped as the movement in which the West gradually reveals itself to itself; it is the coming to truth of the non-West as the West's own self-reflection, its merely derivative "virtual image" (*kyozō*) ("Kindai," p. 135). Although initially forced to posit itself as distinct from the non-West, the West in the course of its historical experience learns that all exteriority is, finally, reducible to itself.

This notion of western immanence allows us to understand that the reflection of Other as self is grounded upon what is believed to be the West's original pre-reflective unity. Only because the West was originally selfsame is it at all capable of reflecting, or mirroring, that which it is not. For the question must be asked: how is it possible for the subject to reflect external objects if it is conceived as absolutely distinct from them? Doesn't there have to be a fundamental identity which obtains between subject and object—or rather, even prior to this, a state of pure seamlessness that predates the very division between subject and object itself? In which case, the emergence of difference would represent a fall from this oneness, such that identity is henceforth reclaimed only by way of that difference, that is, by positing a determinate other *against which* the self equals itself. Yet here as well, although confirming self-identity in its negativity (e.g., the West *is* what the East/non-West *is not*), this other nevertheless remains to some lingering degree yet outside the West's full comprehension. Hence it becomes necessary to inquire into the very possibility of objectivity, given that the West regards this latter as significant only insofar as it enables the subject to come into being. It is at this point that the West reflects upon its objective reflections, desiring to know their conditions of possibility. What it finds, of course, is that this op-posite other is really itself posited—or posing—as object, that what seemed to resist its full comprehension was all along itself existing immanently, and so implicitly, unknowingly, within its own borders. In the act of reflecting itself-as-other, the West succeeds in stripping all remnants of alterity from this double and bringing it back into itself. Here we can make out a strange temporality: the "bringing back" on the part of the West, its proper return-to-self, aims at a point of unity that can only have existed (it is imagined) in the past. Yet that past is attainable now strictly through continued reflection, a reflection whose goal of absolute self-identity obviously lies in the future. In other words, that world history which takes the West as its *telos* desires to arrive at the past precisely by way of its "infinite advance." It is in this sense, Takeuchi suggests, that westernization must be seen as a movement of return, one which for all its alleged emancipations[22] remains heavily weighed down by nostalgia. In circular fashion, the immediate oneness of the West which ostensibly precedes history is restored through the dialectical interplay between self and other, hence negating the West's own act of self-division. This "cut," as Takeuchi calls it, seems therefore to entirely vanish in the healing process that is self-reflection. Now if this process is necessarily interminable, if for essential reasons the West is incapable of ever reducing history fully to itself, there nevertheless remains for us a kind of responsibility in expressing, or demonstrating, this impossibility. It is perhaps as such an expression that Takeuchi's "Kindai towa nanika (Nihon to Chūgoku no baai)" is best read.

---

22. Then as now, westernization is nearly universally regarded as equivalent to emancipation. As Takeuchi points out, however, these "emancipations" can be conceived only in terms of that violence within which they are historically inscribed: "The form of [Europe's invasion of the Orient] was first conquest, followed by demands for the opening of markets and the transformation to such things as: guarantees of human rights and freedom of religious belief, loans, economic assistance, and support for educational and liberation movements. These very transformations symbolized the progress of the spirit of rationalism" ("Kindai," p. 131).

5. History and the Ways of Knowing

The goal of this final chapter is to sketch out Takeuchi's thinking of history as a movement of discontinuity, one which exceeds all notions of *telos* and progress. For Takeuchi, the notion of historical progress is inseparable from the movement of modernization, or what may also be understood as westernization, the becoming West of the non-West. Significantly, Takeuchi performs a series of reductions in order to demonstrate that historical progress, if it indeed takes place, takes place only against the background of that which ultimately resists it: this relationship between two views of historical movement is represented here not simply in oppositional terms, but rather as the inscription of the universal within the general. Hence progress in history is shown to presuppose the possibility of objective knowledge, and with this in turn a notion of repetition without difference; this repetition is then reduced to something like the singularity of the act, which Takeuchi conceives in terms of a tracing out of ways or paths. Here a bilateral reading of this notion of "ways" is introduced in respect of Lu Xun and Hu Shi, two of the leading figures of the May Fourth movement in China. The result of these reductions is that history in its discontinuity is revealed to be most fundamentally a movement in which man acts, such that even knowledge, which presupposes in some sense a transcendent beyond of history, is seen by Takeuchi to be nothing other than "an *act* of knowing," as he calls it. In which case, all security that successive epistemological acts can lead to progress and, finally, to an overcoming of history must be described as illusory. Action indicates instead that the force of history can never be alleviated or overcome by man, and this is why, paradoxically enough, the singular instant of activity is understood by Takeuchi to be at the same time a passive exposure to contingency and the historically new.

189

THE SUBJECT OF REVOLUTION

"I thought: hope originally cannot be said to exist, nor can it be said not to exist. It is just like ways across the earth. For actually the earth had no ways to begin with, but when many men pass through, a way is made."[1] In order to understand Takeuchi's fascination with these lines from Lu Xun, which conclude the short story "Guxiang" [My Old Home] (1921), and which Takeuchi cites as "unforgettable words" in his 1958 essay "Wasurerarenai kotoba" [Unforgettable Words],[2] it is perhaps necessary to place them at the center of his contrastive readings of Lu Xun and Hu Shi. For Takeuchi, Lu must on no account be understood as a proponent of modernization, or—what amounts to the same thing for him—of westernization. Although vigilantly refusing any return to a past associated with Chinese tradition, Lu at the same time resists thinking of the future within the framework of development and progress. Indeed, it is the misrecognition of this fact that has caused Japanese Sinologists to unjustifiably group him together with such western sympathizers as Hu Shi: "When Japan sees Lu Xun, he is distorted (like everything else) into a thinker of progress (*shinposhugisha*), a superior enlightenment figure. He is distorted in mirror-like fashion into an enlightenment figure that desperately chased after Europe in trying to improve backwardness. . . . In fact, however, Lu is the very opposite of this. He is an opponent of such thinkers of progress as Hu Shi."[3]

Although "opponents," Takeuchi is not however blind to a certain element in Hu's thought which doubtless brings him close to Lu Xun. This element, in contrast to Hu's self-declared project of westernization, is attributed by Takeuchi to the influence of pragmatist philosophy. Takeuchi specifically determines it as derivative of what he calls the "distinctive feature of pragmatism," its assertion "that it cannot be understand as a completed system (*kanketsu shita taikei*)."[4] It is this which he believes makes of pragmatism a "theory of revolution," one which in its articulation of a notion of "discontinuity (*danzetsu*) with the past" logically "opens up infinite possibilities for the future."[5] Takeuchi's meaning here seems to be the following: insofar as historical time cannot be conceived as linear, measurable according to a continuum which extends progressively or sequentially from point A to point B, it is in fact impossible to maintain the selfsameness of

1. *Selected Works of Lu Hsun*, trans. Yang Hsien-yi and Gladys Yang (Peking: Foreign Language Press, 1956), vol. 1, p. 75; *Lu Xun xiaoshuoji* (Hong Kong: Jindai Tushu, 1967), p. 91. Translation slightly modified.
2. In *TYz*, vol. 2, pp. 359-362.
3. "Kindai towa nanika (Nihon to Chūgoku no baai)," in *TYz*, vol. 4, p. 160. Originally published in 1948.
4. "Ko Teki to Dūi," in *TYh*, vol. 3, p. 342. Originally published in 1952.
5. Ibid., p. 347.

what are commonly referred to as historical "subjects." In order that a subject remain equivalent to itself, it must be capable of comprehending within itself the difference that attends historical time such that the discontinuity which would otherwise threaten its integrity as subject may be now understood in conjunction with its own internal development. That is to say, the positing of discontinuity, or interruption (*danzetsu*), as securely fixed within what Takeuchi calls, in reference to the philosopher Nishida Kitarō, "the *continuity* of discontinuity (*hirenzoku no renzoku*) within the flow of history,"[6] allows one to incorporate difference as situated within the same, hence providing a kind of bridge by which to think a consistent unity capable of spanning past and future. The subject's discontinuity with itself would in this case yield to a conception of the subject as capable of grounding such discontinuity, such that the break between past and future that is "the flow of history" would function merely to predicate difference upon a ground which remains itself essentially unaffected by those differences.

Now if Takeuchi's and, at a certain moment, Hu Shi's understanding of discontinuity is directed precisely against this notion of subjectivity, it is because subjectivity can only be conceived as a "completed system." "Discontinuity with the past" necessarily disturbs the subject's unifying systematicity by exposing this subject to a future which, beyond its control, *resists* at each instant (*shunkan*) appropriation as part within a coherent whole. Rather, the future in "opening up infinite possibilities" incompletes or de-systematizes the subject by thrusting upon it a multiplicity of forces which it receives primarily passively, and which *themselves* ground the subject's attempts to actively utilize these forces in its desire to repeat itself as ultimately selfsame. This is the reason Takeuchi describes this process in terms of "revolution": far from simply referring to an overturning of determinate historical agency (which, it should be noted, Takeuchi *also* calls attention to in his criticisms of both the European colonization of America and the European-American colonization of the "Orient" (*Tōyō*)), what is here essentially at stake is the possibility of any specific identification of agency itself. Taking into account the discontinuity which internally divides the subject, preventing it at all times from its own self-coinciding, action on the part of the self must be described as strictly unidentifiable. Or rather: that if the self can be identified as author of an action, such determination of

---

6. Ibid., p. 340. Our emphasis. The privileging of continuity over discontinuity in this formulation—which, let us note, seems to run counter to other, later instances of this usage—can be read in Nishida's 1917 text *Jikaku ni okeru chokkan to hansei*: "When we say that experience is discontinuous, we already presuppose the continuity of the self; without consciousness of continuity we could not conceive discontinuity. . . . Discontinuous experience is an abstraction; real experience is always continuous because always containing within itself a unifying ideal." *Intuition and Reflection in Self-Consciousness*, trans. Valdo H. Viglielmo et al. (Albany: State University of New York Press, 1987), p. 65.

identity is possible only retrospectively, meaning after the action has already been performed. Yet given the discontinuity of historical time, all *ex post facto* determinations which seek to establish a continuum between the now and the past can do so from its present standpoint only by imagining the past figure of an agent of action with which the self putatively corresponds. It is therefore owing strictly to the success of this operation of the imagination that the security to act as if subjective continuity were guaranteed is conferred. What is however erased in this imagining is precisely the "revolutionary" quality which Takeuchi attributes to the fractured self. The self is revolutionary because structurally discontinuous; there is necessarily always a rupture between the self of the past and that of the future. In this sense, it can be said that the revolution of the self relates above all else to its fundamental passivity vis-à-vis historical time. Before one speaks of "revolution" in an overtly sociopolitical sense—e.g., here, as it informs both the "self-liberation from European colonization" and the "problem of the progressive nature (and its limits) of American capitalism in its invasion of the Orient"[7]—it must be recognized that the self in its exposure to the alterity of history is always already overwhelmed by revolution, and that it has no choice but to participate.[8] As goes without saying, this insight by no means denies the necessity of political revolution as it is commonly understood. Indeed, for Takeuchi the grounding of all political revolution lies in this original incapacity of the subject to maintain or reproduce itself qua itself. What this insight permits rather is a criticism of a more or less implicit voluntarism—which explains historical change as resulting from the force of the will—which so often in the political discourse of revolution functions to reduce this latter to merely a question of subjective desire. The irreducibility of revolution to will or desire is due to what we may describe as the primacy of exteriority over interiority: inasmuch as the will in its capacity to partially determine action remains necessarily powerless to determine the effects of action, which take place externally in the world, its sovereignty is clearly delimited; yet what is referred to here by the term "revolution" designates much more radically a general discontinuity which functions to situate difference at the heart of all repetition, hence exposing the subject who wills or desires to exteriority (or alterity) in the very process of its self-constitution as interior entity. Subjective interiority, then, is revealed to be inscribed within an exteriority that fully encompasses it, and which it must deny in order to stake out its claims to autonomy.

---

7. "Ko Teki to Dūi," pp. 347-348.
8. As Takeuchi writes in the 1953 essay "Nihon no minshū," "Revolution does not succeed without the human revolution that is its support. Revolution facilitates human revolution, and yet human revolution makes revolution possible." *TYh*, vol. 2, p. 62.

Once cleared of these traces of subjective voluntarism, the relation between sociopolitical revolution and the more originary revolution of the self emerges with greater clarity. The necessary grounding of the former upon the latter brings to the fore the political implications of the insight into the self-fracturing structure of the self. Takeuchi is quick to extrapolate these in his articulation of a notion of revolution "in which the force of internal negation constantly springs forth."[9] Recognition of the inherent instability of identity shows itself to be incompatible with any action performed in the name of determinate subjective agency. Insofar as all subjective determinations are themselves necessarily actions, their effect is to paradoxically distance the self from itself in the very gesture by which it seeks to return to itself. The self is forced constantly to act, but in so doing it projects itself forward, away from itself as the source or cause of action into a future consisting only of the effects of its action. These effects are incalculable: although the self exists nowhere else but in its effects, their in principle limitless extension ensures that no determination ever fully determines the self, hence keeping its identity in a kind of floating suspension. Strictly understood, then, this suspension of the self is due not to the impossibility of determination as such, but rather to the impossibility of exhausting, or completing (*kanketsu suru*), determinations. In fact, it is precisely this incompletion which underlies the task of revolution as envisioned by Takeuchi. Because man must passively submit to that law which forces him to act, and because he is moreover powerless to control the effects of his own actions which both determine and indetermine him, the active task of revolution remains throughout governed by the related principles of incompletion and passivity. The revolutionary, Takeuchi suggests, allows this grounding principle of incompletion to guide his activity of incompleting. Hence he realizes the proper endlessness of his own task, for the activity of incompleting is itself productive of effects which can of course never be completed.

Defined more specifically, what we are calling here the activity of incompleting consists in the operation whereby "systems" otherwise imagined to be closed are opened up to their outside. And, as is suggested by Takeuchi's reading of a certain element in Hu Shi, the system most in need of incompleting, and so revolution, is that of subjectivity. It must be emphasized that this activity of incompleting does not proceed according to a notion of activity which opposes itself to one of passivity; on the contrary, this activity sets out to reveal the passive exposure to alterity that at each instant underlies (and ultimately undermines) systematic unity. In other words, the

---

9. "Kindai towa nanika (Nihon to Chūgoku no baai)," p. 164. Referring here to Sun Yat-sen, Takeuchi stresses that revolution resists its own positivity, failing which it immediately calcifies into counter-revolution. This explains why, he continues, the essential component of revolution is "failure." Through failing, revolution in its sustained discontinuity paradoxically succeeds.

active incompleting of subjectivity does not judge this latter on the basis of a set of criteria that is somehow external to it. Instead it performs its task by uncovering from within the effacement of the truth of the self's internal divisiveness, one which was necessary in order to maintain the facade of subjective integrity and wholeness. Now if it is true that the introduction of "discontinuity" and the corresponding dismantling of "completed systems" which Takeuchi associates with Hu leads in principle to such active incompleting, that is, to a kind of "revolution," it is nevertheless also true that Takeuchi condemns Hu for his actual betrayal of this insight. And just as Takeuchi linked this insight to the influence of pragmatism, so too will he ascribe the betrayal of this insight to this same philosophy. For if pragmatism may be considered in certain respects a "theory of revolution," it is also recognized to be not entirely so: "[P]ragmatism, which is in one sense a theory of revolution, is in another sense an extension of British empiricism. Its form is revolutionary whereas its content is not."[10] Hence it is due to the traces of a certain empiricism (*keikenron*) that pragmatism, and more specifically Hu's thought as it is informed by pragmatism, must be judged as falling short of revolution. While laying the groundwork for a thinking of revolution in his endorsement of the notion of "discontinuity with the past," Hu yet carelessly lapsed into a naïve understanding of history as teleological. So it is that "his basic view of history was that society advances infinitely one step at a time, and this can clearly be seen in his works on the history of philosophy and literature."[11] Indeed, insofar as Hu's vision of history is one of universal development and progress, it can be seen how deeply he remains indebted to the principles of historicism (*rekishishugi*), what Takeuchi defines elsewhere as a "theory of stagistic development" (*hatten dankai setsu*).[12]

HISTORICISM AND THE THINKING OF HISTORY, OR THE MOVEMENT TO GENERALITY

In attempting to explain Takeuchi's understanding of historicism, it is important to note a certain hesitation, or perhaps even inconsistency, in his use of this term. When for example in "Ko Teki to Dūi" he identifies a strain of rationalism (*gōrishugi*) in Hu Shi's thought, Takeuchi concludes from this, without further elaboration, that "he did not undergo the baptism of histori-

---

10. "Koteki to Dūi," p. 347.
11. Ibid., p. 343. Takeuchi continues: "For him tradition was, if irrational, something that could be changed; it was not a burden. It was this attitude that made it possible for him to initiate the Literary Revolution, despite the fact that he was a gradualist and so a reformist instead of a revolutionary."
12. "Kindai no chōkoku," in *TYz*, vol. 8, p. 21. Originally published in 1959.

cism."[13] Now it seems clear that Takeuchi is not here suggesting that rationalism must be historicized in the sense of contextualizing it within developmental history. Attempting at all costs to think history *outside of* the notion of development, he appears rather to be pointing to the ahistoricality inherent in Hu's understanding of Reason. What is significant for Takeuchi is the historical situation within which is made an appeal to Reason as itself historically transcendent. Hu neglects to see that that Reason which putatively holds for all people at all times is of necessity produced within history, that history cannot ever be made subordinate to it, just as he fails to inquire into the historical factors which underlie his own recourse to Reason. In this sense, historicism functions as a kind of antidote to the abstractly universal claims made by rationalism. On a more profound level, however, it can be seen that the historicizing project often unwittingly repeats the very abstraction it condemns. This because of its failure to problematize its own capacity to, literally, make sense out of the past. That the past is understood to be meaningfully comprehensible implicitly posits a standpoint whose greater universality allows for the possibility of knowledge of historical objects and events as, in fact, parts within itself. Historical knowledge presupposes a "theory of stagistic development" insofar as the present is thought to contain the entirety of the past, such that historicism becomes identical to self-reflection. In this regard, historical time is determined as the development from the particular to the universal. While historicizing the universalist assumptions of the past functions to shed light on the contingency of their being, nevertheless the very possibility of this historicization assumes a point of view which is no less universal.[14] What historicism effects, then, is ultimately a displacement of universalism from the past to the present: that which posited itself as universal is in time revealed to be but a part within a larger, more comprehensive universality.

For Takeuchi, this largely unexamined relation between part (particular) and whole (universal) can be seen to underlie the historicist project as such. In this regard, the term "historicism" functions to designate both the particularist and the universalist tendencies at work within this theory. On the one hand, historicism refers to the well-known criticism of logical positivism and scientism which departs from the insight that all knowledge is necessarily historical in nature. Such a doctrine rejects the validity of universal laws, which it regards as ahistorical and abstract, emphasizing in-

---

13. "Ko Teki to Dūi," p. 343.
14. As Gadamer observes, this universalism takes the form of the "prejudice against prejudice itself": "*[H]istoricism, despite its critique of rationalism and of natural law philosophy, is based on the modern Enlightenment and unwittingly shares its prejudices.* And there is one prejudice of the Enlightenment that defines its essence: the fundamental prejudice of the Enlightenment is the prejudice against prejudice itself." *Truth and Method* (New York: The Continuum Publishing Company, 1996), p. 270. Emphasis in the original.

stead the concretely perspectival, and so particular, character of human understanding. While this type of historicism is unquestionably important as a corrective to the formalistic traits inherent in any project of science, it nevertheless fails to radically question the concepts of history and historical experience. It is directly because of this failure that it cannot escape a particularistic bias, as evidenced for example in its determination of perspective in terms of shared cultural identity.[15] If, as Takeuchi demonstrates in his reading of Hu, historical time is marked most centrally by discontinuity, then any appeal to the commonality of identity as a means by which to contextualize knowledge must ignore the fundamental threat to identity posed by this insight. That is to say, the unsettling dimensions of this notion of discontinuity are glossed over in order to think historical difference as a mere difference between subjects.

On the other hand, the historicism that Takeuchi refers to also recalls the attempt (denounced, for example, by Karl Popper in *The Poverty of Historicism* (1957)) to discover a set of immutable historical laws according to which events and movements within history may be determined. Among other problems, such an approach remains thoroughly indebted to such traditional distinctions as those between form and content, identity and difference, and ground and grounded: in other words, the difference that is historical time is believed to be governed by, or founded upon, formal laws whose own identity and autonomy are absolute, and which it is the task of the historicist to uncover. In its quest to reveal the laws which underlie historical change, this type of historicism effectively erases the uniqueness or singularity constitutive of each historical instant, an insight which the first type of historicism paradoxically tried to set forth (although, as we have said, unsuccessfully, insofar as it refuses to explore the relation between singularity and discontinuity). It is this resistance to formalization that above all calls attention to the difference that marks historical time, a difference which is however not simply opposed to the identity characteristic of universal laws. Nevertheless, such criticism is by no means to make light of the exigencies of science to formulate laws or principles by which to explain phenomena, without which clearly one falls back into the naïveté of pre-scientific empiricism. If indeed history demands to be thought, then it seems thought responds to that demand most faithfully by acknowledging its own essential limits, limits which emerge as a result of man's thorough inscription within history.

What is called for then is a kind of "science" of history whose concepts are capable of rigorously taking into account their own ultimate groundless-

---

15. Cf. on this point Naoki Sakai's analysis of the culturalist assumptions at work within hermeneutics, in *Voices of the Past: The Status of Language in Eighteenth-Century Japanese Discourse* (Ithaca: Cornell University Press, 1991), pp. 6-7.

ness. Here, we believe, is the meaning behind Takeuchi's criticism of historicism, on the basis of which the dual tendencies of particularism and universalism can be more effectively avoided. This non-historicist "science" performs its task by attempting to formulate, before all else, what may be tentatively described as a general concept of historical difference. As general, such a concept explicitly problematizes what it considers to be merely the unspoken contradiction of the first type of historicism, that is, its necessary recourse to a principle of universality in the very gesture by which it criticizes the ahistoricality of positivist universalism. In other words, the historicist insight that all knowledge is irreducibly historical and derivative of particular historical perspectives is itself offered as a universal truth of something called "history." Given the apparent impossibility of all universal claims to knowledge, how then is the particularity of a historicist perspective able to know, or rather claim to know, that positivist perspective with which it differs, which is of course distinct as particularity from itself? Evidently there must be posited a universal ground upon which particular difference is inscribed qua particular, and which comprehends all particularities as disparate parts within a common whole. Now it is precisely this universal ground that historicism designates as history. Because of its knowledge of the universal truth of history, historicism is able to successfully transcend the particularity of its own perspective and pronounce the falsity of the positivist perspective—a falsity which, paradoxically enough, stems from the latter's inability to raise itself to universality. Here of course is revealed the silent debt to universalism borne by particularism: in order to articulate a concept of historicist particularity, the partiality of perspective which delimits historicism must be overcome so as to assume that omniscience (or transcendentality) necessary to set forth universal truths which are putatively valid for other particularities as well. The limited truths of other particularities may be identified as such strictly against the backdrop of universal truth against which they appear in relief, and which, originally itself a particular truth, is then universally projected upon others.[16] There is thus a necessary relation between knowledge of another as particular and knowledge of that universal ground upon which all particularities are comprehended as ultimately parts of the same. This ground, apparently universal, in fact reveals itself to be but a narcissistic projection of the self. And insofar as the principle of universality allows in its grounding for knowledge of other particularities, these latter are reduced through their knowability to mere parts of (meaning: contained within) the comprehensive self.

---

16. Takeuchi specifically elaborates this logic as the logic of westernization. The West's recognition of particular difference, for example that of the "Orient," is precisely then the appropriation of that difference as part within the whole, i.e., the West's own universality. See "Kindai towa nanika (Nihon to Chūgoku no baai)," especially pp. 129-136.

This explains, in the final analysis, why knowledge of the other in its determined particularity remains always an unacknowledged solipsism.

Now the implicit universalism operative within this first type of historicism gives way to the considerably less subtle universalism of the second type. Here, as we have noted, the task of the historicist lies in seeking those universal laws of history according to which all historical events may be determined. It is evident that these laws must deny their own situatedness within history in order to successfully formalize historical difference, and in this sense what one might call universalist historicism openly violates the primary rule of historicization as set forth by the former, particularist historicism. Doubtless this is true, and yet perhaps this violation is indicative of nothing more than its insight into a certain inevitability of the universalist position in the project of history's conceptualization. In which case, universalist historicism would have admitted to itself what particularist historicism could not: that any attempt to fully conceptualize history must presuppose the possibility of transcendent positionality (which Takeuchi will identify with the *theoria* of the epistemological subject (*shukan*)); and that this positionality, as a point of ideal identity or self-equivalence, exists outside of or above the difference inherent in historical action (performed, as Takeuchi shows, by the agent of action (*shutai*)).[17]

Hence the following question: how can one maintain the rigor of conceptual thought and think history while at the same time acknowledging the incessant exposure of that thought to historical difference? By posing the question in this way, Takeuchi's problematic of revolution is more easily called to mind. This, to recall, is the task of allowing the activity of revolutionary discontinuity to be knowingly guided by that passive discontinuity which by right precedes it. The difficulty lies here not only in thinking the necessary inscription of activity within passivity, but as well—and, indeed, consequently—in thinking the derivativeness of that very thinking itself. For before thinking ever arrives at this truth for which it aims, that is, before it *knows* it as truth, it will have already unknowingly illustrated it (meaning: it will have been forced to illustrate it). Nevertheless, the truth of this illustration which thinking thus unwittingly performs is not apprehended by man in the immediacy of intuition. In actively thinking its own derivativeness,

---

17. This central distinction between knowledge and action, or *shukan* and *shutai*, can be seen to inform Takeuchi's reading of Hu Shi in "Ko Teki to Dūi": "In [Hu's overseas journal] *Canghuishi zhaji*, however, there are few passages that directly touch upon Dewey and pragmatism. But this is all the more proof of how deeply influenced he was by Dewey, as Hu acknowledges in his 'Introduction.' In other words, Hu did not understand pragmatism as a given theory but rather learned it as a method. He did not study 'philosophy,' he studied 'doing philosophy' (*tetsugaku suru koto*).

"What this means is that 'doing philosophy' is the essential nature of pragmatism, a spirit that Hu Shi had fully grasped. . . . Hu did not preach pragmatism but rather practiced (*jikkō shita*) reform of the status quo" (p. 342).

thought does not simply escape from its element of mediation but rather constantly backtracks, transforming itself into its own object *ad infinitum*. In other words, an infinitely regressive movement is opened up by which thought attempts to think its own limits. The operation of thought reflecting upon itself is strictly interminable: thought strives to identify that origin from which it emerges, and yet every thinking of the origin causes it to retreat further away, hence inciting the repetition of this action. What can perhaps therefore be described as the abyssal nature of thought does not give itself primarily as the essential truth of something called "thought." Were this the case, the universality of this insight would remain fixed against the very historical difference that thinking encounters. If thinking is abyssal, it is so only in its activity of constantly differing from itself. The truth of thought does not lie anywhere outside this activity, and this explains why truth cannot but multiply itself, each time differently. Perhaps it is necessary to then remark of this truth that it is most "true" *before* its conceptualization as truth, or rather, that that conceptualization itself is but one instance of thinking's self-differing activity.

Taking as our clue the infinitely regressive, or abyssal, nature of thought, we are doubtless now better able to answer the question posed above regarding the proper thinking of history. Thinking which fails to take into account its own historical situatedness (i.e., the fact that, qua action, it remains at each moment fundamentally exposed to historical difference) was found to maintain itself relatively complacently at the level of universalism. Examples of such universalism include the two types of historicism already discussed, historicisms which were judged to be reflective of Takeuchi's use of this term as found in his criticism of Hu Shi's teleological vision of history. In their place Takeuchi tries to set forth a thinking of history which remains itself fully historical, and which takes as its central task the articulation of what we have called a general concept of historical difference. This general concept contains three distinct moments, each giving way successively onto the other: 1. The formalization of historical difference. Given here the formal law or structure of difference inherent within historical time, according to which all repetition exposes itself to alterity without the possibility of sublation or synthesis, any recourse to teleology is in principle ruled out. No exceptions are capable of breaching this concept, whose universality precedes and is independent of the actual experience of historical difference itself. 2. Yet, as has been shown, such formalization cannot but shelter the concept from that which it directly thematizes. There is in other words a kind of hypocrisy involved in the universality of the concept, since it refuses to follow its own rule from which, however, nothing can be exempt. Which is to suggest, consequently, that *it is the concept itself which demonstrates the necessity of an outside to its own universality.* In marking itself as universal, the concept shows itself capable of accounting for everything except that very marking. But what conclusion can be drawn from this exceptionability to/of the concept? If it is clear that a remainder must always exist outside of universality, this by no means implies any simple escape from conceptual thought (and hence a lapse into preconceptual empiricism). Rather it points only to the essential limits of the operation or function of grounding. This we may determine as the concept's second moment. 3. Upon marking the exception to its own universality, the concept attempts to ceaselessly reinscribe (or reground) that exception, so justifying its claim as universal. Yet given the exceptionability which for structural reasons undermines these attempts, reinscription merely leads to the repetition of this conceptual operation. The concept's reinscription of its outside in the interest of comprehensive, or unexceptionable, universality has the paradoxical effect of multiplying such outsides, and so, consequently, of multiplying concepts as well. Here, conceptual universality reveals its hidden interminability. Not only is the concept unable to ever fully comprehend its own inscription, but it is also powerless to grasp the series of infinite regressions which begin and continue as a result of this incomprehension. Movement of the concept, which began as an active accounting for difference, ends in a kind of free-fall—a free-fall which, significantly, it itself brings about. This properly abyssal movement is what in Takeuchi necessitates a rethinking of the concept of historical difference as now general rather than universal. Hence the concept's third moment: its inscription as universal within a generality which it points to yet nevertheless does not ultimately control.

What however is meant by this distinction between universal and general, and what is its relation to a thinking of history which remains itself at all times exposed to history? The universal, as we have suggested, is inscribed within the general. If conceptual thought is necessarily universal insofar as it appropriates within itself that which it thinks, hence reducing this latter to but a part within a common whole, then generality would refer to that which exceeds the ken of the concept. In which case, what we have called the general *concept* of historical difference can no longer be understood simply as concept; through its generalization the concept is now forced to acknowledge that which invariably escapes its comprehensive unity, such that, if in fact it may still strictly be called a concept, it would designate both the possibility and the impossibility of thinking historical difference.[18] That is to say, historical difference, understood here as the

---

18. Hence Takeuchi's criticism of the concept (*kannen*), which due to its work of appropriation, or internalization (what Takeuchi refers to as "extracting" (*toridasu koto*)), is unable to think that which for structural reasons allows for the possibility of escape from such extraction: "Scholars for whom science consists in the extracting of concepts are merely situated within the concept of science. Writers for whom literature consists in the extracting of characters, and who believe that characters are ultimately extractable, are simply forcing these latter within the

object of thought, yet resists full internalization within the identity or unity of that concept for which heterogeneity serves only to strengthen its own powers of reductive formalization. It should be emphasized in this connection that such resistance against the concept's internalizing force cannot be explained empirically by the sheer abundance of instances of historical difference for which this concept is supposed to account. Were this the case, the concept's deficiency would be understood in merely quantitative terms: due to the overwhelming wealth of external content, finite consciousness is able to conceptually accommodate some but certainly not all of that which it takes for its object. Here the relation between the conceptualized and the non-conceptualized is regarded as no longer a necessary one. The outside which successfully resists internalization within the concept does so simply by virtue of the fact that it exists empirically outside the concept. In other words, the cause of exteriority is found to be empirical rather than structural (or: exteriority is equivalent only to the non-conceptualized rather than, much more radically, the non-conceptualizable). The very possibility of conceptualization is as a result accepted, taken for granted; what is problematized instead is merely the disproportionality between the finitude of formal thought and the infinity of external content.

Given however the inscription of the concept within its outside—what we have called the inscription of the universal within the general—the relation between the conceptualized and the non-conceptualized must be a necessary one. The deficiency of conceptual thought is not revealed by pointing to that which happens to lie simply outside of it, as if the concept could somehow occupy a space entirely distinct from that outside. On the contrary, such a clear distinction between the concept's interiority (the conceptualized) and its exteriority (the non-conceptualized but conceptualizable) is precisely the condition required for conceptualization. As Takeuchi demonstrates through his articulation of the notion of resistance (*teikō*), the positing of an outside of the concept is in fact the necessary starting point of the conceptual operation—meaning, then, that the concept demands resistance against itself so as to then consume it. Insofar as the movement of the concept is one of internalization, the positing of the outside qua outside consolidates as effect the inside qua inside, therefore allowing for the transformation of external difference into differentiated parts fixed within a universal whole. If however the possibility of conceptualization seems to depend initially upon a relation of simple exteriority between the universal concept

---

concept of literature. They do not think of the place (*ba*) which accommodates characters, and which allows them to move. For if they did, their scholarship and literature would no longer be realized" "Kindai towa nanika (Nihon to Chūgoku no baai)," p. 146.

Given what we have called the universality of the concept, it would seem that the general within which the universal is inscribed, which permits both conceptual extraction and the escape from extraction, is what Takeuchi refers to in this passage as "place."

and its other (which is, ultimately, its general Other), then what remains yet unexplained in this formulation is the *impossibility* of conceptualization. Hence the need to rethink the relation between the concept and its Other as in fact not one of simple exteriority but rather one of inscription. For if the concept is understood to be inscribed within the generality of its Other, both the possibility and the impossibility of conceptualization may be accounted for. The internalizing operation of the concept is thus recognized as possible: here, man's ability to think something called historical difference. This possibility of the concept is, we believe, undeniable, and furthermore must be admitted if one is to then go on to grasp the structural limits, or the impossibility, of the concept. This latter is revealed when it is shown that the concept's inscription within the general prevents any absolute distinction between conceptual interiority and exteriority. Or more precisely, the relation of simple exteriority between the concept and its other (or object) itself takes place against a backdrop of generality which threatens at all times to unsettle the fixity of those boundaries.

It should now be clear that the concept's limitations are exposed not through the quantitative excess of its outside, but rather through the structural presence of that outside within its inside. Which is to say, in this context, that general historical difference grounds the conceptualization of that difference in such a way that the concept may in principle always be overwhelmed by that which it determines as its object. In order to be successful, the concept's internalization of its outside must proceed by an economy regulated by the concept itself. This economy is maintained by carefully fixing the boundaries between what belongs to the concept and what does not. Once the concept identifies itself as distinct from its outside, the work of internalization proceeds without in any way compromising the hierarchy between these two poles. That is to say, the active translation of the outside into the inside must not in that very act *externalize* the inside, carry it outside of itself just as it desires its own self-expansion (*jiko kakuchō*). Yet this is precisely what the concept brings about: by exposing itself to the outside in order to effect its appropriation, the concept finds that it is unable to then fully close itself off from it, that it has, as it were, bitten off more than it can chew. The result is an overwhelming of the concept, an inability to distinguish itself in all purity from the difference that is its object. The regulated economy of internalization required for the concept's development gives way, from the moment of its opening to its outside, to a kind of unregulated general economy, whose effect is the disruption of all conceptual interiority.[19]

---

19. See here Georges Bataille, *The Accursed Share*, trans. Robert Hurley (New York: Zone Books, 1991), vol. 1, pp. 19-41; and Jacques Derrida, "From Restricted to General Economy:

The concept encounters its other with the intention of actively negating it, forgetting that this action at the same time passively exposes it to an influx of the Other which it cannot strictly control. This overwhelming of the concept is in fact the effect of the concept's own action, an effect which betrays its original intention. Yet if the effects of the conceptualizing act exceed all calculation, separating the concept from itself in delivering it over to the generality of its Other, this does not however imply the complete annulment of conceptual activity. In discovering the contamination, or the exposure, of the universal by the general, the concept reacts by retreating from what it sees merely as the provisional taint of alterity so as to then reappropriate that difference in the form of another synthesis. If it is true that the concept is never fully capable of accommodating difference without risk to itself, then it must also be admitted that the concept reacts to that threat by reproducing itself in such a way as to make that difference more comprehensible. These reproductions or repetitions of the concept occur, however, through its own self-retreat, its dividing of itself from itself. In this sense, it seems clear that the concept is constrained to obey that law of repetition which stipulates that all such recurrence take place differentially, as repetition with or through difference. The concept attempts to preserve itself by retreating from its corrupted interior, but this very movement irrevocably marks the concept as now something other than what it previously was. Conceptual activity hence produces in its wake a plurality of concepts, each differing repeatedly from the other. It is impossible to speak here of *a* concept, in the singular: concepts in their movement are forced to multiply themselves through their failure to close off difference. Because these concepts are produced only in this movement and exist nowhere apart from it, they do not ever come to constitute one all-encompassing concept, such as would represent the synthesis of all conceptual differences. For that concept would be incapable of resisting its own conceptualizing activity, which, as we have said, generates as effect the retreat from itself and so the marking of ever newer and different concepts. This interminable production of concepts may be considered as the irony of conceptual activity. The original function of the concept is to negate difference, to comprehend it within itself such that it is now no longer difference but rather part of the concept. The concept sets itself up, therefore, as the identity which any determination of difference qua difference necessarily presupposes. In this way, difference is understood as existing in all strictness outside the concept. Interiority is created through positing a relationship of opposition to subsist between the concept and difference, the inside and the outside. In order to successfully negate this difference, to which it is opposed, the con-

A Hegelianism without Reserve" in *Writing and Difference*, trans. Alan Bass (Chicago: University of Chicago Press, 1978), pp. 251-277.

cept must itself be entirely free from it—otherwise the internalization of difference does not raise this latter to the level of the concept but instead reduces the concept to but an instance of difference. And yet, as we have noted, the concept's own activity works to transform it into the very difference which it opposes, so forcing it to *negate itself* in reaction to its betrayal. Inasmuch as this self-betrayal necessarily brings forth in its turn a self-negation (which leads then back to self-betrayal), the concept has no choice but to forever play this game of catch-up with itself, the end goal of which is pure auto-affection, or the absolute elimination of all otherness. In Takeuchi's language, there is in this desire for pure auto-affection merely a ceaseless "chasing after" (*oikakeru*) without the possibility of any final "restoration," or "bringing back" (*hikimodosu*), into itself.[20] It is by comprehending its other that the concept hopes to reveal that this other is only apparently other and in fact latently itself, thus completing the circle that is the concept's self-relation, its dual function as subject and object. Yet the failure of this comprehension prevents the circle from ever fully closing in on itself, producing rather a kind of spiral movement without end. This spiral movement is what we described earlier by the term "free-fall." In short, then, it is the concept's rejection of its own internal difference that forces it indefinitely backward, paradoxically producing difference in the desire to erase difference.

Let us in conclusion briefly summarize this movement of free-fall in its relation to the conceptualization of historical difference. As has been suggested, it is above all the failure of the universal concept to comprehend the generality of external difference which gives impetus to this movement. In order to rigorously think this failure as well as the movement which ensues from it, however, we were forced to make use of a *concept* of historical difference. Perhaps paradoxically, the function of this latter "concept" was to demonstrate the ultimate impossibility of conceptualization. Hence this "concept" was termed general rather than simply universal so as to underline its acknowledgment of the essential limits of the concept in the face of its Other. In the final analysis, of course, all universal concepts are necessarily general insofar as they cannot but participate in that production of difference generated by the desire for identity. In this sense, any distinction between a universal concept and a general concept must be described as false and misleading. Nevertheless, the articulation of an explicitly *general* concept of historical difference was required so as to better understand what for Takeuchi is the complete immersion of thought within historical difference. This fact of immersion is what must be denied by the universal concept, for which the difference of history is not so much rejected as it is incorporated, that is to say, shown in the very possibility of this incorporation

---

20. "Kindai towa nanika (Nihon to Chūgoku no baai)," p. 149.

to be latently (or implicitly) itself. In which case, the revealed truth of history qua concept is understood in much the same way that Hegel conceives absolute truth in terms of a circular movement, one leading from self to other, returning then back to self: it is "the movement of positing itself, or is the mediation of its self-othering with itself. . . . It is the process of its own becoming, the circle that presupposes its end as its goal, having its end also as its beginning."[21]

In speaking however of a general concept of historical difference, priority must be decisively shifted away from the concept to that historical difference which is the aim or object of conceptualization. The fact of the concept's derivativeness vis-à-vis historical difference—which ultimately makes of the concept but an effect of this difference—is perhaps brought out most forcefully by identifying the correct order of belonging as designated by the genitive in the phrase "the general concept of historical difference." Whereas historical difference must be understood to be *of* the concept in the sense of belonging to it, the ambiguity of the genitive can also point to the contrary meaning, that the concept is *of* historical difference. This distinction is not, however, a symmetrical one. For in order for difference to appear as such, as the marked disparity between two terms or entities which are yet putatively identical in themselves, another, more general difference must be presupposed. In this case, the concept's self-identity is affirmed through positing something called historical difference as that which it is not, just as historical difference must differentiate itself from the concept in order to claim identity as historical difference. While neither of these terms—qua terms—can be immediately equated with general difference, nevertheless both must ground themselves upon this difference in order to assert their own self-identity. Strictly speaking, the genitive of the phrase "the general concept of historical difference" belongs primarily neither to the concept nor to historical difference understood as such. Rather it indicates precisely that which underlies, and so resists, any as-suchness, and which moreover cannot simply be thought or named due to the fact of historical difference—a fact that the name "historical difference" which echoes it points to without really identifying. If then one must conclude that the genitive belongs more originally to historical difference than to the concept, it must not be forgotten that it belongs yet more originally to that difference which both of these terms equally presuppose.

It goes without saying here that this general concept of historical difference by no means represents the generalization of the concept in the sense that this latter now comprehends the movement of generality, that this movement is in other words ultimately a self-movement of the concept. As

---

21. G.W.F. Hegel, *Phenomenology of Spirit*, trans. A.V. Miller (Oxford: Oxford University Press, 1977), p. 10.

we have remarked, this general movement is beyond comprehension and so irreducible to any grounding in identity. It is a passive falling back to which thought has no choice but to succumb, a constant withdrawal or retreat which can be described in terms of a free-fall. And yet, at the same time, this vertiginous movement requires the activity of thought as well—a fact which brings to light a kind of complicity or confusion between the passive and the active. This is not to say that thought functions as the fixed departure point for this movement in which it then loses itself, for thought necessarily begins as a response to something Other which precedes it, something which it tries but cannot fully grasp in its intended universality. In this respect, thought is capable only of thinking *that* there is this something Other: this Other exceeds it, constantly marks a line between thought and itself such that thought is unable to determine with certainty *what* it is.

Yet this is a lesson that thought never quite learns. As universal, it pretends to hold itself above the unsettling difference that is history. And as we have seen, it is this denial in the face of its exposure to history that distinguishes the universal from the general. For the universal there is totality, identity, groundedness, the essential truth of the One. The general is that which escapes, or overflows, this comprehension; as such it denotes abyssality (i.e., infinite regress, the movement of free-fall), alterity, and difference. In the very gesture by which it attempts to account for difference, the concept posits itself as essentially outside it. Indeed, the very possibility of conceptualization rests upon this strict division between inside and outside, the properly conceptual and that conceptualizable difference which is its nutrition or fodder. As a result, the concept recognizes anything which opposes it as merely provisional resistance, for if this latter has not yet actually been conceptualized it may nevertheless in principle always be so. What we have designated as the general "concept," on the other hand, articulates the possibility of conceptualization as inscribed within its ultimate impossibility. Which is to say, put differently, that the universal is inscribed within the general. For structural reasons, the concept is unable to fully internalize the generality of its Other within the confines of itself. Hence a general concept of historical difference is forced, against itself as it were, to respect that alterity which is the difference of history. In wishing to think this alterity, the concept unwittingly opens up—or sets loose—a movement of retreat away from itself. This movement reveals the concept to be in fact internally fragmented, exposed to an Other which it allows within itself only to then be overwhelmed by it.

"IT IS THROUGH THE ACT OF KNOWING THAT I DO NOT KNOW"

We have yet to explain the specific manner in which this generalizing movement of the universal concept relates to Takeuchi's understanding of history. This movement was introduced in our reading so as to better determine what is at stake in Takeuchi's criticism of historicism, through which was delineated a thinking of history that remains at all times mindful of its own fundamental exposure to historical difference. It will be remembered that Takeuchi attacks Hu Shi on precisely this question of history, and this suggests that the latter's thinking of history represents in some way an insufficient response to history's limiting effect upon thought. According to Takeuchi, Hu fails to consider the radical implications of the insight into the "discontinuity" which marks historical time. This discontinuity necessarily affects the status of thinking itself, and with this any determination of man as subject. For it is the idealizing operation of thought which functions to raise difference to the level of subjective (*shukanteki*) identity, hence ensuring the possibility of the subject's continuity (or repetition) as itself. Without this idealization, of course, the subject could never hope to distinguish itself from that difference which threatens always to unsettle it, and which it is forced to posit as existing strictly outside or opposite itself, in the form of object (*taishō*). In this respect, historical discontinuity undermines the subject by exposing it to a properly unthinkable, or unsublatable, difference, thus compelling it to repeat itself as in fact Other to itself. By definition, the subject is understood to be capable of grounding (sub-) that difference which it encounters, and this it does through its ability to *think* difference, hence rendering it as part of that identity which is itself. Yet this very act of grounding cannot deny its own thoroughly historical character. And insofar as history is marked by discontinuity, thought's grounding necessarily takes place upon a kind of non-ground more original than itself, and over which it has no control.

   Now although Takeuchi links this notion of historical discontinuity with Hu Shi, he claims that Hu proved ultimately unfaithful to it in his view of history as teleological. For Hu, the difference of historical discontinuity is reduced to something that can be grounded, something that is, in other words, thinkable or comprehensible by the subject. Difference is not therefore simply denied from the outset;[22] on the contrary, its presence is openly

---

22. Were this the case, there would of course be no subject-object distinction, since reality would be entirely reducible to the *thought* of reality. This idealism was criticized time and again by Hu, who in this sense carried on the tradition begun by such American pragmatists as William James and John Dewey. See here especially Hu Shi's 1919 essay "Shiyanzhuyi," in *Hu Shi wencun, san ji* (Shanghai: Yadong Tushuguan, 1925), vol. 1:2, pp. 75-145.

recognized as testimony to the subject's initial non-coincidence with itself. Insofar as difference resists the subject, it is evident that the latter is not immediately selfsame—for the subject is in a sense forced to share itself with its Other. Nevertheless, if the subject is not immediately selfsame, this is not at all to say that it cannot become so mediately. Selfsameness thus offers itself as a goal for the subject, a goal whose realization is held to be possible. Yet the means by which this goal is realized seem at first glance to contradict the goal itself, since these require that the subject sacrifice itself and actively engage that difference which threatens or haunts it, so that ultimately, as it were, "the identity of itself with itself becomes explicit for it."[23] This only apparent paradox may be summarized as follows: although the subject opposes difference since difference prevents it from fully *being* itself, it at the same time requires difference in order to actually *become* itself, for only through relating itself to that difference will the subject come to reveal that difference to be in truth the subject itself.

It is here that one sees clearly the necessary relation between difference and teleology, as well as the manner in which these two require a notion of subjectivity as their point of convergence. As Takeuchi doubtless realized, the notions of difference and teleology are for Hu Shi only superficially contradictory with one another. On the one hand, Hu is forced to think difference and its intractable resistance to thought. On the other hand, however, he insists upon seeing this difference as in principle always utilizable by the subject, which in actively working through difference shows itself to be capable of greater self-expansion. Which is to say, then, that difference exists ultimately in the service of identity. It is reduced to a means by which to arrive at a goal, the goal of course being the full incorporation of alterity within the sphere of the subject. Thought functions in this sense as the tool of translation *par excellence*, for only by thinking difference does one effectively negate it, thus raising it to the level of identity.[24] As we have discussed, it is by thinking difference that the subject comes to see through its false appearance; in truth, difference is revealed to be nothing other than the subject itself. Hence the subject's progress (*shinpo*) necessarily coincides with the gradual elimination of all otherness. Significantly, Hu will regard

---

23. *Phenomenology of Spirit*, p. 105. If at this point we make reference to Hegel in discussing Takeuchi's reading of Hu Shi, it is because Hu's understanding of history as teleological represents for Takeuchi a kind of Hegelianism. No doubt Takeuchi saw in Hu's project of westernization an attempt to actively translate this understanding into practice.

24. This instrumentalist (or experimentalist) understanding of thought as a "tool" used by the subject to comprehend difference is put forth by Hu Shi as follows: "Thinking is useful precisely to the degree in which the anticipation of future consequences is made on the basis of accurate observation of present conditions, functioning thereby as a tool (*gongju*) with which to respond to the future." "Shiyanzhuyi," p. 138.

It should be noted here that Hu borrows much in this passage from Dewey's *Democracy and Education* (New York: Macmillan, 1916), pp. 393-394.

this movement as not simply expressive of man's individual development, in the fashion for example of a *Bildungsroman*. Instead, the individual's process of development is implicitly presented as a kind of microcosm, one which can be said to reflect the development of mankind as a whole. For only in this way is Hu able to speak of history in any authoritative sense, not merely as referring to the development of isolated individuals, but rather as a universal process marked most centrally by ongoing progress. As Takeuchi writes: "his basic view of history was that society advances infinitely one step at a time." Although historical time is riven by discontinuity, this latter is nevertheless judged to be incapable of seriously endangering mankind in its determination as subject. On the contrary, as subject, mankind represents the universal synthesis of that discontinuity which it encounters in the process of its development, and which serves merely to enhance that development. In other words, history names the ongoing subjectivization of the world by man; it names the process in which thinking encounters increasingly less and less resistance by its Other.

It is helpful to read this difference between Takeuchi and Hu Shi concerning the proper understanding of history as a difference between two types of movement—or *undō*, as Takeuchi often writes. For Hu, history is to be described as a movement of progress and development, the proof of which can be seen in the presence of ever expanding reserves of knowledge about the world. This movement reflects the subject's gradual internalization of difference, such that the terms "internalization" and "progress" become here perfectly equivalent to one another.[25] Takeuchi, too, regards history as a movement, yet this movement is by contrast one in which knowledge (or thought) is fundamentally disabled. Or rather: insofar as knowledge does not simply take place "in" history but is itself thoroughly historical, it is unable to ever fully ground itself. History is conceived of here in terms of that "discontinuity" associated with, precisely—if paradoxically—Hu Shi. Because of the discontinuity of historical time, all repetition must be understood as taking place by way of difference. As a result, the movement of history is radically unlike that continuum which alone makes possible the idealizing operation of thought. Movement is not cumulative but rather disjunctive; it "opens up infinite possibilities for the future," as Takeuchi writes, thus constantly exposing itself to its own becoming Other. The effect of this difference upon thinking is one of generalization, what we have described as the generalizing movement of the universal concept.

---

25. This particular "law of movement," as Takeuchi refers to it, expresses itself for example in the desire among nation-states to "become colonizers so as to escape their own colonization. . . . Lu Xun referred to such kind of self-expansive life force as Japanese 'diligence.' When it appears at the level of consciousness, this diligence is seen as the kind of modernization that takes place through the infinite approach toward the advanced nations." "Bunka inyū no hōhō (Nihon bungaku to Chūgoku bungaku II)," in *TYz*, vol. 4, p. 122. Originally published in 1948.

Now if it is in fact this generalizing movement of all conceptual thought or knowledge that allows Takeuchi to understand history in a way markedly different from Hu Shi, it is also that which brings him close to Lu Xun. Let us recall here that Takeuchi distinguishes between Hu Shi and Lu Xun precisely on that point which concerns the notion of historical progress. To wit, Hu in his project of China's "comprehensive westernization" shows himself to be, in Takeuchi's words, a "thinker of progress." This epithet cannot however in any sense be applied to Lu (and this to the contrary of that general consensus reached by Japanese Sinologists), for whom, it is suggested, history can be in some way conceived outside the binary of advance/retreat (*zenshin/kōtai*).[26] It must be underscored that Lu does not represent for Takeuchi simply a rejection of progress (and so, inseparably, a rejection of modernization, of westernization), for, as he well realizes, any naïve attack against these will almost certainly result in their unwitting reproduction.[27] The point here is ultimately irreducible to either refuting or endorsing progress, since both of these positions alike maintain the *possibility* of something called "progress." In order to effectively explain why history cannot be understood as a movement of progress, one must not be content with adducing empirical evidence in support of the claim that progress is in fact absent. For empirical facts are of no avail when the problem is, precisely, one of explaining the conditions of possibility and of impossibility according to which something like progress may or may not occur. Now if for both Takeuchi and Lu progress is held to be in principle impossible, then this impossibility cannot be indifferent to the status of knowledge, with which, as we have argued, it is necessarily related. Just as in Hu progress is judged possible on account of the possibility of knowledge, so too must

---

26. According to Takeuchi, this disagreement between Hu Shi and Lu Xun on the question of progress extends naturally to their difference in viewpoints regarding the significance of democracy: "Lu Xun did not openly oppose Hu Shi when Hu attempted to introduce democracy into China, and yet inwardly he laughed at Hu's naïve optimism. By that time Lu's 'despair' had already come into being, and this made him unable to maintain the fantasy that China's salvation lay in democracy. Therefore the only thing to do was to write, despairingly, of the absence of salvation." Ibid., p. 124.

27. This of course is the problem of resistance in Takeuchi, one which he credits Lu Xun for thinking the most incisively.

This lesson of resistance which Lu Xun teaches Takeuchi is described by Naoki Sakai as follows: "Above all, here, resistance is that which disturbs the possible representational relationship between the self and its image. It is something that resists the formation of those identities that subject people to various institutions. Yet this does not liberate them; this does not lead to emancipation because people are often subject to what they most fear through the words of emancipation." "Modernity and its Critique: The Problem of Universalism and Particularism," in *Translation and Subjectivity: On "Japan" and Cultural Nationalism* (Minneapolis: University of Minnesota Press, 1997), pp. 175-176.

For a more extended treatment of this problem, see Kan Takayuki, *Takeuchi Yoshimi ron: Ajia e no hanka* (Tokyo: Sanichi Shobō, 1976), pp. 98-138.

Takeuchi and Lu ground their claim of progress' impossibility on the ultimate impossibility of knowledge—that is to say, the movement of generalization in which knowledge falls away from itself. According to Takeuchi,
Lu's teaching comes down to precisely this, not simply that knowledge is
impossible (which in itself is a static truth), but that this impossibility is by
right indissociable from a movement in which it is forced to participate. As
Takeuchi writes of his experience in reading Lu: "It was on this path that I
encountered Lu Xun. My encounter with him was an event. . . . In any case,
what I am thinking of here and now is that my judgment on the relativity of
truth might itself be European. I do not know this. Previously I wrote the
words 'to know,' but this is not a knowing in which I could assert that truth
is relative. *It is through the act of knowing that I do not know* (*shiru toiu kōi
ni yotte wa shiranu noda*). I feel as if I understand what Lu Xun means
when he repeatedly writes, 'I do not know anything.' "[28]

"It is through the act of knowing that I do not know": what can we understand Takeuchi to mean by these enigmatic words, words which he offers here as a kind of key to a reading of Lu Xun? To begin with, Takeuchi
seems to be suggesting that knowledge is incapable of simply transcending
the immediate situation in which it takes place. If knowing is possible, it is
so because of its status as, primarily, an act. We must thus acknowledge that
knowing is possible only insofar as it is an "*act* of knowing" (*shiru toiu
kōi*), and that, as such, the structure of the act by right takes precedence over
any actual content of knowledge. At the very moment of its taking place in
history the act marks its site, what Takeuchi refers to as *kōdō no ba* (the site
or place of action):[29] this site is of course that of the act's performance, and
is, given the "discontinuity" of historical time, necessarily singular, i.e.,
without the possibility of repetition. It is for this reason misleading to speak
of the site of an act's performance as a stage—one thinks for example of the
generalization of this term as it appears in Shakespeare's well-known line,
"All the world's a stage"—since such a term implies the fixity of a spatial
field, one which is believed determinable on the basis of that context which
circumscribes it. On the contrary, here the site does not precede the act but
is instead *created* through the act's radically new and unprecedented emergence in history (which is to say: its actualization). In similar fashion, the
site does not survive the act in any intact or present manner. What remains
of it after the act's passing in the face of historical discontinuity is nothing
more than a trace. Yet insofar as this trace requires in turn activation by
other acts—from within other sites—in order to determine its own identity,

---

28. "Kindai towa nanika (Nihon to Chūgoku no baai)," p. 139. Our emphasis.
29. "Bunka inyū no hōhō (Nihon bungaku to Chūgoku bungaku II)," p. 117. Significantly, this
site is counterposed in the text to a merely observational or theoretical "looking from the outside."

and so through it finally the identity of the original act, it must be described as differing essentially from itself. Because the trace is dependent upon both the act of which it is the remains (which thus precedes it) and the activation which desires to return through itself to that act (which thus follows it), it can be said very literally that the trace is that which is always caught between acts.

This relationship between the act and the trace allows us to better understand the structure of the act, upon which, as we have said, all possible knowledge is based. Just as with Hu Shi we see that the possibility of progress rests upon the possibility of knowledge, so with Takeuchi and Lu Xun do we discover that the possibility of knowledge rests in turn upon the structure of the act, as this term is understood here. Yet if the act enables knowledge, makes it in other words possible, it can also by that same token essentially disable knowledge. For Takeuchi and Lu, it is this latter aspect regarding the *impossibility* of knowledge that is understood to be most characteristic of the act: "It is through the act of knowing that I do not know," not, significantly, "It is through the act of knowing that I know." It is by revealing the dependency of knowing upon acting that Takeuchi and Lu wish to think the groundlessness of knowledge, and through this, finally, the ultimate impossibility of progress in history.

Let us now try to describe the movement of generalization which occurs in the disclosure of knowledge as in fact an act, an act which necessarily leaves behind it a trace of itself. Knowledge of a thing requires that it undergo a kind of transformation, such that it be identified by the knower as identically itself as opposed to something other. Yet insofar as historical time is determined as discontinuous, that is, marked by interruption or difference, any identification of for example X as X and not Y must be regarded as inconsistent with history. Identification on the part of knowledge attributes, precisely, continuity, or repetition, to that which it takes to be its object. By so doing it forgets that the thing is originally devoid of identity, that any determination of it as object occurs through ignoring its properly historical character. In this sense, it can be seen that the object of knowledge is in fact produced by knowledge itself: knowledge pretends to have a relation with something existing outside of it, and yet the very raising of that something to the status of object reveals this relation to be in truth a self-relation, unrelated to the outside. Understood in slightly different terms, we may say that the idealizing operation of knowledge proceeds by representing something as self-identical. This identity is however an *ideal identity*; it does not originally belong to the pre-objectified thing. Identity is constituted in the very act of re-presentation itself, hence allowing the epistemological subject (*shukan*) to view the object as that which is capable of repetition without difference. As goes without saying, the positing of such a subject-object relationship can succeed only by denying the historical situatedness of both man and thing, which on the contrary functions to radically discontinue identity.

As opposed to this pure knowing, the "act of knowing" qua act incessantly marks (or traces) its own historicality. That is to say, it marks the act of re-presentation as repetition with difference, and this it does by leaving in its wake a series of non-identical marks which are literally the remains of knowledge. Insofar as knowledge is an act, the operation by which a thing is raised to the status of an ideal, or repeatable, object must be now recognized as irretrievably corrupted by the act's very singularity. The act is structured in such a way as to constantly betray that "act of knowing" which nevertheless depends upon its support. The subject represents to itself, or internalizes within itself, the apparently repeatable object. Yet this ideal repeatability proves to be merely an effect of difference, that difference which divides and multiplies the epistemological act in the face of its historical situatedness. At each instant of re-presentation the object differs from itself; it is in other words traced through the act of representational knowledge as internally differentiated. As a result, what enters the subject as objective knowledge reveals itself to be in fact a heterogeneous plurality of traces. These traces *mark* the subject, or one could even say that they cut the subject; they disclose it as nothing other than these singular, and so unmasterable, traces of itself.

The profound irony of knowledge as founded upon an act should in this way be clear. In the very act of knowing the outside the subject is forced to expose itself to it. Yet it is this outside exposure that effectively disables the project of knowledge, for once exposed the subject is unable to then fully recoup its losses. In speaking here of what is thus the impossibility of knowledge, however, one must be sure to note the paradoxical role played by the activity of this act of knowing. For in fact this impossibility reveals itself only when man actively attempts to know, when he in other words steps into the outside (which he believes reducible to an object) only to find himself overwhelmed by the outside *through that very step*. There is here a kind of necessary complicity between the act of knowledge and its consequent impossibility. Only through acting to know do I discover that I cannot know—never otherwise. Or, as Takeuchi writes of Lu: "It is through the act of knowing that I do not know." Like the forward motion of progress or development, this act of knowing tends always toward an outside with the objective of returning to the self with that outside now fully absorbed, or objectified. This movement is of course linear, but it is at the same time also circular insofar as the possibility of knowledge of the outside presupposes an original identity between knower and known (or between inside and outside), an identity which the *telos* of knowledge comes to make explicit. This return movement is nevertheless merely the intent of action, it is by no means its effect. While the effect of action can likewise be understood as a movement, it significantly does not realize or end itself upon its return but rather, as we have noted, *generalizes* the only limited circuit of representational knowledge. Takeuchi calls attention to this movement by his use of the preposition *ni yotte*, meaning here "through" or "by way of," "by means of": "*It is through* the act of knowing that I do not know." The strangeness of the line revolves precisely around these two words. *Through* acting to know, I unwittingly expose myself to that outside which I desire as my object of knowledge, but which is in fact irreducible to such. Or again: *Through* acting to know, the outside which I intend to mark as the outside of my inside comes instead to effectively mark me (the self) as nothing more than a plurality of discontinuous marks or traces. In this sense, the "through" can be seen to function as a kind of open passage, one which threatens to overwhelm that economy between inside and outside which it is supposed to regulate. Absorbing despite myself an excess of traces through my act of knowing, I respond by withdrawing from that difference, thereby trying to preserve my identity as self and yet, in that very act, further distancing myself from myself. Needless to say, every act with the intention of remedying this split within the self serves only to exacerbate it. As withdrawal, the act marks repetition as necessarily a repetition by way of (*ni yotte*) difference. My withdrawal from those acts which are mine and yet which once actualized never cease to betray me opens up a movement of generalization in which I am forced to flee from myself.

WAYS

With the foregoing in mind, let us try now to understand the difference between Hu Shi and Lu Xun as a difference between traces. Or more specifically, a difference between reading traces in their relation to the (im)possibility of knowledge. For knowledge can be realized only by way of traces, just as repetition (whose possibility, as we have argued, knowledge presupposes) can occur only by way of difference. As Takeuchi seems to suggest, it is upon this "by way of" that everything ultimately hinges. It is likewise because of this "by way of" that nothing can be simply taken for granted, as for example, here, the possibility of knowledge, and with it the possibility of historical progress. Knowledge and progress are in this case the goals which can be attained only by the means, or the *way*, of the differential traces that is history. It is strictly by passing along the way of these traces that the ideal of the outside can ever be reached, i.e., that space imagined to be absolutely unmarked by difference, that is beyond history. Understood in this sense, the trace reveals itself to be a kind of mediational "way": it is that through which an outside seems to present itself as attainable.

Two different readings offer themselves to us at this point, readings which, following Takeuchi, we may associate with Hu Shi and Lu Xun, respectively. These readings each in their own fashion attempt to think what is at stake in this notion of trace, understood here as way. In the following passages, both Hu Shi and Lu Xun speak of way as *lu* or *daolu* (rendered by Takeuchi as *michi* and *dōrō*), words which can be translated interchangeably as "way," "road" or "path." The first passage is from Hu's essay "Shiyanzhuyi," a work which Takeuchi makes reference to in his "Ko Teki to Dūi." Here Hu attempts to illustrate the process of attaining true and valid knowledge of the world through the example of the way: "I for example walk into a large forest and lose my way (*mile lu*), consequently going hungry for several days because unable to get out. Suddenly I see on the ground several traces (*yinzi*) of cattle hooves [or hoofprints]. The thought occurs to me that if I were to follow these, I would certainly find a place of human habitation. This notion is at this time extremely useful. I follow through with my plan and sure enough escape danger. This notion is therefore true since it was able to deliver me from one part of experience to another. For this reason I have myself verified it."[30]

As is clear, the notions of way and trace are here literalized: the way appears as an actually existing path and the trace a real series of traces. This should not really surprise, for the point Hu is making concerns the "way" in which knowledge is attained. The concretization of this otherwise somewhat abstract notion serves the purpose of illustration. In other words, the acquisition of knowledge through mediation is naturally enough expressed as a real following of a path which then leads to one's destination. Needless to say, the destination here represents that point at which one is finally, both literally and figuratively, out of the woods.

Yet at the same time, this concretization can be described as significant for still another reason. Let us recall that Takeuchi, in his discussion of the influence of Dewey and Deweyan pragmatism upon Hu, characterizes pragmatism as insufficiently "revolutionary," and this because of its naïve grounding in empiricism. The effects of this empiricism upon Hu's thought are in this passage especially clear: the self ("I") is first of all positivized, made into an existing substance, it is placed simply beyond the scope of language and reflection where it is believed to present itself to itself in the immediacy of experience; and further, this self is determined as perceiving in the course of its experience material objects which are likewise positively present, such as are here traces and ways. Things in the world are found to exist strictly independently of the self, just as the self is believed to be independent of them. Objective knowledge takes place, then, on the basis of that perception of the object which presents itself sensibly before one. Now this

---

30. "Shiyanzhuyi," p. 99.

knowledge, as Hu's stated belief in the possibility of verification implies ("For this reason I have myself verified (*zhengshi*) it"), is above all the knowledge of positivism. The meaning of an object which constitutes my knowledge of it may be at any time put to the test so as to determine whether it is true or false, whether, in other words, it corresponds with objective reality as this latter is directly perceived. Meaning is thus empirically verifiable. In and of itself it belongs to the level of cognition, and thus has only a mediate status vis-à-vis the thing itself, which for pragmatism is necessarily the object of sense perception. While its status as mediation enables and indeed requires it to sever ties with the object that is its point of departure, meaning must nevertheless in principle always be able to return to it as it gives itself perceptually.

Now if these remarks are in fact correct, we should be able to abstract here three distinct moments in the coming to knowledge of the meaning of these "traces" which together comprise a "way." 1. The way, or path, of traces is initially encountered as object through perception of its sensible form: "Suddenly I see on the ground several traces of cattle hooves." This object which presents itself before me is at this point too immediate in its materiality. I am yet unable to determine its precise meaning, which requires that I step back from this immediacy and adopt a kind of observational stance in relation to it. Only its bare presence has been registered by consciousness, which now sets out to identify specifically *what* it is, so that it may be effectively utilized. 2. In order to determine what the object is, its immediate materiality must be negated and raised to the level of meaning. Meaning is at first provisionally projected onto the object from outside, that is, on the part of the positing subject, since it does not reveal itself directly. In this case, the meaning of the traces is determined experimentally as that which leads back to human habitation: "The thought occurs to me that if I were to follow these, I would certainly find a place of human habitation." Now the danger here should be obvious. For the possibility always exists that the meaning projected onto the object is simply extrinsic to it, that there is in other words no necessary relation between the object itself (whose immediate presence is at the same time its unintelligibility) and its meaning, which alone is of service to the subject. 3. This danger proves however to be nothing more than a calculated risk, since meaning is understood here to be ultimately verifiable. It is through empirical experimentation that meaning can be determined as either true or false. As Hu writes, "I follow through with my plan and sure enough escape danger. This notion is therefore true since it was able to deliver me from one part of experience to another. For this reason I have myself verified it." Truth is thus realized through the correspondence of the otherwise external or alienated "notion" with the material object itself. The meaning of the traces as that which is capable of leading one back to human habitation is shown to be not at all arbitrary, or merely projected from outside the object without regard to the object itself. Rather it coincides with the meaning that is found to be *inherent within* the object, a meaning which only now reveals itself to man. In this respect, the object may be understood properly as a synthesis of body and soul: it is material and yet at the same time endowed with meaning. Which is also to say: the meaning of the object which constitutes my knowledge of it, and which is at first of uncertain status vis-à-vis the object itself (since I cannot initially be sure whether the meaning projected onto it coincides with its own inherent meaning), never really leaves the object. The return of meaning to the object as explicitly its own meaning is already in principle guaranteed once meaning has been determined to be empirically verifiable.

As a result, the possibility of objective knowledge is for Hu not ever seriously placed in question. Because the subject's knowledge of the object can always refer back to the *experience* of objective reality as to its irrefutable litmus test, it is inconceivable to regard experience as anything but the ground of knowledge. As Hu correctly points out, knowledge is in this context that which "deliver[s] me from one part of experience (*jingyan*) to another." The subject's knowledge of the object thus both begins in experience—from the direct apprehension of the object in its sensible form—and ends in experience—to the empirical verification of the object's meaning. Now once experience has been in this way determined as the ground of knowledge, it will likewise serve as the ground of progress. Both knowledge and progress operate through a kind of forward movement which can be at any time verified experientially. This explains why Hu illustrates this movement through the example of a man progressing upon a way: knowledge of the meaning of the way (of the traces which comprise the way) as that which leads out of the forest is verified with each actual step leading out of the forest. In order to know the meaning of the way, or what it is, one must progress upon it. Yet this progress through which one comes to know the way only in fact confirms it as it originally presented itself in experience. Progress upon the way is experientially verified once it is shown to lead out of the forest. In the same fashion, knowledge of the meaning of the way as that which leads out of the forest is verified once one experiences this meaning to be true. Progress and knowledge in relation to the way are thus possible insofar as the latter is determined to be present in experience.

Such a reading of the way may be fruitfully contrasted with Lu Xun's reading. For Lu, the way is precisely that which does *not* present itself in experience; it is indeed that which somehow disturbs or unsettles experience. Let us refer here to the lines from the short story "Guxiang" which we quoted at the beginning of this essay, lines which Takeuchi himself refers to in connection with his criticism of progress and modernization (or westernization): "I thought: hope originally cannot be said to exist, nor can it be said not to exist. It is just like ways (*lu*) across the earth. For actually the earth had no ways to begin with, but when many men pass through, a way is made." As Lu makes clear, ways are in fact no more substantial than hope. They are shadowy or ghost-like, not ever quite present; they can neither be said to exist, nor can they be said not to exist. The ways that Hu believed to be simply present in experience are on the contrary experienced by Lu as neither present nor absent, but rather somewhere in the middle of these two poles. One could perhaps even go so far as to say here that it is with Lu that the implicit presupposition of Hu's notion of experience comes to light, this being that *experience is determined on the basis of presence*. For only in this way can the dominance of the object go unchallenged. Knowledge of the object will for Hu Shi always be measured against the actual experience of it, as if experience were entirely reducible to the experience of objects. What remains thus unthought in this determination of experience is the possibility of an experience which is not of the object, which in other words precedes the experience of objects qua objects. It is specifically in this sense that a criticism of the notion of experience which informs Hu's empiricism would not simply fall back on a silent rationalism. Instead it would be guided by the need to think a more radical empiricism, one which does not merely reduce the world to the world of objects.

It is because the way is irreducible to a present object that experience is disturbed. Knowledge of the meaning of the way consequently suffers from this disturbance, since it can no longer appeal to the immediacy of experience for the purpose of verification. As goes without saying, pre-objective experience can assure objective knowledge of nothing. In order for experience to be an experience of the object, the object must first be determined as self-identical. So for example the man lost in the forest encounters those traces which together comprise a way: he perceives this "object" directly as itself and not as something other. Yet this identity cannot in fact be materially-based, it does not exist naturally or originally in the world. On the contrary, it is first and foremost an ideal identity which, originating with the subject, is then surreptitiously projected onto matter. In this way, all reference to things in the world as self-identical is possible only after the fact, or retroactively: by right, non-identity—or difference—precedes identity. As a result of this insight into the original non-identity of experience, the appeal to experience on the part of knowledge shows itself to be in truth a self-appeal. That is to say, insofar as knowledge understands experience only on the basis of identity, the meaning of the object determined by knowledge is verified not by experience itself (which, as we have argued, is properly devoid of objects), but rather by knowledge masquerading as experience.

In experience objective identity breaks up into something like "traces" or "ways," which themselves help to create the effect of objective identity. These are not in and of themselves positive but are instead, significantly, *produced* through the very act of knowledge. The act by which I know the meaning of things takes place by productively tracing those things, such that only through this tracing (or "waying") do they become meaningful to me. Here meaning is not considered to be inherent within the thing itself; on the contrary, it requires a kind of "participative thinking" which consists at each instant of nothing more than the encounter between those things and myself.[31] It is for this reason that Lu Xun can speak of the way as neither simply "objective" nor "subjective." Ways themselves do not exist—neither in the world nor in the mind—but are somehow produced through man's participation in things: "For actually the earth had no ways to begin with, but *when many men pass through, a way is made.*" Hence in the example given by Hu Shi, the way comprised of traces which seems to present itself before man as an object is now shown to lose its simple objectivity. Given the necessity of man's participation in things, one can in this context speak only of ways of ways, or traces of traces. Objective knowledge is by right grounded upon these ways, but insofar as ways are produced only through the act of knowing (*shiru toiu kōi*), the object can never be self-identical—it is at each instant dependent upon action in order to then be what it is. In which case, ways can be understood not only as the ground of objective knowledge, as that which in other words makes knowledge of objects possible, but, even more fundamentally, as that which testifies to the impossibility of such knowledge.

It seems evident that, for Takeuchi, this impossibility of objective knowledge is understood in conjunction with the notion of ways as articulated in Lu Xun. Hence it is not surprising to find in his writings on Lu constant reference to this notion, as if, in some sense, ways were at the very heart of Lu's teaching. In for example "Kindai towa nanika (Nihon to Chūgoku no baai)," Lu is associated with "those who break ground" (*kaitakusha*).[32] Several pages later the line appears, "It was on this way [or path: *michi*] that I encountered Lu Xun."[33] And in "Bunka inyū no hōhō (Nihon bungaku to Chūgoku bungaku II)," we read that Lu sought a "roundabout way" (*mawarimichi*) to modernize, whereas "Japanese culture has tried to modernize strictly by approaching European culture."[34] Finally, in the opening pages of the 1953 text *Ro Jin nyūmon* [Introduction to Lu Xun] Takeuchi writes: "I believe that an introduction to Lu Xun must begin by trying to walk alone upon the way (*michi*) that Lu Xun has walked. Here there can be

---

31. See M.M. Bakhtin, *Toward a Philosophy of the Act*, trans. Vadim Liapunov (Austin: University of Texas Press, 1993).
32. "Kindai towa nanika (Nihon to Chūgoku no baai)," p. 128. This term, which appears throughout Takeuchi's work in reference to Lu Xun, has the more common meaning of "pioneer," "trailblazer" or even "settler."
33. Ibid., p. 139.
34. "Bunka inyū no hōhō (Nihon bungaku to Chūgoku bungaku II)," p. 120.

no guides, neither teacher nor elder. One must walk alone. . . . Lu Xun cannot be grasped on the basis of any existing knowledge (*kisei no chishiki*); rather one must experience (*taiken*) what he experienced."[35] Perhaps even more illustrative are Takeuchi's direct quotations from Lu's work. From "Deng xia manbi" [Some Notions Jotted Down by Lamp-light] (1925): "But are we all like the men of old, to be content for ever with 'the good old ways'? Are we all like those classicists who, dissatisfied with the present, long for the peaceful days of three centuries ago? Of course, we are not satisfied with the present either, but that does not mean we have to look backwards, for there is still a way (*daolu, dōrō*) forward."[36] Or from "Nala zou hou zenyang" [What Happens after Nora Leaves Home] (1923): "The most painful thing in life is to wake up from a dream and find no way (*lu, michi*) out. Dreamers are fortunate people. If no way out can be seen, the important thing is not to awaken the sleepers."[37]

Ways are neither present nor absent: they can neither be said to exist, nor can they be said not to exist. Nevertheless it seems that everything depends upon them, foremost among these being the possibility of objective knowledge and the possibility of progress. In the act of knowing, a way or trace is inscribed upon things, and it is this that allows for knowledge of its meaning. Yet insofar as this meaning derives from an act which it cannot transcend, it can never be other than singular, just as the act is itself necessarily singular. As we have said, meaning is produced, emerging only in the encounter (or the exposure) between man and things in the world. This production of meaning takes place through a kind of "groundbreaking," to use Takeuchi's term: the border between man and the world is at each instant opened up, or breached, and in that breaching meaning occurs. This however is not to say that the thing in that groundbreaking act gives itself to man as such. For through the very act in which meaning is traced or wayed, the thing itself retreats. Because of this retreating, the way invariably marks the thing in its difference and singularity. Objective knowledge must nevertheless assume the possibility of the thing's self-identity, an identity which in turn assumes the possibility of pure repetition, or repetition without difference. But the singularity of the way is precisely that which disallows

35. *Ro Jin nyūmon* (Tokyo: Kōdansha Bungei Bunko, 1996), p. 11. Takeuchi seems here to be making implicit reference to Lu Xun's 1926 essay "Xie zai 'fen' houmian," from which we quote the following lines: "Yet it would be even more difficult if I had to guide other people, for I myself am yet uncertain what route to take. There are doubtless in China many 'elders' and 'teachers,' but I am unlike such people. Nor do I trust them. The only destination I know for certain is the grave, and yet this is something that everyone knows, and for which all guides are unnecessary." In *Lu Xun zuopin quanji* (Taipei: Fengyun Shidai, 1993), vol. 6, p. 326.

36. *Selected Works of Lu Hsun*, vol. 2, p. 136; *Lu Xun sanwen* (Beijing: Zhongguo Guangbo Dianshi, 1992), vol. 1, pp. 434-435.

37. *Lu Hsun: Writing for the Revolution* (San Francisco: Red Sun Publishers, 1976), p. 101; *Lu Xun sanwen*, vol. 2, p. 127.

such repetition, hence revealing the ultimate groundlessness of objective knowledge.

Bibliography

Abe Kōbō. *The Woman in the Dunes*, trans. E. Dale Saunders. New York: Vintage Books, 1964.

Agamben, Giorgio. *Infancy and History: Essays on the Destruction of Experience*, trans. Liz Heron. London: Verso, 1993.

Bakhtin, M.M. *Toward a Philosophy of the Act*, trans. Vadim Liapunov. Austin: University of Texas Press, 1993.

Balibar, Etienne and Immanuel Wallerstein. *Race, Nation, Class: Ambiguous Identities*, trans. Chris Turner. London: Verso, 1992.

Bataille, Georges. *The Accursed Share*, vol. 1, trans. Robert Hurley. New York: Zone Books, 1995.

Beardsworth, Richard. *Derrida and the Political*. London: Routledge, 1996.

Benveniste, Emile. *Problems in General Linguistics*, trans. Mary Elizabeth Meek. Coral Gables: University of Miami Press, 1971.

Borch-Jacobsen, Mikkel. *Lacan: The Absolute Master*, trans. Douglas Brick. Stanford: Stanford University Press, 1991.

Butler, Judith. *Subjects of Desire: Hegelian Reflections in Twentieth-Century France*. New York: Columbia University Press, 1987.

Cornell, Drucilla et. al., ed. *Deconstruction and the Possibility of Justice*. New York: Routledge, 1992.

Dazai Osamu. *Sekibetsu*. Tokyo: Shinchōsha, 1973.

Derrida, Jacques. *Dissemination*, trans. Barbara Johnson. Chicago: University of Chicago Press, 1981.

_____. *Edmund Husserl's* Origin of Geometry: *An Introduction*, trans. John P. Leavey, Jr. Lincoln: University of Nebraska Press, 1989.

_____. *Limited Inc*, trans. Samuel Weber et. al. Evanston: Northwestern University Press, 1993.

_____. *Of Grammatology*, trans. Gayatri Chakravorty Spivak. Baltimore: Johns Hopkins University Press, 1976.

_____. *Spurs: Nietzsche's Styles*, trans. Barbara Harlow. Chicago: University of Chicago Press, 1979.

_____. *Writing and Difference*, trans. Alan Bass. Chicago: University of Chicago Press, 1978.

_____, and Maurizio Ferraris, *A Taste for the Secret*, trans. Giacomo Donis. Malden, MA: Polity Press, 2001.

Descombes, Vincent. *L'inconscient malgré lui*. Paris: Les Éditions de Minuit, 1977.

Dewey, John. *Creative Intelligence: Essays in the Pragmatic Attitude*. New York: Henry Holt and Company, 1917.

_____. *Democracy and Education*. New York: Macmillan, 1916.

_____. *How We Think*. Buffalo, NY: Prometheus Books, 1991.

Dillon, M.C. *Merleau-Ponty's Ontology*. Evanston: Northwestern University Press, 1997.

_____. *Semiological Reductionism: A Critique of the Deconstructionist Movement in Postmodern Thought*. Albany: State University of New York Press, 1995.

Freud, Sigmund. *An Outline of Psycho-Analysis*, trans. James Strachey. New York: W.W. Norton & Company, 1949.

Gadamer, Hans-Georg. *Truth and Method*. New York: The Continuum Publishing Company, 1996.

Gasché, Rodolphe. *The Tain of the Mirror: Derrida and the Philosophy of Reflection*. Cambridge: Harvard University Press, 1986.

Grieder, Jerome B. *Hu Shih and the Chinese Renaissance: Liberalism in the Chinese Revolution, 1917-1937*. Cambridge: Harvard University Press, 1999.

Hall, Stuart et. al., ed. *Modernity: An Introduction to Modern Societies*. Cambridge: Blackwell Publishers, 1996.

Hegel, Georg Wilhelm Friedrich. *Faith and Knowledge*, trans. Walter Cerf and H.S. Harris. Albany: State University of New York Press, 1977.

_____. *Phenomenology of Spirit*, trans. A.V. Miller. Oxford: Oxford University Press, 1977.

_____. *System of Ethical Life and First Philosophy of Spirit*, trans. H.S. Harris and T.M. Knox. Albany: State University of New York Press, 1979.

Heidegger, Martin. *Basic Writings*, ed. David Farrell Krell. New York: Harper & Row, 1977.

_____. *Being and Time*, trans. John Macquarrie and Edward Robinson. San Francisco: Harper & Row, 1962.

Honda Shūgo. *Monogatari sengo bungaku shi*. Tokyo: Shinchōsha, 1975.

Hu Shi. *Hu Shi wencun*. Shanghai: Yadong Tushuguan, 1925.

Ichimura Hiromasa. *Zōho "nazuke" no seishinshi*. Tokyo: Heibonsha, 1996.

Isomae Junichi. *Kiki shinwa no metahisutorī*. Tokyo: Yoshikawa Kōbunkan, 1998.

Izumi Aki. *Nihon rōman-ha hihan*. Tokyo: Shinseisha, 1969.

James, William. *Pragmatism*. New York: Longmans, Green and Co., 1910.

Kan Takayuki. *Takeuchi Yoshimi ron: Ajia e no hanka*. Tokyo: Sanichi Shobō, 1976.

Kant, Immanuel. *Critique of Pure Reason*, trans. Norman Kemp Smith. New York: St. Martin's Press, 1965.

Karatani Kōjin. *Origins of Modern Japanese Literature*, trans. Brett de Bary et al. Durham: Duke University Press, 1993.

Keene, Donald. *Dawn to the West: Japanese Literature in the Modern Era*, vols. 1-2. New York: Henry Holt & Co., 1984.

Kitagawa Tōru. *Sengo shisō no genzai*. Tokyo: Dentō to Gendaisha, 1981.

Koschmann, J. Victor. *Revolution and Subjectivity in Postwar Japan*. Chicago: University of Chicago Press, 1996.

Lacan, Jacques. *Écrits: A Selection*, trans. Alan Sheridan. New York: W.W. Norton, 1977.

Lacoue-Labarthe, Phillipe. *Heidegger, Art and Politics*, trans. Chris Turner. Cambridge: Basil Blackwell, 1990.

_____, and Jean-Luc Nancy. *The Literary Absolute: The Theory of Literature in German Romanticism*, trans. Philip Barnard and Cheryl Lester. Albany: State University of New York Press, 1988.

_____, and Jean-Luc Nancy. *Retreating the Political*, ed. Simon Sparks. London: Routledge, 1997.

Liu Qingfeng, ed. *Hu Shi yu xiandai zhongguo wenhua zhuanxing*. Hong Kong: The Chinese University Press, 1994.

Lu Xun. *Lu Xun sanwen*. Beijing: Zhongguo Guangbo Dianshi, 1992 [trans. *Lu Hsun: Writing for the Revolution*. San Francisco: Red Sun Publishers, 1976].

_____. *Lu Xun xiaoshuoji*. Hong Kong: Jindai Tushu, 1967 [trans. Yang Hsien-yi and Gladys Yang, *Selected Works of Lu Hsun*. Peking: Foreign Language Press, 1956].

_____. *Lu Xun zuopin quanji*. Taipei: Fengyun Shidai, 1993.

Mishima Yukio. *Sun and Steel*, trans. John Bester. New York: Grove Press, 1970.

Miyoshi, Masao and H.D. Harootunian, eds. *Postmodernism and Japan*. Durham, NC: Duke University Press, 1989.

Nakagawa Ikurō. *Takeuchi Yoshimi no bungaku to shisō*. Tokyo: Orijin, 1985.

Nancy, Jean-Luc. *Corpus*. Paris: Éditions Métailié, 1992.

_____. *The Experience of Freedom*, trans. Bridget McDonald. Stanford: Stanford University Press, 1993.

_____. *The Inoperative Community*, trans. Peter Connor et. al. Minneapolis: University of Minnesota Press, 1991.

_____. *L'oubli de la philosophie*. Paris: Éditions Galilée, 1986.

Nishida Kitarō. *Intuition and Reflection in Self-Consciousness*, trans. Valdo H. Viglielmo et. al. Albany: State University of New York Press, 1987.

_____. *Last Writings: Nothingness and the Religious Worldview*, trans. David A. Dilworth. Honolulu: University of Hawaii Press, 1987.

_____. *Zen no kenkyū*. Tokyo: Iwanami Shoten, 1999 [trans. Masao Abe and Christopher Ives, *An Inquiry Into the Good*. New Haven: Yale University Press, 1990].

Nishitani Osamu and Sakai Naoki. *"Sekaishi" no kaitai: honyaku, shutai, rekishi*. Tokyo: Ibunsha, 1999.

Oda Makoto. *Sengo bungaku to Ajia*. Tokyo: Mainichi Shinbunsha, 1978.

Olson, Lawrence. *Ambivalent Moderns: Portraits of Japanese Cultural Identity*. Savage, MD: Rowman & Littlefield, 1992.

Sakaguchi Ango. *Teihon Sakaguchi Ango zenshū*. Tokyo: Tōjusha, 1975.

Sakai, Naoki, ed. *Nashonaritī no datsukōchiku*. Tokyo: Kashiwa Shobō, 1996.

_____. *Translation and Subjectivity: On "Japan" and Cultural Nationalism*. Minneapolis: University of Minnesota Press, 1997.

_____. *Voices of the Past: The Status of Language in Eighteenth-Century Japanese Discourse*. Ithaca: Cornell University Press, 1991.

Takeuchi Shigeaki. *Sengo shisō e no shikaku: shutai to gengo*. Tokyo: Chikuma Shobō, 1972.

Takeuchi Yoshimi. "Ajia ni okeru shinpo to handō: Nihon no shisōteki jōkyō ni terashite." In *TYz*, vol. 5.

_____. "Bōkoku no uta." In *TYz*, vol. 7.

_____. "Bungaku ni okeru dokuritsu towa nanika." In *TYz*, vol. 7.

_____. "Bungaku no jiritsusei nado." In *TYz*, vol. 7.

_____. "Bunka inyū no hōhō (Nihon bungaku to Chūgoku bungaku II)." In *TYz*, vol. 4.

_____. "Fujino sensei." In *TYz*, vol. 1.

_____. "Goshi bunka kakumei." In *TYz*, vol. 3.

_____. "Hōhō toshite no Ajia." In *TYh*, vol. 3.

_____. "Hyōgen ni tsuite." In *TYz*, vol. 7.

_____. *Kindai no chōkoku*. Tokyo: Fūzanbō Hyakka Bunko, 1979.

_____. "Kindaishugi to minzoku no mondai." In *TYh*, vol. 2.

_____. "Kindai towa nanika (Nihon to Chūgoku no baai)." In *TYz*, vol. 4.

_____. "Kokumin bungaku no mondaiten." In *TYh*, vol. 2.

_____. "Ko Teki to Dūi." In *TYz*, vol. 5.

_____. "Kotoba mondai ni tsuite no kansō." In *TYz*, vol. 7.

_____. "Nihonjin no Chūgokukan." In *TYh*, vol. 3.

_____. "Nihon no minshū." In *TYh*, vol. 2.

_____. "Nihon to Ajia." In *TYh*, vol. 3.

_____. *Ro Jin*. In *TYz*, vol. 1.

_____. *Ro Jin nyūmon*. Tokyo: Kōdansha Bungei Bunko, 1996.

_____. "Seiji to bungaku no mondai (Nihon bungaku to Chūgoku bungaku I)." In *TYz*, vol. 4.

_____. "Seikatsu to bungaku." In *TYh*, vol. 2.

_____. "Shisōka toshite no Ro Jin." In *TYz*, vol. 1.

_____. "Son Bun kan no mondaiten." In *TYh*, vol. 3.

_____. "Waga kaisō." In *TYz*, vol. 13.

_____. "Wasurerarenai kotoba." In *TYz*, vol. 2.

Taylor, Charles. *Hegel and Modern Society*. Cambridge: Cambridge University Press, 1979.

Tsurumi Shunsuke. *Takeuchi Yoshimi: aru hōhō no denki*. Tokyo: Riburo Pōto, 1995.

Yamanouchi Yasushi et. al., ed. *Iwanami kōza: shakai kagaku no hōhō*, vol. 2. Tokyo: Iwanami Shoten, 1993.

Yoshimoto Takaaki. *Yoshimoto Takaaki zenchosakushū*. Tokyo: Keisō Shobō, 1968.

Index

abandonment, 12, 26, 46
Abe Kōbō, 153
action, xiii, 1, 24, 27, 52, 99, 102,
107-109, 115, 120-122, 172, 183,
189, 191-193, 198, 211-214, 219-
220
address, 67-74
Agamben, Giorgio, 130
Akutagawa Ryūnosuke, 41
alterity, xi, xiii, 2, 3, 15, 19, 26,
38, 40, 44, 46, 53, 66, 84, 86, 90-
91, 96, 99, 103-104, 109, 115,
132, 134, 144-146, 155, 160, 172,
174, 180, 186-187, 192-193, 199,
203, 206, 208
American Occupation, 55-57,
157
Ampo, ix
anxiety, xiii, 32-47, 49, 52, 72,
82, 89, 92-93, 96, 103-104, 115,
117, 141, 161, 166, 186
appropriation, xi, 3-4, 10, 17, 20,
40, 62, 70, 72-73, 86, 124, 134,
155, 160, 174, 187, 191, 197, 200,
202
Asian Studies, xii, 1, 2, 5, 6, 44

Bakhtin, M.M, 219
Balibar, Etienne, 68

Bataille, Georges, 156, 175, 202
Benveniste, Emile, 109-110, 123
binding, xiii, 81
body, 11-12, 14, 18, 22, 72, 87-
99, 103, 108, 113-114, 125, 177,
183
Butler, Judith, 166

chaos, 13, 41
Chinese Communist Revolution,
viii, 53
Chinese literature, 37-38, 87, 183,
186
community, 58, 62, 67-85, 158
concept, 25, 30, 32, 41, 100-103,
167, 177, 199-207
consciousness, 25, 28-29, 39, 51,
89, 91-94, 99, 103, 107-108, 112-
115, 131-132, 163, 166, 168, 170,
172, 174, 178-182, 201, 216
contamination, 12, 166, 183, 203
continuity of discontinuity, 29,
35, 49, 81, 191
corporeality, xiii, 11, 18, 50, 52,
66, 86, 88, 91, 99

Dazai Osamu, 146
death, 2-8, 50, 70, 76-77, 90, 108,
111, 177-182

CORNELL EAST ASIA SERIES

Order online: www.einaudi.cornell.edu/eastasia/CEASbooks, or contact Cornell East Asia Series Distribution Center, 95 Brown Road, Box 1004, Ithaca, NY 14850, USA; toll-free: 1-877-865-2432, fax 607-255-7534, ceas@cornell.edu

6-04/.7M pb/SB

www.ingramcontent.com/pod-product-compliance
Ingram Content Group UK Ltd.
Pitfield, Milton Keynes, MK11 3LW, UK
UKHW041836020425
457001UK00001B/17